Slaying
the Mermaid

Also by Stephanie Golden

The Women Outside:
Meanings and Myths of Homelessness

Slaying
the Mermaid

Women and the Culture
of Sacrifice

STEPHANIE GOLDEN

Harmony Books

NEW YORK

The publisher gratefully acknowledges permission granted by the publishers and the Trustees of Amherst College to reprint from *The Poems of Emily Dickinson,* Thomas H. Johnson, ed., Cambridge, Mass.: The Belknap Press of Harvard University Press, copyright © 1951, 1955, 1979, 1983 by the President and Fellows of Harvard College; and permission to reprint from *The Complete Poems of Emily Dickinson,* Thomas H. Johnson, ed., copyright © 1929, 1935 by Martha Dickinson Bianchi, copyright © renewed 1957, 1963 by Mary L. Hampson by permission of Little, Brown and Company.

Copyright © 1998 by Stephanie Golden

Published by Harmony Books, a division of Crown Publishers, Inc., 201 East 50th Street, New York, New York 10022. Member of the Crown Publishing Group.

Random House, Inc. New York, Toronto, London, Sydney, Auckland
www.randomhouse.com

HARMONY and colophon are trademarks of Crown Publishers, Inc.

Printed in the United States of America

Library of Congress Cataloging-in-Publication Data

Golden, Stephanie.
Slaying the mermaid : women and the culture of sacrifice / by Stephanie Golden. — 1st ed.
Includes index.
1. Women—Psychology. 2. Women—Religious life. 3. Self-sacrifice. I. Title.
HQ1206.G666 1998
155.6'33—dc21   97-53285
CIP

ISBN 0-517-70812-4

10 9 8 7 6 5 4 3 2 1

First Edition

Author's Note

FOR WOMEN PARTICULARLY, THE ISSUE OF SACRIFICE CANNOT BE SEPA-
rated from the equally treacherous question of suffering, which our
culture has struggled with for centuries. My friend Leslie was fortu-
nate, therefore, to discover her own answer to the question when she
was still a teenager. The formidable headmistress of her private girls'
school, teaching the book of Job in an ethics class, asserted that suffering was a virtue in itself. Leslie couldn't see it, and said so. The
headmistress argued the point, but nothing she said satisfied Leslie.

"That was the beginning of my independent thinking," she told
me. "I had a lot of respect for that woman, and it took courage to confront her. Rejecting suffering was what freed me intellectually."

My own first encounter with the question of suffering was more
emotional than intellectual, and my reaction more muddled than
Leslie's. This book took shape out of that reaction, and through the
writing I came to understand why this question is so important for
women that, all by itself, rejecting the virtue of suffering could give a
teenager her intellectual freedom. In our culture, suffering is a crucial
component of the sacrifice expected of women—as mothers, in
romantic relationships, in our work lives—a type of sacrifice that
both diminishes and confines us.

The expectations regarding women's self-sacrifice are quite specific, which is why this book is entirely about women and not men. Of
course men make sacrifices too, but differently, and the effect is not so
disempowering. A woman's self-sacrifice typically involves suppress-

ing her own needs, limiting her sphere of action, and diminishing her sense of self. A man's self-sacrifice is more likely to be balanced by an element of self-assertion. Even though he may have to repress his feelings in order to bear up—for example, to do work he dislikes in order to support his family—his sacrifice tends to bestow a positive sense of identity that builds up his self rather than diminishing it. Nor—most decisively—is that self shaped by centuries of tradition holding up as a model the image of an exalted, self-abnegating angel of compassion.

This book combines personal experience, research, and interviews with thirty-five women who described the sacrifices they had made in their lives, or had seen other women—usually their mothers—make. Their definitions of sacrifice varied considerably, but common themes emerged which made it clear that sacrifice occupies a large space in women's lives. Even a few women who were nervous about the interview because they thought they would have nothing to say turned out to have plenty—and I discovered after collecting as much material as I could use that there was an endless world of other stories out there.

I am grateful above all to these thirty-five women who were willing to speak so openly to me, for their stories are the flesh of this book. Their lived experience gives substance and meaning to the images I've drawn from myth and popular culture; it also endows with present-day significance the otherwise seemingly remote facts of history. I feel, too, a personal benefit, a sense of enlargement, from my encounter with the wisdom they distilled from their experience. To protect their privacy, I've changed their names (with a couple of obvious exceptions) as well as specific identifying details.

This book owes its existence to the inspiration first of my agent, Theresa Park, who saw before I did that I could write it, and second of my editor, Shaye Areheart, who—knowing more than anyone I've ever met about the care and feeding of authors—lavished upon me during the writing the most exquisitely effective moral support.

Author's Note

Dina Siciliano, Barbara Marks, and the other staff at Harmony and Crown provided a level of practical support that most authors only dream of.

Over the years that my ideas were germinating, they received extraordinary fertilization from the two other founding members of the Compassionate Action Meditation Group at New York's Open Center, Don Salmon and Rita Nickle. I thank Don in particular for opening up to me the profoundest meaning of the word *sacrifice*. I am deeply grateful also to David Kirby, and the Buddhist tradition he is part of, for the gift of a practice that truly made it possible to transcend the limitations of the linear mind.

The idea of "women and sacrifice" reminded Jim Hughes of Maude Callen, and he kindly rooted around in his basement to find for me a copy of photographer W. Eugene Smith's research notes describing her. I would like to thank Smith's son Kevin Smith for permission to quote from this unpublished typescript in Chapter 10. I am also grateful to Suzanne Stutman for allowing me to use the lines from her poem about pain that appear in Chapter 8.

Bonnie S. Anderson and Phyllis Deutsch, who read sections of the manuscript, continued to offer the priceless intellectual and emotional support that sustains my entire project as a writer. Barbara Winslow clued me in to Verdi's *Traviata* and provided other leads to good sources (and often the books themselves). Alix Kates Shulman has been a wise-woman mentor for me ever since my struggles with my first book.

I thank, too, the members of the Columbia University Seminar on Women and Society for their very helpful comments on an early version of Chapter 1 and, for various forms of assistance, Sherron Courneen, Vivian Goldstein, Rod Morrison, Susan Perlstein, Sonia Jaffe Robbins, Laura Seitel, and my brother, Clifford E. Schwartz.

Finally, I thank those whose friendship itself supported this work: Irene Davidson, Meeta L'huillier, Margit Reiner, Harriet Serenkin, and Mary Valmont.

Author's Note

The events at the shelter for homeless women described here have been haunting me for years. This writing finally lays them to rest, while leaving me with a lasting appreciation of the type of community created there, in which sacrifice can be experienced as transformation.

Contents

Slaying
the Mermaid

1

Sacrifice and the
Feminine Ideal

I FIRST CONFRONTED THE QUESTION OF SELF-SACRIFICE YEARS AGO, when I began volunteering at a shelter for homeless women, run by nuns. The atmosphere there of intense Catholic spirituality, which amplified ordinary altruism to extreme levels, precipitated a crisis so disturbing that it sent me on a quest to understand the complex implications of sacrifice in our culture: how it bears upon our individual lives and on our social acts.

The affair began innocuously, soon after the arrival of a new volunteer named John. One day, as Sister Elizabeth stood in the living-room doorway, eating a piece of dried fruit and watching several residents sitting together, John came up behind her. "I believe so much in self-discipline and fasting," he remarked. "Look at these broken women, look at their faces. Couldn't you give up eating sweets out of love for them?"

"Of course I could" was Elizabeth's immediate response. "I love sweets," she explained later, and the idea of giving them up for the sake of the homeless women "was part of my whole spirituality—denying myself so others might benefit." Besides, she said, John's challenge played into deep-seated, pervasive feelings of guilt, of never measuring up to her own expectations, never believing she had done enough.

Talking among themselves shortly after this incident, the five sisters who ran the shelter discovered that John had been speaking in the same way to each of them separately. To Sister Catherine he suggested that everyone stop eating meat and fish, because killing animals was an act of violence; the shelter, he said, should be totally nonviolent, dedicated to creating peace in lives that were victimized by violence. He asked Sister Monica if she couldn't finally quit smoking. Each day he would take one of them aside and harass her about some issue that pressed on her own weak point.

Thus began an insidious campaign to gain control over the nuns, a relentless siege of psychological manipulation and coercion. John was forever preaching at them, two sisters complained to me at the time; he always had the last word and had to be right. His "first victory," as Elizabeth viewed it, was prevailing on them to make the house vegetarian. On the surface this change seemed benign, for the food served to the homeless women suddenly improved drastically. But the underlying issue was "who was going to have power," and in pursuit of this end John eventually pushed the nuns themselves to the point where—in the middle of a very cold winter—they were subsisting on nothing but fresh fruit and water. ("I was ravenous all the time. I could never eat enough, I was so empty," Elizabeth recalled.) This diet—touted by John as both healing and more spiritual, and accepted by the nuns as a form of fasting—weakened them mentally as well as physically, diminishing their resistance to his continued assaults.

Once, after they had made a painful decision to force a violent, uncontrollable woman to leave the shelter, John painted her as Jesus

Christ and Sister Monica as Pontius Pilate. "Don't you realize it's bitter cold out there?" he repeated over and over, wearing them down until they questioned a decision they had originally felt quite clear about. In the same way he criticized every other decision they made that signaled an unwillingness to give without limits. He also castigated them for their reluctance to let go of relationships and achievements that were personally dear to them. He told Catherine, for example, that she wasn't really living in poverty and never could, especially because she wouldn't give up social work school and her goal of becoming a professional. Heaping psychological abuse on them when they questioned him, sowing doubt in their minds about one another, he broke down their faith in their own perception of reality, and within a few months had created a virtual mini-cult within the shelter—which yet remained invisible to most everyone else, including me.

I had no inkling that something strange was going on until the day things actually came to a head. Late on that typically chaotic Monday, when the constantly ringing phone and doorbell vied with the endless demands of the shelter residents, I was waiting impatiently for the nuns to emerge from a meeting upstairs. They were still the fountain of strength I depended on for practical advice and also for the moral energy it took to respond to the desperately needy homeless women. But the sisters had been mysteriously absent all afternoon.

When they finally appeared, each vanished into the swirling needs of the residents and other volunteers wanting help. Seizing my chance, I cornered Sister Sara at the foot of the stairs. But for once she didn't give me all her attention; her eyes had a faraway look.

In their meeting, she confided, the nuns had reached a momentous decision. They had founded the shelter out of a mission to aid the most outcast members of society, whom they saw as the shopping bag ladies camped out on the sidewalks in their neighborhood. In accordance with their vows, the nuns lived in the shelter with the homeless women, ate (until John changed their diet) the same food, and wore mostly the same donated clothing.

But now, Sara informed me, they had decided to go still further in order to truly "become one with the homeless." They would renounce absolutely everything that differentiated them from the homeless, or that prevented their being able to give themselves totally to the homeless. This meant vacations, except the kind that, as she put it, "fill us up again for more giving"; it meant friends; and it meant families.

"I've been loved, and I'm not poor," declared twenty-eight-year-old Sara fervently, explaining her decision to say good-bye to her family and separate from them forever. "Instead of writing to me," she would tell her mother, "write to someone who *is* poor and love *them.*"

For a moment I was speechless. "That's a lot to ask of someone," I said finally.

"Yes," she responded, "but how else are people going to really help the poor? There are so many poor." Sara seemed to feel that by removing herself from her mother in this way, she was leaving a space that some homeless person could fill—and that by this act she was leading others toward similar acts. "Instead of standing on the sidelines and talking about it," she added, "why not *do* it?"

Why, indeed? Sara had touched a sensitive spot in me. Was I doing all that *I* could do for the poor? I came to the shelter once a week, but the rest of the time I led my regular life; *I* hadn't taken a vow of poverty. Yet every Monday I saw women in desperate straits that tore my heart out. How much should I be giving? More time? More money? Part of my apartment? I had been struggling to find a line beyond which I didn't have to give more; and now Sara had wiped all the lines away.

Yet I found myself resisting her logic. "What you're doing is really kind of inhuman," I told her, "though I can see how you feel it's necessary. But do you realize what an extreme act it is?"

She shook her head.

Sacrifice and the Feminine Ideal

"When I leave here in the evening," I went on, "I always ask myself how it is that I'm going to a home and these women have none. I've always felt that conflict, but I can't do what you're doing."

"Until you do you'll always feel that conflict," Sara answered.

I hesitated. For a split second I felt a vacuum in the air, like an indrawn breath. "Then I might just have to feel it the rest of my life," I heard myself saying. My vocation, I added, was being a writer, for which I needed solitude; and there were other things I wanted and couldn't give up. It was as though another part of me, with a knowledge the first part didn't have, had decided to speak up.

I have never forgotten the disturbing, even horrifying experience of looking into Sara's eyes as she told me how she planned to cut herself off from her mother. They were impersonal, as though she had passed beyond the everyday human realm of family feeling. For Sara, however, this renunciation was simply the next step in the spiritual path the nuns were following.

By definition, nuns embrace sacrifice: they take vows of poverty, chastity, and obedience. And for this group, creating the shelter was not just a form of social service but part of their spiritual vocation. Since their goal was to "be with" the homeless women, inviting them into the shelter also meant inviting them into a spiritual community in which the nuns and the homeless were one. To Sara it made sense to renounce everything that stood in the way of this oneness.

But I went home that night and cried. In part, I think, my tears were a compensation for Sara's own failure to feel the pain of what she was doing (I kept thinking of how her mother would react when presented with the instruction to love some poor person in Sara's place). But they also represented relief—at having found out that for me, at least, there was some sort of line.

I didn't know yet that the drastic decision to renounce everything in order to "become one with the homeless" had originated with John. It was, in fact, the prerequisite to the grand finale of his whole scheme. For John believed that he could read the signs of the times, and that the Second Coming was at hand. His plan was that he and the nuns would walk out onto the streets, with the poor leading them, and proclaim this to the world, with the help of TV coverage.

At the last moment, the nuns awoke from their brainwashed state and told him to leave the shelter, but the experience was shattering. It left them empty inside, literally self-less, and left the rest of the shelter community (including me) profoundly shaken. Several sisters were so devastated that they couldn't remain at the shelter. Although other nuns arrived to keep it going, the heady and potent "community of spirit" that the five original sisters had created was eventually replaced by a more conventional social service operation.

Even though I wasn't directly involved, John's takeover reverberated in me for years, as though it had activated a harmonic chord in my psyche that wouldn't stop vibrating. Having become connected to the nuns' intense community of spirit despite not sharing their religion, I felt implicated in its loss. Having also believed in their strength, I felt undermined by their vulnerability to John's assault. And having subscribed to their nonprofessional approach to the homeless women, I was left struggling to validate it.

As I rethought the whole experience, what emerged as key was the nuns' propensity for self-sacrifice. This was the vulnerable point at which John had first applied pressure; and the self-doubt engendered by his condemnations of them for initially resisting his demand that they give themselves totally to the poor was what enabled him to consolidate his power.

Still, religious indoctrination in the virtue of self-sacrifice couldn't be the whole story, for I had had no religious training at all, yet I too tortured myself over the question of how much to give. And despite being a thoroughly secular, nonobservant Jew, I had certainly bought into the nuns' vision of their mission in an uncritical way that meant I must have shared with them some blind spot that had nothing to do with Christian ideology. It seemed to me that comprehending John's ability to destroy the initial vision of the shelter, with its unique success in reaching out to frightened, wary homeless women, would require an inquiry into the fundamental meaning of sacrifice.

My ensuing research revealed that the nuns' ideal of renunciation was only a magnified version of a mandate that is widespread in our culture, exerting particular pressure on women; the enlargement simply enables us to see the details more clearly. In urging more and more sacrifice on Elizabeth and the others, John took advantage of an imperative that stretches back centuries to the central image of Western culture: the suffering Christ on the cross. As nuns they were particularly attuned to this image, but few of us are unaffected by its legacy, for it permeates our culture.

Christian Virtue and Women's Role

It was Christianity that made self-sacrifice the "first principle of the moral world": "The crucified Christ put on Christians' conscience an unlimited obligation to sacrifice self in all things," while by extension self-deprivation, pain, and suffering became associated with virtue, nobility of character, and spiritual edification.[1] Whereas other traditions, such as Buddhism or Jewish mysticism, found God in "joy and tranquillity," prominent traditions within Christianity—especially the Protestantism that shaped American culture—emphasized pain and suffering. Martin Luther, for example, asserted that "God can be found only in suffering and the Cross."[2]

Some scholars have suggested that Christianity's emphasis on self-sacrifice grew out of the need to counteract Western men's tendency toward overweening pride and self-assertion, which separated them from God or the larger, cosmic whole. But self-sacrifice has never been an appropriate ideal for women, whose fault is, rather, excessive self-denial and an inability to assert themselves except on behalf of someone else.[3]

Certainly the valuation of suffering affected men and women differently. Originally, the sexes were equally prone to seek out suffering to achieve spiritual goals. The Christian saints of the fourteenth century, for example, are famous for their extreme acts of piety. While men were more likely to relinquish wealth and possessions, and women more likely to mortify their bodies—fasting, refusing to sleep, flagellating themselves—both sexes engaged in all these practices.[4]

This equivalence reflected the equal economic importance of women's and men's work in maintaining the family and society. But beginning in the eighteenth century, industrial development increasingly moved production of household items, which for centuries women had manufactured, out of the home. Economic growth led to an increase in wealth among middle-class families that freed more and more women from working in a family business, working for wages outside the home, and even from performing heavy household labor within it.[5]

As a result, women's and men's roles increasingly diverged, until by the nineteenth century they were totally distinct. Women and men came to be defined in terms of the separate "spheres" they occupied: the home for women, everywhere else for men.[6] No longer required to work, middle-class women acquired symbolic functions: as elegantly dressed evidence of their husbands' financial success and as guardians of morality. While men engaged in the aggressive, brutish behavior of the business world, women were entrusted with preserving the spiritual virtues that their men had to ignore to function effectively in the marketplace.[7] Since Western Christian culture identified virtue and morality with self-sacrifice and renunciation, sacrifice became women's responsibility.

By the middle of the nineteenth century, as Chapter 4 will show, self-sacrifice had come virtually to define the feminine character. Woman, wrote the French historian Jules Michelet, whose 1859 book *Woman* was enormously popular in the United States, was "the altar." Her ability to sacrifice herself for a man "places her higher than man, and makes her a religion."[8] A perfect woman was "always ready to concede her own pain lest others should suffer," wrote the American moralist T. S. Arthur in 1845. And an essayist in the periodical *Christian Wreath* affirmed that while "man lives for himself...woman lives...for all.... She cannot be said to live—even for herself. She is forgotten in the unfoldings of her duty."[9] We still embrace this notion of woman as self-sacrificer, which coexists uneasily and unstably with the more recent concept that women *should* live for themselves.

The epitome of this ideal was the "Angel in the House," the pure, devotedly self-renouncing middle-class wife and mother, subject of a long poem published between 1854 and 1862 by the English writer Coventry Patmore. "A rapture of submission lifts / Her life into celestial rest," he exulted.[10] Notice how his language, like Michelet's, paints domestic self-sacrifice as a form of ecstatic spirituality: this merging of the mundane and the celestial is central to women's relation to the practice of sacrifice.

"In those days," recalled Virginia Woolf acidly seventy years later, "every house had its Angel."

> She was intensely sympathetic. She was immensely charming. She was utterly unselfish. She excelled in the difficult arts of family life. She sacrificed herself daily. If there was chicken, she took the leg; if there was a draught she sat in it—in short she was so constituted that she never had a mind or a wish of her own, but preferred to sympathize always with the minds and wishes of others.

Woolf goes on to recount how, in order to become a writer, she herself had to slay the Angel, who hovered over her as she sat at her desk, cautioning her not to say what she truly thought.[11]

Woolf presented this description of the Angel in a speech to an audience of pioneering young women who were entering professions previously closed to them, such as law and medicine. She ended by exhorting them to persevere in battling the hindrances remaining from the nineteenth century. Another seventy years have passed since she spoke, but we still battle the Angel.

Certainly we did at the shelter, where, I concluded, our critical failure was an inability to come to terms with the limits of self-sacrifice. For me as for these Catholic religious women, and for other women in our culture, the virtue of self-sacrifice—of selflessness—was a lesson that we absorbed imperceptibly as we grew up. It functions like a tinted filter coloring our judgment when we confront experiences that in Western culture are intimately associated with sacrifice: guilt, suffering, and pain.

The takeover of the nuns happened nearly twenty years before this writing. At the time I thought they were caught in a kind of vestigial prefeminist mentality that would wither away as the women's movement widened its influence. Yet as the century ended, all sorts of women were still being seduced by the siren song of the call to sacrifice.

A Contemporary Sacrifice

"Let me tell you what I did to myself to make Bobby happy," said Marilyn, shaking her head ruefully. "For ten years, I put my life on hold so he could play hockey." Founder of a nonprofit arts organization that used theater to build community in New York City neighborhoods, Marilyn helped generate understanding and affection among different age, ethnic, and racial groups that feared and distrusted one another. But while she was developing this work that empowered other people, Marilyn sacrificed her personal life to a sport—and a lifestyle—she hated.

It started when her son Bobby, at five, turned out to be a talented ice-skater. Starting at a local rink in Brooklyn, then progressing to lessons in Manhattan, Bobby soon joined a New Jersey farm team, which toured every weekend and practiced three days a week.

Sacrifice and the Feminine Ideal

Marilyn and Bobby's father Jack were divorced and had joint custody. Under the schedule they had set up, being with Bobby in any meaningful way meant taking him at six A.M. on Sunday to New Jersey, and again on Tuesday after school. He was then in the second grade.

Bobby played hockey through his junior year in high school, and every weekend he toured. "Every other weekend I was on the road," Marilyn said. "If I hadn't done that, I would not have seen him. But it was an unbelievable ordeal. I was always tired; my life was discombobulated. I spent years of time in stinky run-down motels." She had nothing in common with the other parents at the games. "I was the only one without a killer mentality. I saw kids get badly hurt, and I couldn't stand it." She was the only single parent, and the odd woman out; she always felt alone.

Because her work was so demanding, she gave up every other activity. "I had no personal life. All I did was work and take care of my son. It cut me off from the neighborhood community of other parents because Bobby was never here. I never went to his high-school graduation, because he was away. I devoted the best years of my life to doing this ridiculous thing." Nevertheless she was unwilling to give up any of her designated time with Bobby, fearing that if she did so, she would lose him completely, since Jack loved his son's prowess and relished his own weekends on the road with his new girlfriend and the other hockey-obsessed parents.

Marilyn was dynamic and financially independent, and she and her ex-husband prided themselves on their egalitarian beliefs. Yet they wound up playing out a nineteenth-century scenario. "I was noble and self-sacrificing about joint custody," she remembered. "Even in working out our schedule, I was accommodating." She was sure that if instead they had had a little girl who wanted to be a figure skater, her ex-husband would have never given her the support he gave Bobby; figure skating would not have appealed to him as ice hockey did, and he lacked that self-sacrificing impulse. "Jack would have said it wasn't worth it; he wouldn't have paid fifty percent of the costs as I did. I went along with it and tried to encourage Bobby to do what he wanted to, though it meant sacrifice to me and my life. Jack would never have done that."

Recounting this experience still brought Marilyn to the verge of tears, even though Bobby was now in college and her days of touring were well past. If giving up her life so that her son could play hockey was noble and right, why did she feel so wounded? And if she found it so painful, why during those ten years couldn't she obtain some relief? Why did she continue to pay half the costs, when Bobby's father made much more money than she did? Beneath these questions lies a more basic one: why, for women, does self-sacrifice often equal self-betrayal?

"Burnt Toast Syndrome"

Women's propensity for excessive self-sacrifice is so well known it's a cliché, a staple of magazine articles and self-help books. We're so used to it that we take for granted much behavior which, viewed from a normal perspective (that is, try to imagine a man doing it), appears morbid. "Think of all the women who wear clothes they don't like because their husbands like them," my friend Bonnie suggested. "I myself used to buy—and eat—calf's liver, which I loathed, because my husband liked it." That hit close to home: I used to never wear pants because *my* husband hated them.

Bonnie and I are hardly unique. Magazines are full of advice for women like Karen, who "changed her whole style of dressing in the name of love," getting "gussied up" in "makeup and jewelry and high-heeled shoes" to please "the new man in her life," even though her own taste ran to "neutral tones, low-heeled shoes; jeans and sweatshirts at home." Or Rhoda, who after her marriage broke up found herself "crying in the supermarket because I didn't know what I wanted to eat. We always ate what *he* wanted."[12]

Sacrifice and the Feminine Ideal

The harmful effects of self-sacrifice are so widespread among women that Christiane Northrup, M.D., an expert on women's health, has given them a diagnosis: "burnt toast syndrome." This is "not a disease itself," she writes. "But it can *cause* many serious female health problems. It occurs in women who always put others first— and settle for what's left. Like the burnt piece of toast. Or a husband always working late. Or a life spent in service to others."[13] Dr. Northrup links many common physical symptoms such as lumps in the breast, uterine fibroids, and even cancer and heart disease to years of self-deprivation, of sacrificing one's own aspirations and putting the needs of others first.

In the same way, women also jeopardize their financial well-being. Too many women "sacrifice their careers for their husbands" and therefore don't develop pensions or savings plans that can assure their future in case of death or divorce, explains Phyllis Wordhouse, a certified financial planner and financial educator. "Because women are the nurturing sex, they want to make sure everyone else in their family is secure before they think about themselves."[14] Even financially comfortable women may lead lives of constant self-denial, refusing to spend money on themselves not only for simple inexpensive pleasures, but for things they really need. These "self-depriving women" are "momentarily soothed by feelings of being ennobled through self-sacrifice.... The fantasy of virtue through martyrdom is a powerful motivator for repeated self-depriving behavior."[15]

Women also often sabotage themselves professionally, undermining their careers to protect the feelings of a lover, husband, parent, or sibling who reacts to the prospect of their success with humiliation or resentment.[16] More subtly—yet more tellingly—they may do this even when there is nobody to protect. Carmen, who had a doctorate in education from a prestigious institution, was selected for a national fellowship that would bring her to Washington, D.C., to study federal education policy. But the very day she was supposed to move to the capital, she decided not to go—for it meant leaving behind the bilingual education program she had created at her school, which, as she put it, "was my baby." She called Washington and spoke to the national director of the fellowship program, a woman who told her, "You're doing something that only women do." Women, the director explained—she had never known a man to do this—become attached to projects or jobs as if these were their babies, and can't let go. Consequently they block the personal growth they could achieve if they were willing to move on. "The minute I heard that," Carmen said, "I realized I was sacrificing my own development for an institution that had no commitment to me." She changed her plans again and rushed to Washington.

Self-abnegation may go still deeper. Many women consciously and deliberately sacrifice their own feelings—as when they fake orgasms because they're more concerned with their lovers' pleasure than with making sure they experience pleasure themselves. "Many women still have no concept that their bodies and their sexuality exist for themselves—no concept that their lives can be lived for themselves," remarks therapist Harriet Goldhor Lerner. They think of this "pretending" as something "done in the service of enhancing another person at the expense of the self." "To be worthy of being called 'a good Black woman,' sisters must be self-sacrificing and long-suffering," writes Susan Taylor, the editor of *Essence*. "These are the messages our culture continues to send us."[17]

Women absorb these messages early. Journalist Peggy Orenstein, who spent a year talking to eighth-grade girls, found that they were already completely indoctrinated by "the lessons of the hidden curriculum," which emphasize niceness, teaching girls "to value silence and compliance, to view those qualities as a virtue." The girls responded by developing an ideal of a relentlessly selfless "perfect girl" who is both "perfectly nice" and "perfectly smart." But to become this girl they had to squelch all their negative feelings. The result: anorexia, panic attacks, thoughts of suicide—at the age of thirteen![18]

Sacrifice and the Feminine Ideal

Books and articles offer psychological and social explanations for why such girls turn into women who are, as one book's title puts it, "too good for their own good."[19] Experts point to dysfunctional family dynamics and "toxic parents"—mothers who give mixed messages, perfectionist fathers. They invoke social messages instructing women that their nature is to be nurturing: "cultural teachings...that women should strengthen men, and our bond with them, by relinquishing our own strength." Some writers point to the greater social power of men, which compels women to hide their true feelings "as a matter of self-preservation."[20] Academic researchers have further documented how women's willingness to sacrifice their careers—taking jobs that are less remunerative and less fulfilling than they might otherwise be able to get—for the sake of their family responsibilities arises from an early socialization that emphasizes connectedness and the value of caring for the needs of others.[21]

Yet none of these explanations has successfully disposed of the Angel in the House. Adults like Marilyn continue to sacrifice themselves in contradiction of their own principles, while young girls turn into new Angels. The truth is that women won't be able to stop sacrificing in these self-defeating ways until they learn what appropriate sacrifice really is. To date, however, they have no models to work with, for while the experts reject the inappropriate types of sacrifice described above, no one has identified a more developed or evolved form that can benefit other people without betraying the self.[22]

Constructive sacrifice is harder to recognize in our individualistic, rationalist culture, because it occurs at what might be called a collective, or transpersonal, or even spiritual level of experience. Because Western culture defines humans as rational, autonomous beings, set apart from the rest of the cosmos and set against one another, our perceptions are shaped by a mental splitting-off process that separates mind from body, man (associated with mind or spirit) from woman (associated with matter or flesh), and self from other. Despite paying lip service to the value of community, we don't profoundly acknowl-edge the validity and virtue of interconnectedness.

One casualty of this splitting-off process is constructive sacrifice. As Chapter 4 will explain, sacrifice was originally a method for achieving a sense of expansiveness through creation of a larger unity. But that aspect of it was lost, and we were left with the familiar Chris-tian ideal of self-sacrifice, with its valuation of pain and suffering for their own sake. It was this truncated version that came to define women's nature.

This book pulls together a range of approaches—historical, soci-ological, psychological, anthropological—to construct a comprehen-sive, integrated concept of sacrifice that points beyond simple analysis of a problematic female behavior to our culture's fundamental modes of thinking and perceiving. For it is not some essence of female nature that causes women to be overly self-sacrificing, but rather a basic component of psyche and society.

Slaying the Mermaid

So far, in laying out the destructive aspects of sacrifice, I have deployed psychology, sociology, and history. Now, to uncover its lost constructive aspect, we move into the realm of myth, for myth extends our individual experience out into that of the collective. We have seen that women today are still haunted by a phantom that tor-ments them, as the Angel in the House did Virginia Woolf, and ought to be laid to rest. Slaying her requires seeing her clearly and under-standing her thoroughly, so I am going to raise this specter here, although in an incarnation more suited to our time.

To those who know only the Disney movie version, Hans Chris-tian Andersen's Little Mermaid may not initially seem the most logi-cal embodiment of the sacrificial spirit. But the film leaves out some gruesome elements of Andersen's original tale. In order to acquire human legs so she can go on land and make the prince fall in love with her, the mermaid obtains from a sea witch a magic potion. Drinking it, the witch warns her, will make her feel "as if a sword were going through your body." And once she does have legs, "every time your foot touches the ground it will feel as though you were walking on knives so sharp that your blood must flow." Andersen dwells on the pain and bleeding of the mermaid's feet as she dances for the prince and climbs mountains with him: "But she suffered it gladly," he assures us.[23]

The mermaid's sacrifice, however, is more than an expression of her devotion to the prince; it is also a quest for transcendence. When she learns from her grandmother that, unlike humans, mer-people do not have immortal souls, she is possessed by a longing for one. "I would give all my three hundred years of life for only one day as a human being if, afterward, I should be allowed to live in the heavenly world," she sighs. As it happens, this is possible, but "only if a man should fall so much in love with you that you were dearer to him than his mother and father." If he married her, "then his soul would flow into your body and you would be able to partake of human happiness," the grandmother explains.[24]

Despite the mermaid's devotion, the prince marries someone else, which dooms her to death according to the terms of her bargain with the witch. Rejecting the opportunity to save herself by stabbing him with a knife her sisters have obtained for her, she throws the knife away, sacrificing her own life instead. But because she has "suffered and borne [her] suffering bravely," instead of dying she is transformed into a "daughter of the air," a spirit with a transparent, ethereal body. She now has the chance to obtain an immortal soul by doing good deeds.[25]

Transcending the preoccupations of the flesh to connect to a realm of ultimate truth is, of course, the purpose of penitential practices like those of the Christian saints. This vision of salvation, in fact, is what makes the idea of sacrifice so potently seductive. It is not to a transcendent reality that the mermaid tries to connect, however, but to a mortal man; her salvation will come by means of his soul flowing into her body. Human women, too, have been said to need an intermediary in this matter; as Milton put it in *Paradise Lost,* "He for God only, she for God in him." The reason the prince's soul can flow into the mermaid is that she is empty. Her own self was emptied out when she sacrificed her true nature as a sea creature to live on land in pursuit of a fantasy.

In religious terms, "salvation" means deliverance from sin and other evils of life into knowledge of ultimate truth, or God. But people also seek a secular version of it: we all want to be released from feeling bad or unhappy into a sense of being virtuous and justified in the world, or of achieving a satisfying fullness of being. Whether religious or secular, the goal is to feel connected with the source of goodness. The danger, for most women today, lies in seeing that source as another person.

Sacrifice, of course, is a time-honored way to achieve salvation. In true spiritual sacrifice, the individual self merges directly into an authentic, impersonal source of goodness; the secular version may involve dedication to some work or service perceived as greater than the self. But if, like the mermaid, one simply hands the self over to another limited human being, one sacrifices it without transcending or achieving anything. One does achieve a delusion of transcendence—a voluptuous feeling of noble martyrdom. But this type of martyrdom does not have noble consequences.

Like many women, the mermaid confuses spiritual transcendence with the exalted devotion that is idealized as a pattern for human love (recall the spiritualized language of Patmore and Michelet). She embodies women's tendency to seek salvation through sacrificing the self for another person instead of through self-transformation. Nor does this confusion necessarily involve romantic love: the nuns accepted John as an intermediary in their mission to "the poor." In either case, women tend to identify so closely with the virtue of being self-less that we literally lose ourselves in giving, as though having and being make us uncomfortable. And as we start to disappear, Western culture cheers us on.

Sacrifice Versus Power

The image of the Little Mermaid joins the glorification of suffering and self-sacrifice to the loss of the self and a corresponding relinquishment of personal power. For beyond individual questions of guilt, the desire for transcendence, and indoctrination in an ideal, the fundamental issue underlying sacrifice is power. In the following chapters we will see how the valuation of sacrifice spirals through different levels of our lives, intertwined with the issue of power.

Most often, self-sacrifice is a practice of the powerless. "Christianity is pre-eminently the religion of slaves…slaves cannot help belonging to it, and I among others," wrote the twentieth-century French philosopher Simone Weil, whom we will meet later, for she provides another spectacular example of highly dubious self-sacrifice.[26] Weil too elevated suffering to a transcendent value; but this was because she believed that in a society like ours, built on great inequalities of power, for the powerless suffering is the only path to transcendence.

Chapter 9 will explore the implications of this social imbalance. Here I want to emphasize how destructive self-sacrifice destroys what power people do have. After her sacrifice, the mermaid becomes a cripple, unable to walk without pain, literally lacking a secure footing. In the same way, once the nuns acceded to the sacrifices John demanded, they lost their own firm standpoint and became pushovers for his absurd dictates. And it was Marilyn's initial sacrifice of her needs that left her in a powerless position, so that her subsequent actions were dominated by her fear of losing Bobby.

Indeed, inappropriate sacrifice winds up subverting all sorts of personal and social ventures, from intimate relationships to social service missions to political movements. "I got to see Bobby," Marilyn recalled of her excruciating weekends on the road, "but he told me later how much he resented it because I was such a drag." One observer at the shelter noticed that as the nuns became more involved in John's scheme, they spent less and less time actually ministering to the homeless women they had dedicated themselves to serving. And I have known advocates for the homeless so possessed by the spirit of sacrifice that they practically became homeless themselves. Naturally this severely limited their resources, making their advocacy less effective. Their major achievements were a monumental self-righteousness and the ability to induce guilt in other people—hardly a socially beneficial motivator.

Because our culture places so much value on sacrifice and suffering, people who feel aggrieved, like those advocates, are likely to cling to their victimhood as a badge of merit and become enraptured with their own suffering. Anger and resentment do generate a surge of energy that provides an illusion of power and strength, but ultimately these emotions are counterproductive.

Amy, a community activist, habitually did much of the "grunt work" that nobody else in her community group would take on. Sitting before her computer one day, putting together a summary of the group's bylaws, she grew resentful, even though she had volunteered for the task. With the resentment came a surge of adrenaline, and it occurred to Amy that what looked like sacrifice or selfless service on her part might actually be a form of addiction to that adrenaline rush. To experience the rush, she needed something to provoke her resentment, which was why she took on these tedious tasks. As a consequence, her activism was tainted and her energy wasted.

Amy conjectured further that her "addiction" to the adrenaline rush was somehow tied to chronic pain she suffered from a whiplash injury. She had, in fact, discovered the connection between sacrifice, physical pain, negative emotion, and the ability to act effectively, which Chapter 9 will explore further. Here I simply note that pain— as philosophers and scientists both have remarked—is an isolating experience that cuts us off from human community and the empathy engendered by connection.[27] Yet originally, sacrifice was not about suffering.

Sacrificial rites are among the earliest forms of worship known. They were intended to create communion between the human and the divine, a connection whose beneficial power strengthened not only individuals but the whole community. Over time, this expansive, empowering, collective meaning of sacrifice—in which whatever is forfeited is not lost, because as part of a cyclic movement it returns in the form of other benefits—has largely been forgotten. My project here is to reclaim it, translate it into modern, secular terms, and build a new interpretation upon its ancient meaning.

The process begins with a shift in consciousness that alters our perception of previously unquestioned behavior. This happened to Amy when she realized that her own self-sacrifice was rooted in physical pain and the energy rush of resentment, not in the inherent necessity of the tedious jobs she took on. All at once the rationale she had constructed for performing them fell away, leaving her free to evaluate the importance of each task and make a choice about it. Once her inner feeling of compulsion was gone, so was Amy's resentment, and the energy bound up in resentment was released for more productive, satisfying work.

Various stimuli can trigger this kind of perceptual shift. It may occur spontaneously, like Amy's, or through imaginative identification with a mythic figure like the Little Mermaid, as it did for me. And it can also happen when new knowledge strips away the accumulation of centuries of cultural imprinting. The following chapters offer historical information, analysis of contemporary examples from popular culture and everyday life, and powerful mythic images, all as tools readers can use to reconceptualize their own experience.

There can hardly be a single woman in our culture who hasn't struggled with the conditioning that tells her she's no good unless she consistently disregards herself to put other people first. "It's so ingrained," one friend remarked, "you do it with your *dogs.*" Sacrifice should be a choice, not an obligation; it should enlarge the self, instead of diminishing it. Accordingly the following pages develop a model of sacrifice that balances autonomous individuality with the awareness that our own welfare can flow from the well-being of others.

2

Queen for a Day:
The Rewards of Virtue

"I WANT A HOUSE AND SOME FOOD," THE YOUNG WOMAN IS SAYING, barely above a whisper. Young, pretty, blond, she wears a styleless straight skirt and dark shirt with a pale cardigan—you can't see the colors, for this is a grainy black-and-white TV image. What's clear is that she's gripped by an affliction so enormous she barely knows where she is.

It's March 1956, and Mrs. Ellen Brewer is contestant number three on today's episode of *Queen for a Day*—the "Cinderella show" that grants the dearest wish of the most pathetic among five hard-luck women who each weekday afternoon provide nonfiction soap opera to a nationwide audience. Number one has asked for power tools for her laid-up father-in-law. Number two wants a washer-dryer so she won't have to keep doing the laundry for her five children by hand. Fairly humdrum requests—in fact, number one tried to spice hers up a bit by claiming that the tools would give her father-in-law "saw-curity."

But Mrs. Brewer is of another order. A mother of four, whose truck driver husband is in the hospital (he had an accident and then pneumonia twice), she gazes at Jack Bailey, the show's avuncular host, with the teary helplessness of a little girl waiting for Daddy to make it better. He has to prompt her for each desperate detail of her tale of woe.

"We live in a trailer camp and we haven't paid our rent, and the man come over last night and said we have to be out by tomorrow. We don't have any money," she adds, in a rising wail. "My mother and father live with us, and they're not able to work." The camera repeatedly cuts to her hands, ceaselessly wringing a handkerchief.

"If you're elected our queen, we'll get you the food, and we will get you the house, and you had a smile a minute ago, well, you put that back on," admonishes Bailey jocularly. She smiles reflexively but her mouth can't stretch the whole way; it trembles and, as she returns to her seat, her expression relapses into wistful misery.

Number four, up next, asks for a secret meeting with her real mother, who gave her up for adoption—to be arranged without the knowledge of the mother's husband, who doesn't know she ever had this baby. As number five approaches Bailey, Mrs. Brewer can be seen behind her, sniffling into a handkerchief. Number five would like a new bicycle for her boy. Since his old one broke, she's been getting up at four in the morning to take him on his paper route. He gave her the money to come here today—which is his birthday, she adds gratuitously, trying to extract maximum pathos from a not very pathetic situation.

So it's not surprising that when the moment of judgment arrives, Mrs. Brewer wins hands down—or, more precisely, hands up, since the contest is decided by the volume of audience applause registered on an "applause meter" superimposed over the contestants' faces. Still apparently overwhelmed by her inner vision of imminent disaster,

Queen for a Day: The Rewards of Virtue

Mrs. Brewer barely reacts as the female attendants drape a fur-trimmed cloak around her shoulders, set a tiara on her head, and hand her a bunch of roses. But when Bailey announces that she'll be taken to a supermarket to "shop to your heart's content" and that the show will find her a house and pay the rent for six months, her mouth opens and she gasps, then smiles, shaking her head in disbelief.

As Bailey begins to recite all the prizes she'll receive in addition to the granting of her wish, the camera, which has been glued to her face, tears itself away to display these items, as much a part of the show as the contestants. Among much else, there's a vacuum cleaner, a sixty-seven-piece set of china, a dinette set (the audience oohs), a sewing machine ("Ooh! Ahh!"), and a refrigerator (Mrs. Brewer herself gasps over this one). With all the gifts announced, the attendants seat her on a throne, and the camera resumes its tight close-up of her face, which now wears the dazed yet hopeful expression of a dog unused to not being kicked. The audience applauds wildly.

Queen for a Day started out on radio in 1945, became a local TV show in Los Angeles in 1950, and went national in 1955, airing at four-thirty in the afternoon. Its formula, allowing viewers to identify with the contestants' real-life sob stories and then wallow vicariously in the flood of consumer items that compensated the winners for their pain, was irresistible. Within a few months, *Queen* was the number one daytime show, watched by 13 million. It lasted until October 1964.[1] For many women of that time—and their daughters who watched it after school—it remains an icon.

"That was one of my favorite shows," recalled Diane, a forty-two-year-old theater director and performer. "I loved its high emotional intent—the women suffering, trying to outdo one another in who suffered more. I liked to cry—I think it was an identification with my own suffering from having lost my mother."

Diagnosed with breast cancer when she was four months pregnant with Diane's youngest sister, her mother, a devout Catholic, chose to delay treatment, which would have meant an abortion. But in her seventh month, her doctor decided the baby must be born by cesarean so she could have surgery. The cancer went into remission but returned a year or two later, and she died at thirty-five, when Diane was five.

"To me that's the ultimate sacrifice: my mother sacrificed her life for the life of my sister," Diane said. Her mother had a choice, for the Church permits abortion to save the mother's life. However, Diane pointed out, "the social pressures put on a woman at that time, the onus of abortion, and the notion of what a good woman does—the priority of the life of the child—were all very important." Her mother's death left her with a "terrible legacy that I have to consciously fight against," of "putting other people's needs in front of my own." Coupled with a Catholic education which taught her that "the world is a bad place, and somebody's got to be like Christ and make it a better place," this legacy left Diane believing that, even though all her own needs would never be met, she should be taking care of other people's.

Diane's painful legacy and the vulgar, blatantly exploitative *Queen* are linked by that central fifties image: woman, the devoted mother-martyr. The crowning of Mrs. Brewer, whose suffering on behalf of her family the TV camera conveyed so voluptuously, was a response not just to her obvious need but to her equally evident virtue—for, as we'll see, her suffering was a badge of her goodness. As Diane recognized, the show's equation of suffering with virtue carried a kind of emotional exaltation that is a modern version of Michelet's and Patmore's spiritualized language of female self-sacrifice, quoted in Chapter 1. In our secular time, however, the queen receives an earthly rather than a heavenly crown. So Mrs. Brewer got not only what she really needed—the house and food—but a shower of consumer goods to reward her virtue.

The women who appeared on *Queen for a Day* were the mothers of the baby boomers—of Diane, and myself as well, who were in our forties and fifties as the nineties drew to a close. Unlike daughters in most historical periods, a lot of us looked at our mothers and said,

"Not me!" But like Diane, most baby boomers did not completely escape their legacy. And their own daughters, while in many respects freer yet, still, when they came face-to-face with the blinding light of the sacrificial ideal, were also often transfixed before it, like a rabbit on the road at night.

Asking women about sacrifice presses a button that makes their eyes light up: "Women are the *agents* of sacrifice!" exclaimed one, when told what my subject was. Another insisted that this was the "central characteristic" of women in our culture. Asked to elaborate, however, everyone had a different notion of what "sacrifice" is really about.

The Vital Substance

Most definitions of sacrifice for women cluster around the idea of motherhood. The essence of this notion was best expressed by Bernice, whose story typifies the trajectory of middle-class women who came of age in the fifties and early sixties.

Bernice described herself as "a displaced homemaker in an Armani suit." Married for twenty-nine years to a top movie executive, she lived "a grand hello-from-Hollywood life" before her divorce. She had a second home on the ocean; traveled around the world several times; ate expensive meals at three-star restaurants; entertained celebrities, domestic and international. But Bernice is not a member of the Hollywood First Wives Club, for she was the one who walked out of her marriage.

"I was my husband's partner," she recalled, "fused at the hip. We were Mr. and Mrs. America and their three children. I thought that was oneness. I was an extraordinarily good caretaker, and he let me." When people asked what she did, Bernice told them she was a juggler: "I juggled my life and everybody else's, juggled my day so that when my husband and the kids came home, I was there. But I didn't know that what I was sacrificing was myself."

Her husband was "particularly needy of me: I'd take an art class, he'd call me there three times. He performed in the world very well, but when he came home he literally sucked at the breast." Bernice went to the Cannes industry festivals twenty-three times. After the fifteenth time she told her husband, "I can't do this anymore." But he said, "I can't go without you. Please." So she went, because she was "still holding his hand." Yet more and more she felt that she "needed to breathe my own air."

Once her children were grown and gone, she felt she had to stop being "mother" and "tap into 'woman'"—get a job, start a business. "Why didn't I? I think it was that mother role, that self-sacrificing, of my generation. At one point—the kids were already in college—I was invited to join a group of women who were meeting from five o'clock to seven to learn to meditate. My husband didn't even get home until seven, seven-thirty, but it was still a major breakthrough to do this thing *for me.*"

Bernice's husband, unable to comprehend why she was leaving him, fought her in court for four and a half exhausting, demoralizing years. One day, soon after their settlement was finally signed, she "looked down at my rather pendulous breasts. I called a friend and said, 'Give me the name of your plastic surgeon.' Ten days later I had a breast reduction. I was ending that period of mothering, nurturing everybody else."

This is the essence of the mother: pouring out her vital substance to nurture others. But such nurturing is not restricted to literal mothers. Wendy, an artist and performer, was single and young enough to be Bernice's daughter. Whereas Bernice's family was essentially normal, Wendy's was floridly dysfunctional, centering around her older sister's mental illness. In this family's belief system, Wendy's caretaking was considered essential to her sister's happiness and well-being. "The burden of being her friend, let alone her only friend, was almost unbearable," Wendy said. "I became transfixed by the idea that I was being asked to lie down and give my sister a transfusion of all my blood in order to help her be healthy and well. It would have been fine with everyone even if I had died. And it became clear, too, that nobody really expected her to get well from that transfusion, that in some complicated way this involved sacrificing both of us." To survive, Wendy wound up estranging herself from her family.

More often, women let themselves be drained in commonplace ways. Marsha, a fifty-year-old technical writer, happily married, passionately recounted her acute resentment at pouring her energy into taking care of friends who didn't reciprocate. "Taking care" might mean months of helping a friend with cancer—running errands, visiting her at home and in the hospital—or simply going out of her way to keep a date with her cousin's son in order not to hurt his feelings. The sick friend recovered but no longer took any interest in Marsha's own needs or problems; the cousin repaid her consideration by canceling a later plan on a whim, blithely assuming that "Marsha won't mind." She did, but she couldn't say so. "When I get depressed," she explained, "I feel I only exist to help other people, and that all my friendships have to be based on my taking care of them."

When I broke a dinner date with her because of a bad headache, "I couldn't even let you know how I felt," she confessed later. "That's what I think of as sacrificing my needs for someone else. Though my need was so strong for you to understand how I felt and to apologize, I still felt you were in pain and I had no right to impose my needs on you. I wasn't worthy."

Marsha thought she might be modeling herself on her Jewish mother. "When I was growing up, I don't remember my mother ever, ever being sick. I remember her crying when my grandparents died. But she was just always there and always able to take care of everyone. She never had a cold, she never had temperature. As an adult, when I found out that some of my friends' parents had headaches or colds, it shocked me. Mothers don't get headaches, mothers don't get colds."

Women's thinking about sacrifice almost always wends its way back to this source. The most frequent single reaction among the thirty or so women I talked to was epitomized by Anne, who said, "When you asked about sacrifice, I thought about my mother." For some the reaction was, "She sacrificed so much for me and I'm so grateful"; for others, "I looked at what she did and swore my life would be different." A few said their fathers had sacrificed, too (though never quite in the same way). But nobody said, "When I think about sacrifice, I think about my father."

The Mothers' Legacy

Whether a mother's sacrifice was a support or a burden, the awareness of it bit deep into her daughter. "My mother's generation were caregivers and nurturers," Anne explained. "This was the woman's role: she takes the broken chair"—like the Angel in the House, who took the leg of the chicken. Anne's father had food allergies, and at restaurants her mother would order for herself not dishes she liked but food that Anne's father could eat, to provide extra for him, since he would be unable to eat part of his own serving.

"My mother lived through her children. She had nothing else," Anne continued. "This was her decision—it wasn't out of necessity. I and my siblings resented her because our friends' mothers did needlepoint, or painting by numbers, or they golfed—they had something that was their own. Our mother had nothing; it was all her children." The children, in turn, were supposed "to make her happy by fitting the mold." Anne found this "a heavy burden to carry. When I was a teenager, I thought I'd never get married or have children, partly because I didn't want to be like my mother." When Anne did marry and have a son, she thought through the issues carefully, and as we will see, she did it differently.

For Christine's mother, too, "motherhood is the only real accomplishment. Her work"—as a seamstress—"is only in the interest of taking care of her children. She was a terrific mother—we're in awe of what she did." Separated from Christine's father when Christine was two, her mother, an immigrant from the Caribbean, not only raised and supported her three children alone, but deliberately gave up a sexual and romantic life for their sake. Her son by her first husband had been treated badly by Christine's father, and, determined to spare her children the stress of having another stepfather, she never again had a man in her life.

"Being Catholic, it never occurred to me when I was younger that it was odd she didn't remarry, because you can't get divorced," said Christine. But later she realized that her mother could have had a boyfriend. "I felt flattered and loved that someone would make that kind of sacrifice for me. Now I'm at the age she was when her marriage broke up, and I don't know if I'd be willing to do what she did." At the same time, Christine felt "an incredible burden of her children being everything to her. The message was: 'You now have to give up your life for me.' And in a sense we have—we've given up our romantic, sexual lives for her."

A strand of ambivalence threaded through Christine's account, for she saw that her mother's sacrifice had bound her and her siblings into a web that prevented them from developing independent emotional connections. Christine and her sister were approaching forty; her brother was in his late forties. Her sister and brother still lived in their mother's house, and none of the children had ever married. Although for the sisters this was at least partly due to the scarcity of marriageable black men, it was unusual for a heterosexual black man her brother's age not to have married or fathered children. This was not a price Christine paid happily.

Not so Claudia, a thirty-nine-year-old office manager, who asserted roundly, "I'm single as the day I was born, and I like it like that!" The impact of her mother's experience as a single parent "slapped me full in the face, and I said no. Watching my mother was how I learned the word *sacrifice*."

Claudia's mother had been taken out of high school to keep house and care for her ill mother while her two brothers and three sisters were allowed to continue in school. She fell in love with Claudia's father, "the one man who paid attention to her, thought she was witty and intelligent. It was a time when twenty-three-year-old white women didn't get involved with much older black men. People were supposed to be married when they had kids, and she wasn't."

Her family disowned her and Claudia's father left her; she scraped by, working as a typist. "It was hard for her every single day. We never had a year that was good, when everything worked out. She never had success, never had time to take care of herself," though she gave money to her brothers and sisters when they needed doctors. And it was she who cared for her father in his last years.

Claudia remained fiercely loyal to the memory of her mother, who died in 1995, and adamantly resolved not to get caught in the same trap. Her mother, she said, let herself be defined entirely by others: first by her parents, then by Claudia's father, and finally by her children. "She really had nothing of herself that defined her. It takes you so long just to find yourself—that's why I've shied away from being involved with someone else." Claudia did not want to be "redefined every time I'm in another relationship as my mother was. I think it's because of her that I didn't feel pressure to be self-sacrificing myself. I don't think I've ever had to sacrifice anything." But to me, Claudia's satisfaction in having preserved her independence felt chilling; again, a mother's sacrifice had cut her daughter off from other intimate relationships.

Moira, too, while still a young girl, saw her mother caught in a trap, and made it her business to escape the same fate. She grew up in a suburb of Dublin, one of eight children in a culture that laid out an inflexibly predetermined path for women:

> I saw the sacrifices my mother made, by denying a huge
> amount of herself, her intelligence and creativity,
> because she had child after child after child. She'd gone

into a convent as a young woman; it was a way of resisting her eventual fate. The convent was one of the few
opportunities a woman in 1930s Ireland had to develop
herself, and I think there was a part of her that wanted a
spiritual, creative life. But she couldn't manage it, and
she came out, married my dad, and had eight children.
She thought of marriage and having children as a vocation: you just sacrificed everything, the children came
first.

Intellectually she didn't develop. She'd a fine intelligence, and a real love for opera and classical music.
When she entered the convent, she'd given away her
piano, and we couldn't afford a really good one, so we
never had a piano. She always talked about sacrificing
her piano. Her first child was born within a year—there
was never a chance to get that piano back.

As a teenager in the fifties and early sixties, Moira looked at her
mother—cooking, cleaning, and doing laundry for eight children,
without even time to read—and thought, Why do women have to do
this?

We had a tradition that a girl who was getting married
would lay out her whole trousseau in the upstairs
bedroom. Sexy underwear, long white first-night underwear—it was assumed you were a virgin. And there'd
always be the swagger coat—a fifties-type model, usually made of gorgeous Irish tweed. It was a very loose
coat so you could have baby after baby after baby, and it
never looked as if you were huge.

I said to my mother, "I will never wear a swagger
coat!" In that Dublin suburban neighborhood, a swagger
coat symbolized that this is the only life women have. It

was a complete, horrible sacrifice of everything—going by my mother—that was my reality. I looked around and didn't see any role models. But I really believed, There's got to be a better life.

She found it: she left Dublin forever and became an artist— although that entailed its own sacrifices, as we will see.

An account of self-sacrificing mothers wouldn't be complete without a Jewish mother, or at least a Jewish-style mother. "My favorite example of self-sacrifice is my mother," said Wanda, born in Poland, the daughter of a nominally Catholic mother and a Jewish father. Her mother was a brilliant student who planned to study biochemistry at the university. But both her parents died, and she went to work instead to support her two younger siblings.

When she married Wanda's father, she decided that because his career as a physicist had great potential, she would be the one to stay home. Because they had little money, "she never expressed a desire to do anything for herself." Wanda painted a picture of a woman who in any circumstance put her family—especially the children—first and herself last, even to unreasonable lengths that "bordered on martyrdom" when she refused to take care of her health.

All this time, she's going to live with pain because we don't have money for a doctor. She had skin cancer; it took years to get her to have it taken care of. Now it's her varicose veins, which she's had since she was in her twenties. She almost fainted every summer from the pain. No, we don't have the money now; it can wait till later. It was the same with her heart disease. My father probably didn't know about it because she never complains. It's a cultural thing: that's what's expected and she wouldn't question it; she lives for her family. Her son needs a jacket, so she can wait to go to the doctor.

Queen for a Day: The Rewards of Virtue

Although Wanda's mother was obsessed with making sure everyone else ate,

> She herself sometimes doesn't eat enough, and she eats the least expensive food, and keeps what's good and expensive for my brother and me. Both my parents used to do this, but even though we're better off now, my mother still does it. She's gotten a little better, but we still have a family joke: how can you be eating, you already ate this week?

Wanda's Polish Catholic mother rather resembles my Russian Jewish grandmother, who ate the leftovers off everyone else's plates and refused to take even the most innocent opportunity to give herself pleasure: self-sacrifice seemingly for its own sake, to the point of absurdity. "The Jewish mother is really an Eastern European mother," Wanda suggested. "Self-sacrifice is what that cultural context expects of women." If so, the Eastern European mothers, of various ethnicities, brought from the old countries seeds that mingled with native varieties, forming healthy hybrids that flourished in the American climate.

Wanda loved her mother deeply and considered her sacrifice heroic. "I don't condemn her for what she's done. If she hadn't, none of us would be where we are." Joyce, a singer who worked for a nonprofit organization and came from a southern African-American family, saw herself even more broadly as the culmination of a historical advancement.

> In my family, each generation wants its offspring to do better. I have the luxury of doing and being whatever I feel like because my grandmother's generation sacrificed so much. They gave up pursuing their dreams so they could give us things they didn't have. They worked

really hard to give us choices. To my grandmother, having a job, no matter what it is, was more important than finding the right job. It wouldn't have occurred to her to think she didn't like what she was doing. Being happy wasn't a goal, but it is for me. My mother, too, gave up her dream of being a writer. She was expected to get a job, so she did. We don't have stay-at-home women in my family. So she became a teacher. She learned to love it, but there was definitely a settling there.

Joyce's mother and grandmother enabled an entire family to move into the middle class. Wanda's mother made it possible for her husband to devote himself to his career and her children to develop theirs. Sarah's mother also helped keep her immigrant family afloat. The first-generation daughter of poor Russian Jewish immigrants in New York, she sacrificed her desire to be a journalist and instead learned accounting—even though she "hated it with a passion"— which she taught at vocational high schools. Later, when she married Sarah's father, a scientist with a mystical bent who was unhappy working in industry, she provided the support that enabled him to finish a Ph.D. so that he could do pure science at a university while also making a good salary. Only later, when her children were grown, did she get a Ph.D. herself. As Sarah put it, "She allowed him an enormous amount of time with his muse while she kept the universe going. She wanted him to be happy, and his sense of what women give was shaped by the fact that she's given a lot to make his life good." This outlook determined his reaction when Sarah herself, in her mid-forties, decided to live with a man. They felt considerable trepidation, since each had been single until then. "Doesn't he know," inquired her father, "that the woman always gives up more?"

To Laura, a corporate manager, this "enabling" that women do is malignant. A divorced mother of a college-age daughter, Laura defined sacrifice as "putting other people first when you don't want to." Women, she maintained, are conditioned from an early age to do this, and if they don't, they feel they're not good. "Good women enable others. Bad women enable themselves." Her words are echoed by a *Mademoiselle* article advising women "how to break the yes habit." Many of us, the author asserts, are "always putting someone else's needs before our own.... In my house," she confides, "saying no signaled that we were (gasp) selfish, the worst sin of all."[2]

Neither Laura nor *Mademoiselle* was condemning all forms of sacrifice. The question—especially for women, to whom enabling becomes second nature—is, When is sacrifice appropriate? And how do we decide?

To answer these questions we need criteria to judge by, and I propose two. In all the accounts above, from women of widely varying backgrounds, two basic issues appear. The first involves the question of choice. Did the woman act consciously, deliberately? Or was she blindly impelled by her cultural conditioning? As Maria, whose family is from Puerto Rico, put it: "What is it we learn from our mothers and grandmothers and aunts about sacrifice that we do routinely, without being clear if it's something we want to do or not?"

The second issue is the question of what, exactly, is being sacrificed. Anne and Claudia believed their mothers had given up their entire beings and had no self left. Wanda and Moira lamented the loss of creative or professional potential that diminished their mothers' self-development. But to Joyce, who recognized the historical necessities that shaped the choices of a black family in the South, though her mother and grandmother had lost potential, they were not diminished; to her, what they did made them larger.

The interplay of these two components—the degree of choice and the effect of the sacrifice on a woman's sense of self—is key to evaluating all the sacrifices that the following chapters describe. I begin by looking at sacrifice in the context of personal relationships. The next chapter widens the focus to the workplace and the larger community.

"If They're Happy, I'm Happy"

For me, the hardest stories to hear were from women who had spent years so submerged in husband and children that they resembled the Sleeping Beauty—only it was the prince's kiss that had put them to sleep in the first place. When they awoke, it was to a poignant awareness of the time they had lost.

At forty-six, Denise looked back over the previous twenty-five years and sighed. Since 1967, when she was sixteen and worked part-time as a dental assistant, she had wanted to be a dentist. But instead she married young and gave up college to become a dental hygienist. Her struggling Jewish parents said it was "a great profession for a woman because it wouldn't prevent her from being married and staying home with the kids. I was making these choices to please everyone and live up to family expectations. I really didn't want to do any of this stuff."

Denise's first marriage broke up; in her second marriage,

> I became Susie Homemaker, the June Cleaver role, cooking and cleaning and being transportation engineer. Not looking for anything that makes me happy, but thinking if they're happy, then I'm happy. If I can make them brilliant in school, then I'll be satisfied. If I cook a gourmet meal, with candles, for Bill when he walks through the door, then I'm successful. But I was hating every minute of it toward the end, and I didn't know why.
>
> My whole life was raising the children, making sure everybody thought they were perfect. I would make their Reeboks white, and then I would buff them. If the shoelaces on their sneakers got dirty, I would take them out and put them in the wash and bleach them. But inside I felt like an erased blackboard.

Queen for a Day: The Rewards of Virtue

For Denise the sacrifice was more than just the possibility of being a dentist. It was also that "on many levels I was sacrificing my feelings, my joys and my pleasures, for other people, because I thought my role was to please everybody, to really be a doormat. If I did everything for the person I was married to or for my children, that's making me a whole person. So it was not only putting my life on hold, but not knowing what makes me happy."

To blot out her increasing anger and unhappiness, Denise began drinking. What finally woke her up was breaking her arm while she was drunk. Eventually she got sober, separated from her husband, and went back to work. But what had put her to sleep in the first place?

> For my entire childhood, until I was about twenty, my mom would tuck me in bed every night and tell me that I was a princess and that one day Prince Charming would come on his white horse and carry me off to his castle, and I'm going to live there happily, forever and ever. So when I fell asleep I should dream about what it would be like living in that castle. That was what I went to sleep to, every night, for a very long time, and my dreams were always beautiful.

They amounted, in fact, to the same dream of salvation that led the Little Mermaid to sacrifice her own life for the prince. Its potency can be measured by the fact that Denise never stopped feeling betrayed by her mother's promise—"I'm still very disappointed. I bought that story, and I still buy it"—even as she made sure her own daughter grew up with no such dreams.

Nor was Denise that unusual. Up and down the economic ladder, girls believe in the same fairy tale. In 1975 sociologist Lillian Rubin interviewed fifty white working-class and twenty-five white middle-class families and found that, as girls, most of the women had "the dream of the knight who comes to sweep her off her feet…or the prince who rescues Cinderella from ashes and cruelty."[3]

Such a fairy tale is like a jeweled frame around the icon of the devoted mother, surrounding her with an aura of sanctity that holds across cultures. "In the Mormon community, family is all that's important," Mary Ellen told me. "There's a lot of pressure for women to marry and have families." At forty-one, she had been married for twenty years and had four children. But one morning about six months earlier, she had woken up, looked across the room at her husband, and suddenly felt unsure whether she had stayed with him all this time "because I wanted to or because I felt I should have."

Sacrifice, Mary Ellen thought—like Denise—could be "just going along with what you think society expects of you" without stopping to figure out what you really think and feel about who you are. Although "I felt I had talent enough to do anything I wanted," she had devoted herself to raising her children and working in her husband's business. But now her sudden doubt sent her off by herself for a few days to reconsider. It was "scary" because she feared she would find she was "hollow inside." And indeed she "came to see that for a few years I was just doing what people around me expected. You can become a nonperson; you can take sacrifice to the utmost degree, and sacrificing can be very destructive." Nevertheless, in the end Mary Ellen concluded that

> I had everything, there was nothing out there greater than what I had. Part of sacrifice is being able to do what's right, rather than what you want. By giving up a few things I thought I'd rather have had, but doing what I felt was right, I have so much more than I ever could have dreamed. For a lot of years I guess I did sacrifice my own self-expression or time and energy for my family, but in the end I found that there was nothing else I could have done to give a greater return. If you give up some-

thing you want to get something better, is that a sacrifice?

Mary Ellen's assertion that she had on balance not made any real
sacrifices was not quite consistent with her awareness of how easy it
was to become a nonperson; but how much her conclusion could be
attributed to her true feelings and how much to the powerful precepts
of Mormonism, whose prescriptions for women are both exacting and
compelling, I couldn't judge. But whether or not her renewed dedication to her family represented a rationalization or a real understanding, one sacrifice she did make all those years emerged clearly.

Having had a bad relationship with her own mother, whom she
never loved, Mary Ellen confided, "I guess I never expected my children to love me. I've done all this all of my life, not expecting a return
from them. But I'm getting it now—'cause my children love me, they
really do. And it's so rewarding, so gratifying, when I never expected
it." The degree of willed selflessness in twenty years of mothering
without any confidence that her affection was reciprocated ranks
Mary Ellen high on any scale of sacrifice, maternal or otherwise.

Paradoxically, as more young mothers began working outside the
home, the devoted-mother icon was burnished even brighter. Increasingly engaged in a workplace whose values were competition, manipulation, and self-interest, women clung in their personal lives to
selfless attentiveness to their children's needs as their paramount
value.[4] Perhaps this was why women's magazines were forever cautioning mothers not to be *too* self-sacrificing.

An article in *McCall's,* for example, describes "Three Sacrifices
Moms Shouldn't Make" for their children: "your hobbies and interests," "your urge for spontaneous fun," and "your marriage (and sex
life)." Such a warning is needed because "many of us," according to
an expert quoted in *Parents,* "learned that a 'good mother' is a woman
who negates her needs, her body, her life, to take care of everyone
else's." Although the author concludes that "there is little precedent

for self-nurturing motherhood," she does present one mother's rather modest good example. One morning, this woman's mother-in-law found her sitting at the table, eating a nice breakfast while her toddler played quietly and her baby napped. "She was shocked. 'In the fifteen-year span that I was having babies, I never sat down to breakfast,' she told me. Her voice sounded half disapproving, half admiring."

While exhorting women to remember their own needs, these articles remain careful to avoid the implication that a mother deserves such pleasures as eating breakfast sitting down purely for her own sake. They soothe her conscience by reassuring her that ministering to her own needs will in the end make her a better mother—as though the conditioning to "enable" was so strong that it disabled the pleasure principle.[5]

Perhaps this is why I heard so many extraordinary stories from quite ordinary women. The intensity of their experiences—like Bernice's need to literally amputate her mother-organ to reinforce her determination not to be the nurturer anymore—and the parallels that kept recurring among them ("*I* never sat down and ate breakfast with *my* children," Mary Ellen remarked when I mentioned the *Parents* article) made me wonder if I had not somehow skewed my sample so that I was getting only the extreme end of the spectrum of sacrifice. I found the women I spoke to through social and professional encounters and by what social scientists call the "snowball method," which means asking people you interview to recommend someone else. Naturally those who agreed were those for whom the topic rang a bell; yet there were few for whom it didn't. I began to think the real explanation was that women accept as a norm levels of self-sacrifice that men would not even consider—an idea that was supported by other sources.

For example, among couples who cannot have a baby because the man is infertile, the woman may choose to undergo in vitro fertilization—which involves tremendous emotional stress, invasive procedures, and serious health risks—even though she is fertile and could have a baby by means of the far simpler method of artificial insemination, using another man's sperm. Studying a group of such wives, sociologist Judith Lorber found that some, who already had children of their own, underwent IVF as a gift to the husband; others because they wanted to have a baby by him; and others because they were pushed into it by the husband, whose sense of masculinity was threatened by his infertility. In all these cases, the wife took on the emotional burden of his infertility by referring to herself as infertile, too.

Lorber compares the results of her study to an earlier one of kidney donors of both sexes, which found that women were less likely than men to be ambivalent about donating a kidney. In addition, male donors' reactions after the operation tended to be more extreme than women's, apparently because for them it was a more extraordinary event; women took the act "more for granted as part of their duty *as women."* Suggesting that childbearing prepared women for "suffering pain to give life to another," the authors of the kidney study concluded that "women are more altruistic than men."[6]

My own interviewees' stories, I suggest, are not unusual; they are normal. As anthropologist Mary Catherine Bateson comments, one "vulnerability that women raised in our society tend to have" is "the quality of self-sacrifice, a learned willingness to set their own interests aside and be used and even used up by the community." She adds that "women are taught to deny themselves for the sake of...marriage," while "men are taught that the marriage exists to support them."[7]

With that in mind, consider Suzanne Hall, wife of James Hall, a prominent Jungian analyst left quadriplegic by a stroke when he was fifty-seven. Intensive rehabilitation enabled him to feed himself and type on a computer keyboard. With the aid of constant caregiving, he continued his professional life. After he left the hospital in 1992, most of that care was provided by Suzanne Hall. "He wears an electronic chime around his neck that he uses to call her when he slips in his chair. She wipes the corners of his mouth when he drools. She drives him to meetings and stays to take care of him." At night, she spends two hours putting him to bed.

Although trained as a therapist herself, Suzanne Hall never felt "worthy of her husband" and "focused her life on their two daughters" and a charismatic church. She knew he was repeatedly unfaithful—in fact, he took another woman on a trip to Europe—and was about to divorce him when two women he had had affairs with lodged ethics complaints against him. So she stayed, "for the sake of his career."

The New York Times Magazine, where this account appeared, published two letters responding to it. One asserted, "She is the real hero.... She must have an enormous amount of kindness, forgiveness, love and loyalty to 'be there' for this man still." The other writer, a minister, was appalled by the "bitterness" evidenced in her comment "God has punished him in ways I never could." That, he chided, was not "the true gospel of love and forgiveness."[8] To the first writer, Suzanne Hall embodied the devoted-mother icon, in its commonly enlarged meaning of mother-as-general-caretaker; to the second, she was a false version of it. But for both, the icon itself still shone brightly in its glittering frame.

Struggling to Break Out

American women from a variety of ethnic and racial backgrounds grow up with different versions of this icon suspended before their mind's eye. One quite literal example is a powerful Mexican religious and cultural symbol deriving from an apparition of the Virgin Mary near Mexico City in 1531. This image of a brown-skinned woman wearing a blue mantle covered with stars and standing on a crescent moon held by an angel, known as Our Lady of Guadalupe, is ubiquitous in Mexican-American culture. As a role model of the long-suffering, perfect, self-sacrificing mother, she has helped enforce a traditional stereotype of Mexican and Mexican-American women as

Queen for a Day: The Rewards of Virtue

"violated, submissive, passive, and even masochistic," according to theologian Jeanette Rodriguez. As Mexican-American women enter the work force, their traditional training to be meek and quiet conflicts with the requirement that they be assertive and articulate on the job. By reinterpreting the Virgin of Guadalupe "as one who empowers" those experiencing injustice, Rodriguez hopes to provide a way for Chicanas to rethink their self-image so they can reshape their roles in society to better meet their own needs.[9]

Indeed, this is the classic pattern of immigrant families: as the younger generations encounter mainstream American culture, their values shift and their behavior changes. Young women brought up to revere the devoted-mother icon try to redefine or even smash it—even as they may still feel compelled by it. Three stories from immigrant daughters show how this can happen.

"Even though I'm a woman of the nineties, I saw the world through my mother's eyes," Narrisa told me. "I was living by her being able to sacrifice what she needed for her children and her family." Thirty-four, a social worker turned health advocate in New York City, Narrisa was born in Puerto Rico and raised in what she called a "typical Hispanic culture" in which women's role was to serve men: "My mother had me and my sister cleaning up after the boys." As a child she was taught that a woman had to "settle." If your husband was a good provider, if he didn't hit you or drink, you swallowed your dissatisfactions and accepted the way things were without complaints, since God would always "give you what He felt you were entitled to. If in the process you had to give up something, God was taking inventory of what you gave up and your long-term reward would be bigger."

Narrisa vowed she wouldn't be like her mother. "Her life was my father," yet she was constantly fighting with him and being humiliated by him. But once Narissa married, "that little girl who didn't want to be like her mother got lost in trying to become that Spanish wife I was conditioned to be. My mother would visit us and he'd walk in—she'd say, 'He's here! Go serve your husband.' I'd do it. That's just the way we were reared; when my father walked in, my mother served him." She expected to match the standard set by her mother, "this woman in control; a cold never got her down. I can't remember her ever being sick."

After a few years, Narrisa was disturbed to realize that she wasn't happy. She wanted emotional satisfaction in her marriage, but her husband, also Hispanic, expected only to provide for and take care of her in a practical way, as his father had done for his mother. Narrisa's feelings, her career and goals, didn't matter; he never learned the names of the people she worked with, or her likes and dislikes—but she knew his. And "sexually, there was nothing going on. It was just getting him taken care of."

An additional factor was shaping Narrisa's feeling about herself. She had been born with polio, which left her with a disability that made walking somewhat difficult, and her parents feared she would never find a man to take care of her. She shared this fear, even though it was she who did most of the caretaking in her marriage. "I settled for this person—he was a wonderful person, but he wasn't right for me—because I didn't think I could do better," Narrisa confessed. "I didn't feel I was being loved as I wanted to be. I wanted to be beautiful, I wanted to feel good about myself, I wanted to be empowered and recognized for being smart, and I never was." Toward the end she "allowed him to shush me in front of people; he'd say I didn't know what I was talking about"—just as her father had done to her mother.

It was this "settling" that Narrisa saw as her sacrifice. Like Denise, she disregarded her feelings, her needs, her sense of self-worth for a notion of marriage imposed by her culture—and in her case, for an unexamined assumption about the limitations imposed by her disability. Eventually Narrisa left her husband and got her own apartment—a monumental achievement that required resisting her family's objections, "accepting that I was different," and redefining her notions of success and failure, her idea of marriage—which she now saw as a partnership—and her religion. "I really had to find the God part inside of me. That God part came out of the courage I was able to find" to finally smash the icon of the "Spanish wife."

For Marian, another immigrant, the sacrifice lay not in adhering to traditional norms but in breaking them. Born in Antigua among the working poor, Marian saw her mother raise twelve children, help her father, and run her own business as a baker. Working so hard, Marian believed, contributed to her mother's early death, when Marian was fourteen.

> I've always felt, That's not going to happen to me. I'm not going to be having all these kids, and I'm not going to be just a housewife—not that there's anything wrong with that, but it was seen there as that's all you are. I never felt I wanted to settle just for that position.

After her mother's death, Marian lived with an older sister until she came to the United States at seventeen. Although she cleaned and cooked, and took care of her sister's children in Antigua and then every summer in New York, Marian felt perpetually obligated, as though her life no longer belonged to her.

> I felt I had to sacrifice my life and my goals to go to school and to save money so I could give back to her what I felt she had done for me after my mother died. Every time I'd get a paycheck—I've always worked and had my own apartment since I was seventeen—I had to send her money, I had to send her packages. It took me a long, long time and ten years of therapy to understand that I had my own life, and because she did that for me I wasn't obligated.

To her family Marian was "the smart one" who went to college and must be doing well because she was in America. They expected her to send money and goods back home. "She's not married, doesn't have any kids, her life is better, and therefore she should be able to sacrifice more for the so-called family."

> To pursue my goals, I had to make a tremendous sacrifice and risk losing any kind of connection with my family. I had to decide, Well, look, I realize it's just me. When I decided I wasn't going to be a yes person, or I wasn't going to feel obligated anymore, that's when the relationship came apart.

Marian became a social worker and psychotherapist, but at the cost of her relationship with the sister who had cared for her after her mother's death. Despite different backgrounds, she and Narrisa shared with Bernice and Diane, who grew up in mainstream American culture, an underlying assumption that their lives belonged to someone else. When they became unwilling to sacrifice those lives anymore, they had to give up that someone.

The fact that this did not happen to Theresa was due to her distance from the pressure of tradition, as well as to her own energy of character. Theresa's mother was Japanese and her father, Korean. "A lot of Western women have inherited the Judeo-Christian notions of sacrifice and virtue, but there's an equally strong strain in Confucian philosophy," the source of the idea of the woman's role in Japan: "the subjugation of woman to man, and the importance of service to family and to society. That's every bit as much a virtue in Confucian society as it is in Christian society," she explained. Her mother, raised in the cultural norms of Japanese society in the 1930s and 1940s, gave up her career as a social worker when Theresa's father, who worked for the United Nations, was posted overseas.

Queen for a Day: The Rewards of Virtue

She basically gave that up to be a housewife, which she found terribly frustrating and stifling. In that significant way, she made tremendous sacrifices, but in all the small ways, too—cooking the things my father wanted to eat, we could only go to the restaurants my father wanted to go to—everything revolved around him. Her role was very simply defined, and that was to be selfless and nurturing.

As a girl, Theresa received "contradictory messages" from her mother.

She wanted to make sure I was independent and strong and had the kind of nurturing she never had from her mother. But on the other hand, my family environment was so geared toward trying to keep my father happy that the unconscious message came across that somehow his needs were more important than ours.

The adolescent Theresa sensed that there was "something wrong with that picture" and became rebellious. "I absorbed a lot of the internalized frustration and resentment my mother felt, and I couldn't stand the way my father treated my mother and the sacrifices she was making." Her own ambitions and expectations were shaped by these perceptions of her mother's experience.

Away at college, Theresa found the support she needed to "deal with issues of ethnicity and being female in a chauvinistic family hierarchy." By the time she went on to law school, she was determined that she would never regret any sacrifices she made herself. "My mother's sixty-four now. There are so many times I look back at her life and think that if she had never married my father, she could have done so much more. I don't want to spend twenty-five years of my life serving somebody who can't see beyond his own needs."

One reason it was "so easy for me to break out," Theresa thought, was her family's cultural isolation.

> Because we moved all over the world, we were never subjected to the larger cultural pressures you find in closely knit ethnic communities in the U.S. In the rest of the family, all the generations are very involved in every single couple's marriage. But we were extremely alienated from every community. My struggle was really with my family—I wasn't shaped by larger societal norms, like my mother. I didn't feel I owed my mother's family or my father's family anything.

After working briefly as a lawyer, Theresa became a literary agent. At twenty-nine, and in a relationship with a man who was "completely different from my father," she had clearly escaped the kind of trap that restricted her mother. Still her struggle left her with some strong feelings about women and sacrifice; for Theresa is my agent, and it was her immediate, enthusiastic response to that topic that made writing this book possible.

Caring for Parents

Traditionally, it was women who cared for ill or incapacitated elderly family members. Today, although we talk about the "sandwich generation"—middle-aged people caught between the needs of their young adult children and their own parents—the caregivers to the elderly are still mostly their daughters and daughters-in-law. In one study, although these women in the middle said they believed that women and men should share equally in caretaking responsibilities, and that working women should pay someone to care for elderly parents instead of giving up their jobs, they were the ones who provided the most assistance to their own mothers, relinquishing free time and leisure activities when necessary. Some had actually quit their jobs to care for their mothers.[10]

Among women I spoke to, responses to these pressures depended on their distance from traditional cultural values. At the same time, these values shaped the meaning they gave to the sacrifices that care-taking entailed.

When Alicia was in her early thirties, her mother had a second stroke. Alicia left the apartment she shared with three other women and moved in with her mother and stepfather. "There were things about her care that didn't just require physical help but also an intimate knowledge of who she was," Alicia explained. "She needed a daughter, and I'm her only child. Especially because I'm a single daughter, my parents are more my responsibility than that of my stepfather's daughter, who has several children. It would have been more of a sacrifice for her to do this than for me."

This response grew out of Alicia's upbringing. Her parents, immigrants from Panama, had raised her according to their own cultural norms. "There's a lot more emphasis on the family as a unit, as opposed to an emphasis here on the child. I experienced more of a focus on your responsibilities to your whole family, particularly to your parents and grandparents but even to the larger family." Although Alicia was born and grew up in this country, her parents taught her that their ways were different from those of her school friends. "The messages I was getting from school were that the idea of growing up is to go away from your family. I never have gotten that from my family—that was always the American thing that 'they' do."

While Alicia's family expected her to move in, her American friends expected her to hire a nurse and were horrified when she told them what she was doing. "What will happen to your life?" they asked. And Alicia acknowledged that if she had not made this commitment, she might have moved away from New York. For their part, although her parents felt pleased "that I was doing the right thing, I could see the furrow lines around their brows," for now they wondered "whether they had been right to teach me this other way with no society to support that"—that is, no extended family around her. But, Alicia added:

> I think there's a connection between what seems like an act of great sacrifice and what a person needs to do for themselves. I did a thing to help someone I loved at a time that she needed it. I also, it turned out, did something to recover for myself truths about the relationships in the family that I would never have had an opportunity to do otherwise, at a time in my life when that was important work. What looked from the outside like such sacrifice was something for me, my own heart and soul.

For Joyce, not yet faced with the need to make a decision about caring for a parent, the issue was nevertheless a live one. She saw it, as she did the question of sacrifice in general, in terms of a generational shift.

> Both of my grandmothers live with their children, one with my dad, one with my mom. My mom doesn't really want my grandmother in the house with her, but there was never a question. My grandmother always said, "Soon as I get to the point where I can't take care of myself, you all put me in a home." She didn't want to infringe on my mother and my uncle. But a year after my grandfather died, she was down at my mom's house. And whether it would be my mom or my uncle—never a question. That's a sacrifice. My mom is in the prime of her life, and she's got my grandmother to deal with. There are times she wants to go out of town. "Why don't

you come up here to visit?" "I can't leave your grandmother."

For me, there'd be a choice. If I didn't want my
mother with me, I'd put her in a nursing home in a second. I really like my mom, so I could see it'd be fun to
have a brownstone, she could be in the garden apartment. But for me there's a choice there, and it would be
my choice, whereas I think with my mom and my
grandmother, it was my grandmother's choice. It was
just expected, and I think my mom feels that that was
her duty.

Yet, like other women caught on the cusp of change, Joyce still
felt a tug toward the old ways. Even as she asserted her own freedom
of choice, she stressed the contrast between the culture she had come
from and that of her white friends.

A friend of mine was talking about her grandmother,
who was younger than mine and more mobile, but in her
mind there was no question that she had to be in a nursing home. In my family that's just not an issue. Our
across-the-street neighbors, their matriarch stayed with
them until she died. It's just done.

In Ruth's case, though, the nursing home did not cancel the need
for sacrifice. Ruth, a high-school teacher, was the only child of parents
who retired to Florida when she was in her early thirties. Although
her parents did not have a close relationship with each other, Ruth
"loved them dearly individually rather than as a set. We were always
a very lively threesome."

When her mother was diagnosed with Parkinson's disease in the
early 1980s, "I steeled myself for the fact that I was going to be her
caregiver," since her father had health problems of his own. When

her mother became unable to manage the household, her parents returned to New York and moved into a Jewish nursing home in the Bronx.

> I had to look after them. It's hard to talk about sacrifice, because it just was a matter of course. I knew there were other things I wasn't doing, but I never felt I was consciously making a choice. I couldn't abandon my parents—I had made that promise to them and myself when I was a kid.

Ruth's job teaching some of the least successful students in the New York City school system was "incredibly demanding and exhausting."

> The times that I did get close to falling in love or did develop relationships, the one thing that came first was my work, because I had always been told I had to support myself. I loved teaching, and I wanted to do well, and that required being in bed by ten-thirty in order to have the energy I needed. I had to spend one day of the weekend grading, I had to keep studying to make sure I knew the material I was teaching, and then I had my parents at the nursing home to look after. So I never married and I never had children. I just didn't feel like there was any emotional energy left over, and I wasn't going to do one thing less well in order to have children for the sake of having children—although it's a source of sadness to me.
>
> Yet I don't feel resentful or remorseful. How can I complain about my life? I've had such an interesting life and used my time within the parameters of the choices I had. I made the decisions that made sense to me. There

were times I felt put upon, overwhelmed, and I felt like my emotional resources were so depleted that I really don't know where the patience and kindness that I had to find in myself to continue to be a good teacher came from. It's kind of miraculous that I wasn't so totally emotionally exhausted by the needs of the children I worked with that I could actually go in day after day and then go spend a whole day with my parents, who needed and needed and needed. But somehow it was there.

Ruth's story is a completely ordinary one. What stands out is the state of mind she brought to the sacrifices her commitments entailed. She made them but she did not lose her self.

Balancing Acts

Along with the heartrending stories came a few from women who had evolved ways to balance the pulls of competing needs. A few even consciously confronted the Little Mermaid and slew her.

Anne, as we saw, emerged from childhood determined not to be like her mother. Shortly after first meeting her husband, Joe, she made him breakfast. "You're such a nurturer," he remarked, and she got furious; to her, that was "the ultimate put-down." Still, her mother's state of mind was deeply ingrained in her. When she and Joe began to live together, they decided to buy a reclining chair, mostly because Anne had a back problem. In the store, he liked one style; she wanted a particular color. The only model that came in that color also had extra support in the small of the back, but did not come in the style Joe liked. "Joe said, 'You decide,' and I chose the one he liked, without back support, even though it was my back we were buying it for." It took her a couple of years to realize what she had done.

Anne did not become pregnant until she was thirty-eight, having given the decision to become a mother careful thought. Quite a few people felt impelled to warn her, "You're giving up so much! Your life won't be your own."

> I said, "I don't care if I never go to another fancy East Side restaurant in my life, or a Broadway show—I've done that. It won't be a sacrifice that I won't do those things." Maybe my point is, I don't see certain things as sacrifice if I've thought them out and prepared myself ahead of time. But by others it's evidently considered a sacrifice.

For Anne's birthday one year, her husband arranged to take her to a lunchtime concert. But her son was in an accident and had to see a doctor whose only available appointment was for that same time. "I was very excited about the concert, but I readily gave it up. I didn't feel it was a sacrifice—my child comes first—but I felt had I been a twenty-two-year-old mother, rather than forty, I probably would have resented it." That is, once Anne had developed enough of a self to know what her needs were and satisfy a number of them, she could freely let them go when her son needed her.

This was also Laura's strategy.

> I made a conscious decision that I was not going to have a child until I wanted one, until I was ready. And I didn't. I was involved in the women's movement, in the antiwar movement, and I was married nine years before I decided I wanted to get pregnant. That was because the war was ending, and I decided I could do it at that point. And it was wonderful—it was a victory then to get pregnant. I was getting what I wanted—it was like ordering when you're hungry.
>
> And so I enjoyed the pregnancy tremendously, I enjoyed my child tremendously. My need to be in a hun-

dred different places wasn't as great as for people who have children right after they get married.

Sarah, too, became a parent later, but at more of a price. Despite a satisfying career as founder and director of a not-for-profit theater, she felt "pain and deepening sadness that accompanied everything I did because I didn't have a family and wasn't a mother." At thirty-nine, she gave up her theater—which required almost all her time—to pursue an adoption search, and several years later adopted a daughter.

"People always say I'm so brave, so generous, so selfless, because being a single mother is so hard," she told me. "And I say, 'Parenting is hard.'" Like other women she knew who became mothers late, Sarah saw herself as lucky. But to many, she appeared as "very self-sacrificing." Like Anne, she noted:

> When you come to it late, you do it differently. You've explored many of the options life has put in front of you—been a working person, developed friends, gone to the theater, the movies, traveled—and now you're looking at your résumé and saying, "This isn't enough." I could forgo another promotion at work, a bigger house, three or four nights out a week. I would be happier if I was making an investment in a child. I'm not giving up self-development or self-fulfillment—as a matter of fact, I'm pursuing them through nurturing a child.

Although giving up her career was painful—"I feel there's a large part of me that's been amputated"—she felt "such joy in being a mother that I'd never change my decision." Sarah noted, finally, that a man of her age most likely would not have had to sacrifice his career to become a parent; he could have found a younger woman to have a child with and not had to do it all alone.

Sarah's adult choices are consistent with her reaction as a child to the story of the Little Mermaid.

> My feet hurt all the time when I was little—I had flat feet—and I didn't like it. For me that story was embedded in the idea that you give up your life and walk in pain for a man, and I had a visceral child's reaction: "I wouldn't walk in pain forever for anybody."

Still, she remarked, "I always suffered for the things I wanted and felt I had to work doubly hard for them." The difference was that her sacrifices were made in pursuit of goals that were hers, not someone else's; she did not give her life over to the prince. Now, she concluded, "I'm happy to be with a man I want to give support to so he can be happy, and who supports me. It's a choice, and I'm not walking in pain because of it."

3

Global Responsibilities

"ONE REASON WOMEN DO WELL AT WORK IS BECAUSE THEY ENABLE the one above them to do well," observed Laura, recalling an incident at her company which illustrates that women don't leave their conditioning at home when they walk out the door. A male department head asked each of ten employees, six of whom were women, to write a marketing plan to bring in more revenue. These employees spent a long time developing thirty-page plans "with some wonderful ideas in them." The department head then assembled the best of these ideas—giving no credit to the authors—into a report of his own that he submitted to his managers. "That director actually received a bonus for revenue ideas that weren't his, weren't attributed, and certainly he didn't share the money," Laura concluded indignantly.

What particularly struck her was the difference in the women's and men's reactions to being ripped off this way. The men "had a healthier psychological response, which is that they actually felt cheated in a way that was good for their egos." But the women couldn't get as angry, for on some level they believed "the boss had the right to take their ideas, because the boss was the boss, and women are trained to give. Somewhere deep down, being trained to be enablers got in the way of the anger, being righteous. Women feel it's their job to make their bosses happy, and they're very happy when their bosses are happy."

This picture was familiar to business consultant Renée Karas. "Women bring with them that self-sacrificing attitude that they're going to put the other one forward," explained Karas, president of Winning at Work, a leadership development program for women in business. "They're socialized to enhance the effectiveness and power of others, and they play this out in the workplace. They see themselves in secondary, nurturing roles—her word *enabler* is a good one—in enabling roles, endlessly giving, without expecting anything for themselves. They're just happy to have a job, happy to be wanted."

In Catherine's office, women's enabling was complemented by employers' expectations. "Boy!" she exclaimed when she heard the word *sacrifice*. "Could I tell you stories!" A fifty-seven-year-old Irish Catholic mother of four, and for the past fifteen years a single parent, she had worked for thirty-three years at a large bank, starting as a keypunch operator and rising to vice president. "I made all the sacrifices, I've been there round the clock at times, I've been there on weekends. I've really paid my dues there, yet I haven't been compensated the way a man would be compensated. If a man does it, he'll make twenty or thirty thousand dollars more. It's just expected of women."

"So much of it is perception," was Karas's response to this complaint. "It's what you assume others are expecting of you. We don't know what would have happened if she had gone to her boss and said, 'I know you want to get this done, and I'm really glad to work on it, but I would need a bonus in order to do it.'"

Global Responsibilities

Catherine's assumption that her self-sacrifice would be recognized and rewarded was complemented by the bank managers' traditional expectation that women always put the needs of others first. Participants in a focus group Catherine attended complained that a woman who had a baby was perceived as having "deselected" a career at the bank. A woman who became a single parent (through divorce or widowhood) was seen "almost like a part-timer" because now she had twice as much responsibility and couldn't give her all to the bank. Yet men who became single parents got special privileges, such as leaving early on Friday if their children had only a half day at school.

Karas explained that "subtle forms of discrimination" against women—such as not being offered opportunities to travel, or to take on big projects—occur because their bosses assume that they have "global responsibilities" for child care or elder care beyond the job that would make additional work too great a burden. By contrast, the employer assumes that a man puts his career first, so the idea that other responsibilities would impinge upon his work does not arise.

But, Karas noted, "The women's movement has had an impact." Women under thirty-five have grown up assuming they will have a profession, and their expectations are higher; consequently, they are "much more respectful of their own needs." Many employers' old-fashioned assumptions caused such dissatisfaction among these women that they were leaving corporations "in large numbers" to start their own businesses.

But an act that for a white woman signifies liberation, for a woman of a different race may be another form of sacrifice. According to Antonia Cottrell Martin, a consultant, genealogist, and founder of the Foundation for African-American Women, black women from both middle-class and poorer backgrounds—who may have made tremendous sacrifices to get graduate degrees—"often walk away from the traditional corporation because it's so stressful and difficult to be there."

Slaying the Mermaid

People continuously judge them. If you're black, you're "less than," certainly "not as competent as," "not as pretty as"... and it's said to you so often that you don't meet the standards, that in order to stick it out you have to go into some delusional place. Women from Wall Street or corporate law firms, or any arena where they have to act like any other worker, make tremendous personal sacrifices by shutting down emotionally, not allowing the bad things to disturb them, just focusing on the work they do.

Ultimately, in order to preserve their self-esteem, many leave to become entrepreneurs—now sacrificing income, security, and the use of their hard-won credentials.

In the creative professions, people of both genders and all backgrounds are likely to sacrifice financial security, but here again women's training in nurturing and enabling has an additional pernicious effect. Diane spent much of her professional life working with collective theater groups that presented plays dealing with social problems. Her reaction to her mother's sacrifice, reinforced by a Catholic upbringing that stressed the necessity of "doing good works" and the virtue of self-sacrifice, led her to focus "not on myself as an artist but on how I can be useful in this group." She found herself "working too hard for not enough money," or sometimes, when people needed her expertise, for no money at all.

In a similar way Wendy felt that if she was going to "commit the audacious disloyalty" of distancing herself from her family, "it had better be to take care of someone else's needs." Disregarding her talents for painting, dancing, and storytelling, she taught and then did social work. Later she worked in community theater, where she could use her artistic skills. Still,

there was a time when I would not have put up much of a fight about being unpaid or underpaid for that kind of work. I'd have heard my mother's voice telling me, "What makes you special is how helpful you are, how people can count on you to be there for them, how people get so much comfort from you." I don't like that voice. I'm still angry at her for telling me that. Now I want to be paid for my work and my time.

Moira, characteristically, seems never to have had that self-sacrificing impulse. From the age of twenty-one, when she left Dublin for Paris to become a famous artist, she focused single-mindedly on her work. But doing so, she believed, required that she sacrifice having a husband and children. She married briefly in the 1970s, but "for me," she said, "marriage was very difficult. Was it just my limited belief system? I couldn't see a traditional man support somebody like me, who would put my work and my career first before anything else—actually support me the way women have always supported male artists, have their children, go out, get a job, and really put the woman artist first."

"You weren't willing to settle for half and half?" I asked.

"No," she responded. "Because I couldn't do things halfway. If you're really committed as an artist, you're committed."

The women described so far made sacrifices unwillingly or unwittingly, or escaped doing so only through conscious struggle. But none of their stories demonstrates the pervasiveness of the sacrificial ideal so pointedly as the experience of someone who successfully upended it, then encountered so strong a reaction that she questioned her own judgment.

"In my life I feel extremely fulfilled," Julia declared at the outset of our interview. "I love my work, and I love my family. I've had a very unusual opportunity not to have to make a big sacrifice and also not to feel any of the guilt or hesitation a lot of women feel about not being home." She saw sacrifice not as necessarily negative but as a way to get what one wants. Editorial director of a university press, Julia was married to an architect who took off three years from his career to care for their daughter after her birth. "I went back to work after a very short time but felt really great because Gary was home with her."

By the time their son was born, Gary had switched careers to computer design, and to avoid another career break for him, they found day care and a baby-sitter. But Gary remained the backup parent, the one who went home if the baby-sitter called or picked up their daughter if she got sick at school. When their son was one and a half, Gary began freelancing. He remained the parent involved with the micro-details of the children's lives—went to school bake sales, knew which day they had ice-skating. For Julia, his availability made "a huge psychological difference in my ability to focus on my job. I don't have to bear that responsibility. If I miss stuff because I'm taking a trip, I don't feel like no one's there."

What they hadn't realized was how unusual their arrangement was, and they were unprepared for the reaction. People assumed that Gary's involvement with his children meant he wasn't a serious professional; potential employers cast a suspicious eye on the three-year gap in his résumé. For her part, Julia—who couldn't keep play dates straight and never knew when ice-skating was—sometimes felt that "people assume I don't have a strong bond with my children." And Gary's greater involvement with the children's daily lives struck some as positively abnormal.

> When my daughter was in day care—she was about one and a half—she fell down one day and started screaming for her daddy. He wasn't around, so they called me and I went. The teachers had never heard a kid screaming for daddy when she bumped her head. That seemed to be, in child development, the moment when the child reaches out for the mother, and they thought it was this really big deal—everyone was talking about it. I couldn't understand why.

Global Responsibilities

Then I told a friend about it, and she said, "Didn't you feel terrible that she didn't call for you?" Her kid always called for her, in the middle of the night or whenever. I hadn't—but then I started to think, Is there something the matter with that?

In the same way, when Julia came home from a business trip,

everything's normal, they look up and say, "Oh, hi." But they don't come racing down the hall, with tears in their eyes, and throw themselves into my arms—which many women describe to me as the scene they face when they get home from a trip. In our culture a lot of women think that's normal. I worry that some of my editors here aren't traveling enough. One in particular says, "I can't—my son is too upset when I leave, and I don't have anyone to stay with him."

Julia deplored the prevalent model of selfless mothering.

Everything you read tells you that loving your children as a good mother, by its very definition, means sacrifice. Who says that love equals sacrifice? Is that what you want to teach your daughters? Do you want them to see you as having to sacrifice all other aspects of your life in order to show that you love them, or do you want them to feel that you love them because you love your life?

There are no alternative models, Julia observed; "everything is couched in this sacrifice paradigm."

For example, my daughter says, "Why do you have to go to work today? I want you to stay with me and go to a museum." We're expected to say, "I really wish I didn't have to work, 'cause I'd always rather be with you." But is that true? A lot of times you wouldn't rather stay; in fact, after the weekend you're excited about going back to the office. But second, is that really what you want to say to your child about the way you love them? Is it just as helpful to say, "I do love to be with you, but I also love to go to my work"? There's a limited vocabulary, particularly for how to talk about relationships with children, that doesn't involve the sacrifice model.

Poverty and Sacrifice

Like culture and race, poverty redefines sacrifice. In poorer families there is likely to be so little margin once survival is assured that women's needs vanish even more completely than is true for middle-class women. As part of her pitch for being elected "Queen for a Day," contestant number five described her day to Jack Bailey. When she got home from taking her son on his paper route,

> "I get their breakfast, get him off to school, and then I do all the housework that is possible before I go to work [at eleven] and put in my eight hours [at a hospital cafeteria]."
>
> "Boy, you never get but about five minutes to yourself!"
>
> "And then I come home and I prepare their supper, and then I relax about thirty minutes before bedtime."

One of Lillian Rubin's working-class informants recalled her mother's similar life.

Global Responsibilities

My mom did domestic work, and it always seemed like she never stopped working. She'd come home and clean the house, and cook dinner, and clean up the dishes, and fix our lunches for the next day. It seemed like no matter what time you woke up at night when we were little, Mom was still up doing something....

And you know, she was never late with a meal....My mother always taught us that you shouldn't keep a man waiting for his supper after a hard day's work. You know, it's only recently that I began to realize that she worked hard all day, too, and nobody *ever* made supper for her. No wonder she was always in a bad mood.[1]

In Puerto Rican culture, Maria told me, sacrifice is "ingrained" in women. As a girl growing up on New York's Lower East Side, she had to clean and cook after school, then wash the dishes after dinner; all her brother had to do was take out the garbage. Her stepmother cooked with her after working all day in a factory, while her father read the paper. Eavesdropping on the women's conversations, she heard about emotional needs unmet, husbands' unfaithfulness, and their belief that a woman "had to stand in the husband's shadow to help him develop." In church, too—her family was Baptist—"we had to affirm that the husband was the head and spiritual leader of the household."

The man came first no matter what his gifts were. Choices made for the family had to center around the man, not necessarily what the children or mother needed. It was important that the man appear good, whether he was or not. So if the husband was limited, then the limitations for the woman were even greater. I know some very bright women my age who didn't go to school, didn't develop themselves professionally, because the husband was limited. In order to develop, they had to divorce. The generation before me would not even have done that.

Women's needs also came after those of children; and poverty increased their sacrifices. "Everybody around me was very poor when I grew up," Maria recalled. "Some ways women coped were by getting a factory job and leaving the kids alone, not going to the doctor when they needed to, not buying medicines. It's a greater hardship—that adds to the sacrifice."

The rule that "you learn to sacrifice and give your life for others" did not apply to men. "I've never seen the man expected to sacrifice for anything. By the time he's seventeen, eighteen years old, the family accepts that he's going to be a man and they have to let him find his way. He has an obligation to be responsible and provide for his family, but not to sacrifice."

Maria herself put "self-development" at the top of her agenda, and managed to evade many of the usual sacrifices. "Washing those dishes," she exclaimed, laughing,

> was how I developed my strategy not to have sacrifice forced on me! I made a plan very early that certain things were not going to happen to me. I was not going to marry a husband who didn't iron his own shirts, who didn't clean, do dishes, cook, shop, and wasn't going to be as concerned about my development as I was about his. It took me a long time to find him, but I got the right husband.

She took advantage of the fact that because her mother had died when she was little, the family felt sorry for her and she "could get away with more." Ultimately she got away with a master's in public administration, and became director of services for older adults at a not-for-profit social service agency.

Work and the Wider World

For some people, work goes beyond making a living or even building a career. They aspire to large-scale social change. Chapter 9 will discuss sacrifice in relation to social action more broadly. Here I want to show how women's self-sacrificing role plays out in this arena as well.

Perhaps the last occupation one might associate with altruistic self-sacrifice is that of politician. But when the politician is female, the association is surprisingly appropriate. My first inkling of this came in speaking to Joan Millman, a Democratic Party district leader for a state assembly district in Brooklyn. She noted that, at the city and state levels she was familiar with, male elected officials usually had other incomes from law, insurance, or real estate and did "very well financially," while women were more likely to "do that job full time, and they tend to take it very seriously. And they're not getting rich that way." Asked why, she speculated, "It may be that the women take it as more of a public trust. When you take on the responsibility of doing this job of serving the public well, it is an enormous task and does take a lot of time and energy. It is a sacrifice."

Further, she went on, female politicians who were married with children felt far more guilty "for shortchanging the family life." During the summer one male district leader sent his family off to a vacation house, allowing him "to do more politicking"; his female colleague, unwilling to be away from her children, took only two weeks off with her family, "while she worries about the things she's missing here."

Single herself and employed full time, Millman did her political work in the evenings and on weekends. This cut into her social life. Whereas a man in her position could find a woman to go to a political function with him—or sit at home and wait for him to call when it was over—"guys just don't want to do that. The choice is either not to go out with this person, or not meet what I see as my political obligation to my title."

Given the sacrifice of time and social life—and the fact that, as she said, "there's no money at all involved in this"—what was the draw? First, Millman said, there was the satisfaction of "being able to put the pieces together" to provide the first bus for disabled people in Brooklyn, or to get a car for a neighborhood crime patrol. "That's a very nice feeling to know you could accomplish that." It was also agreeable, she acknowledged, to be a "very minor celebrity" who rubbed shoulders with bigger celebrities. Learning how the political system works had made her into a real cynic, she added, but "one reason I still do it is that I feel very committed to the leadership in our district. There are times when by working all together we do accomplish some good stuff."

Was Millman, like any politician, not simply trying to present herself in the most favorable light? I wondered. But it turns out that a fair amount of research has been done on women in public office, which supports Millman's take on the differences between women and men. What's more, other women's responses to questions about motivation parallel hers, and their behavior supports their claims.

"Our research suggests that an awful lot of the women in public office really do see themselves as being there because they're committed to making the world a better place," said Susan Carroll, senior research associate at the Center for the American Woman and Politics at Rutgers University. It's true, she explained, that since both men and women know they're supposed to care about their constituents, both will "give you a public-service response." But when you look at how these women became involved in politics in the first place, very often you find they were concerned about some specific issue—from drugs or crime to needing a stop sign on their street. "I take that as a better indicator than what they say," she noted.

Women officials also claim, Carroll continued, "that they care less about being out there getting the glory and more about actually creating the kind of change or the legislation they want. Men are more likely to take credit for things and be less concerned with actually achieving policy outcomes." This assertion was so frequent "that it's either an incredibly prevalent stereotype or it has some validity."

I would say: both. First, we've already seen the ubiquity of the devoted-mother icon (and Chapters 4 and 5 will present much more evidence); and second, the women's claim that they're more interested in results than in getting credit exactly parallels what I heard about women in business. It's the politicians' version of enabling—and not necessarily a bad thing, or we might never have gotten some useful legislation, such as the Family and Medical Leave Act, for which a number of women legislators went out on a limb. One was Marge Roukema, a Republican from New Jersey, who voted against her party on this issue. "This may change over time," concluded Carroll, "but generally I'm comfortable saying that women less often than men are motivated by personal ambition and more often by concern about a particular issue, at least in their initial political involvement."

In 1997, six months after I spoke to her, Joan Millman was elected assemblywoman. Her first session in the New York State Assembly reinforced her belief that "the women don't go into it for economic gain. I think their priorities are more to serve."

For their concern these women, like Millman herself, often pay a price. Men coming from careers in business or law, where the hours are flexible or the employer sees an advantage in having them hold office, are more often able to take time off without financial loss.[2] Women, on the other hand, are more likely to enter politics from traditional women's occupations such as teaching, health care, and social work, which are less flexible in terms of time. Thus women are more likely to have to leave full-time jobs to become public officials— although, Carroll suggested, this may change as younger women graduate from law schools, establish themselves in traditionally male careers, and then decide to run for office.

Millman noted that women's orientation to service made it harder for them to raise money to run for office. "Women often get into politics because they've been involved in PTAs or local community boards—they've given public service without getting any compensation for it. So they're surrounded by people who are also volunteers and don't have access to people who give a lot of money." Further, women don't feel they can write checks for large amounts of money without checking with their spouse first—"She doesn't feel it's just her money; it's family money, or her husband's money"—while men not only feel no such constraint but often write checks to male candidates in their offices, where they persuade colleagues to contribute, too. "Where the money is, is not where the women are, unfortunately. That's begun to change, but it's a real problem for many of us," Millman concluded.

Women officials may also pay a career price for choosing legislative priorities "that are still considered more marginal because more related to the life experiences of women," according to Carroll. Men still occupy the "main power positions" and define what's important, so people who focus on "marginal" issues thereby become less important themselves. "But it's a choice women make because they care about those issues," Carroll said.

The sacrifices women in politics make, then, are dictated by both external circumstances and individual priorities. Women who give up a job for elective office, or lose out on chances for a social life, or choose to work on issues that are perceived as "marginal" are put into the position of making sacrifices that men don't have to make. And they're willing to. "One of my colleagues," said Millman, "was considering running for higher office and then her husband became very ill. Thankfully, he's going to be all right now, but they diagnosed cancer, and he was undergoing treatment, and she just gave up all her plans of running. When a man does that, the newspapers write about it because it's supposed to be such a marvelous thing. Nobody wrote about this woman. It's expected that that's what we're going to do."

Other forms of social activism don't offer the rewards of political office to either men or women, but here, too, the same differential holds, with women putting their own needs at the bottom of the list.

Global Responsibilities

Arlene was a thirty-four-year-old activist who had always felt called to "political activity, changing the system, going up against authority." Raised Catholic, she found herself repeatedly returning to religious organizations to do her political work, which involved housing and hunger, among other issues.

Despite her commitment to her work, Arlene had begun to feel a certain dissatisfaction, for it had led her into a style of activity that contradicted her real nature—"introverted, reflective, self-created." Though she had originally "wanted to write, be an artist, be alone a lot," she found herself operating very much in public, something she did not find easy. "My work involves a lot of facilitating groups of people to have discussions, presenting a project to a foundation, calling people all over the country, talking about what they do and how we can help them. I'm very 'on' a lot of the time."

Facilitating a meeting, Arlene noted, really means "bringing out what other people have to say"—that is, enabling. "I'm often doing what's best for the organization, for the project, for other people— not necessarily what I enjoy the most. It feels at times like being bled," she added, echoing Wendy's image. "Not always, but the accumulation of it can definitely feel like something's always being taken from me for the good of the world. It's not satisfying, but it's what needs to be done, so I have to do it."

After fifteen years as an activist, Arlene was finally putting her own needs in the balance, asking, "What's the price, what do I get out of it? Is there a way to do what I really want and not what I feel I should do because it's better to give than to not give?"

Karen, too, was in the process of reevaluating her style of activism. After hearing me describe my topic at a luncheon meeting, she strode up, pressed her card into my hand, and said, "I want you to interview me." A thirty-five-year-old lawyer, Karen was executive director of a nonprofit organization that did education-related legal advocacy work. Self-sacrifice, she said, was "a theme that runs through my life."

But Karen had a different take on sacrifice: she associated it with risk. "They go together. Usually when I've taken risks for a stand, I've sacrificed something important to me, either money or personal security or social ostracism." Since her teen years she had put herself on the line for her politics. "I had an overwhelming sense of my life being a duty to change the world. It was my form of religious excitement," she explained.

In high school Karen was nearly expelled for being a "rabble-rouser" who revealed "some shenanigans about a business deal." At college, after a number of rapes occurred on campus, she mounted a public campaign to improve security for women, in the midst of which she walked her tiny roommate across campus at night without thinking about any danger to herself. Her attitude was, "I don't care if I get in trouble or expelled—this is too important. The idea of another woman getting raped justifies my taking this risk." After an off-campus journalist who had interviewed her about the issue tried to rape her himself, she was "cowed," but only briefly.

Transferring to a school in New York City, she got involved once again in a community issue, this time writing for the campus newspaper about a sewage treatment plant being built in Harlem. "I would walk up there alone at night to go to meetings. I knew the risk but persisted to break the story and reveal the injustice. I had been good, so nothing bad would come to me." She did reveal a major deception regarding air monitoring at the plant. "I triumphed—this gunned me up to do another. Each time I took a bigger risk, I seemed to get bigger returns."

After graduating, Karen took a job at which she worked many more hours than she was paid for—this time as "a challenge to myself to see what I could pull off with limited resources." Later she supported a husband who wasn't working, while also putting herself through law school. At length, angry at losing time from schoolwork to help him, she left him. After law school she worked for a large corporate law firm for two years, then returned to public advocacy, taking a $70,000 pay cut.

But now, she said, she was "on the cusp of changing my whole way of dealing with things." About to leave her job to marry a man in another city, Karen expected to continue her public advocacy, but at less cost to herself.

> Slowly I have been walking away from these high self-sacrifice modes, and the more I do that, the more respect I get. I started wanting back for what I gave. Increasingly I tend to do a cost-benefit analysis of sacrifice rather than impetuously try it. I'm less willing to subjugate my needs to other causes and people. As I'm less personally invested, I'm more professionally successful.

With Karen, Arlene, and the politicians, the arena of women's self-sacrifice expands. In their impulse to subordinate their own needs—emotional and even, in Karen's case, physical—to the welfare of others, they resemble the other women I've described. But in extending the impulse out beyond their personal relationships into social action, they demonstrate how, beyond the sacrifice of money and status that social action often entails, women wind up embodying less traditional but still recognizable versions of the devoted-mother icon.

An Ever-Flowing Fountain

As I said, the women whose stories appear in these last two chapters were all ordinary people living everyday lives. Astonished to uncover such operatic intensity of experience behind their commonplace appearances, I concluded that the amount of self-sacrifice built into normal female lives is in a sense rendered invisible by cultural constructions like the devoted-mother icon, which lead us to take the resulting behavior for granted. But there were women who went beyond even that norm.

Most women I talked to saw sacrifice in terms of giving without receiving an adequate return. They felt themselves in danger of running dry; or worse, that in giving to others, they had lost pieces of themselves. But in a few, the vital substance continued to flow like a fountain, and the self remained intact.

When I called Josephine, whose name had been suggested by an acquaintance, to ask to interview her, she offered to drive to my home to pick me up. I protested that I wanted to arrange the interview in the way that was most convenient for her, but she could only respond by offering to do something for me. "That's what I'm like," she said. I expected to find a woman whose perpetual giving arose from insecurity. But Josephine in person did not give that impression.

She had survived many tribulations: as a child she was legally blind for years, not regaining her sight until she was twelve; as an adult she had other serious illnesses; and worst of all, her twenty-nine-year-old daughter had died of pulmonary hypertension, leaving three children whom Josephine was raising. To the question "What did you originally think of when I mentioned sacrifice?" she responded, "I thought about all the illnesses I had in my life, the people around me that I either had to take care of or they had to take care of me at some point, and all the sacrifices around the recovery." Her voice was quiet, slow, and sad. Illness, loss, and giving were the themes she kept returning to, and clearly they were related.

At nineteen, Josephine had begun working in a hospital emergency room.

> [It] was a shock to me; I didn't know people had so many emergencies. Giving became a part of life—to care for somebody in an emergency, to give somebody a cup of tea, just to rub their back when they're laying in a bed for a long period of time, hold their hand. I found myself totally into finding out what to do to stop that particular suffering. I just wanted to help them stop the bleeding; if

they were vomiting, ease the vomiting; if they were in pain, stop the pain. If they were in an accident, trauma- tized, talk with them and calm them down so they can be treated.

She worked next as a nurse's aide in a larger hospital.

I was meeting people of all different races, all different cultures, all different traditions, with all the different types of physical problems that had to be treated. And I plunged in there and tried to save the world [here she laughed], and when I couldn't save the world, I started praying for them, endlessly. I had a prayer list of my own every day to just make sure I felt freed up from the responsibility. I felt helpless, so by praying I felt that I was doing them the greatest good.

Later she became an occupational therapist, and between that and her daughter's illness, her entire life focused on one theme.

You're giving all this time, you're just giving and giving and giving. You give to your family, you give to your friends, you're giving so much you just don't have time to think about yourself, you don't have time to rekindle your selfness, so to speak. You have to do things, some sort of playtime, to restore yourself.

Crafts and painting pictures, she said, helped her "get back to myself."

One "great sacrifice" was that—like Christine's mother, but unlike her, with evident sadness—Josephine had to give up relation- ships with men, who "couldn't handle" being with someone who had to care for her sick daughter and her grandchildren. "I never anticipated not having male companionship in my life, but I just got caught up with the giving and caretaking. This is a sacrifice on me," she said.

Yet she also felt that not having a permanent relationship allowed her to retain her sense of herself.

> I feel like a whole person because I didn't totally give up my life for some man and negate the other things I thought were important. Having a relationship was important, having someone love you and care for you is very important, too, and maybe I'm missing something, but I feel a bonding relationship shouldn't mean giving up who I am. It's not me hanging out in a bar when I'm not a bar person. It's not me going to work and giving my whole paycheck up to this person. It's not me slaving over the stove when everybody's drinking beer in my living room, and running around serving. If I'm in the kitchen, he has to be there, too. If we're changing Pampers, we're changing Pampers and feeding the baby together.

Despite her sadness, Josephine radiated peacefulness. Sacrifice to her meant all her losses and her life of caretaking, but it was also connected to her faith. Growing up as a Methodist, she took seriously the teachings in Sunday school. "At nine years old I started to try to develop that discipline of loving, giving, sharing, and having a humble heart." Clearly this early practice had flowered into her adult life, so it was not surprising to hear her say she felt blessed despite all the pain she had been through; each trial "made me even more grateful for my life than I was before." In addition to all her other giving, Josephine worked in her church, "wanting to give back some of the good that's been given to me. You can give on many levels; it doesn't have to be out of your pocket, it doesn't have to be your clothes, it doesn't have to be your food. You can just give someone a helping hand, a little direction, and that could change somebody's life. The sacrifice is little next to the reward of giving." For Josephine, then, sacrifice rode on the stream of faith, a fact whose meaning will become clear later when we consider the nature of appropriate sacrifice and its relation to transcendence.

To their various experiences of sacrifice the women I've described attributed a range of meanings. As much as these different reactions are rooted in personal character and circumstances, they are also shaped by centuries of history. Each story told here will look less individual and more conditioned when set into its cultural context.

4

A Good Woman Is a Sacrificing One

FOR INNUMERABLE YOUNG CHILDREN, THE HEROINE—IF I MAY CALL her so—of Shel Silverstein's picture book *The Giving Tree* is a model for a quite literal form of self-sacrifice. The tree (to which the author gives a female gender) loves a little boy who comes every day to climb into her branches, eat her apples, play hide-and-seek. These innocent games make boy and tree both very happy. As the boy grows older, however, he becomes interested in girls and neglects the tree. When he is old enough to want to buy things, the tree offers him her apples to sell to make money. He accepts, making the tree happy.

As the "boy" ages, the tree grows sad because he stays away for long periods, returning only when he is dissatisfied and wants something. In his young adulthood, the tree gives him her branches to build a house. "Then you will be happy," she says. But apparently he never is, for he returns again in a discontented middle age, wanting a boat in which to go "far away." She offers her trunk so he can build one. He cuts it down, leaving a stump.

Finally, in old age, he returns once more. The tree wishes she could give him something but is now "just an old stump." The "boy" responds that all he needs is "a quiet place to sit and rest." So she invites him to sit on her. "And the boy did. And the tree was happy."[1]

This is not exactly a sentimental story. It has an ironic edge, furnished by the hero's selfishness and failure in life (evident in Silverstein's drawings of the miserable aged "boy"), as well as by the tree's satisfaction in finally having him to herself, despite his defeat (shades of the woman whose self-sacrifice is really a form of possessiveness). Yet most people apparently take the story straight. *The Giving Tree,* first published in 1964, remains one of the most popular children's books in print.

"That's a great book!" exclaimed a toy store saleswoman whom I asked about it. "A beautiful book!" echoed her colleague. They sold it in both English and Spanish. But a children's librarian thought it was "odd that people take this literally." Disliking *The Giving Tree* herself (she considered Silverstein "mean"), she never offered it to readers, but people came and asked for it; it was especially popular among religious Christian families. "It's a classic," confirmed a bookstore manager. "It just keeps going and going." Adults bought it for boys as well as girls, he said, and even for one another. "It sparks something in people," commented a clerk at another bookstore.

Sparks what? Perhaps the spark rekindles the votive flame before the old devoted-mother icon, creating such a sentimental glow that the vast audience for this little book is able to ignore the irony, the meanness, and the fact that the tree's selflessness not only destroys her but fails to make the boy happy. Each time a parent gives this book to a child, the flame is lit anew: little girls learn what female creatures are supposed to do for "boys," and little boys learn what to expect from them. For both, a model of behavior that has grown up over centuries is reinforced. Various strands of cultural history are wound together in this model, and this chapter will untangle them. To do that, and to lay the groundwork for later consideration of constructive forms of sacrifice, I must return to the original meanings of sacrifice itself.

Sacrifice and the Circuit of Life

People tend to use the word *sacrifice* in a general way to mean giving up or renouncing something for the sake of a higher goal or value; thus the self-sacrificing women in the previous chapters disregarded their own needs in favor of other people's. But the word originally referred specifically to an act of worship. *Sacrifice* derives from the Latin *sacrificium,* which combines *sacer,* "holy" or "consecrated," and *facere,* "to make." That is, it refers to a material object that is "made holy," or set aside to be offered to a divinity. This offering might be a slaughtered animal, a plant, or a fluid such as wine, milk, or honey. It was conveyed to the divinity in various ways, such as by burning or pouring over an altar. The offering might also be eaten by the worshipers in a communal meal in which the divinity participated or was present in the food. In some cultures, including ours, this act of offering came to be understood as a more internal or symbolic type of sacrifice involving a self-giving, or inner devotion, to the divinity.

Sacrifice is an extremely ancient, worldwide practice, and many theories have attempted to explain its origin and nature. It has been described, for example, as a method of creating communion both among the people who sacrifice and between them and their god; as an expiation of sin; as a gift or tribute creating a reciprocal obligation on the part of the god, to promote the fertility of the land or the well-being of the community; as a means of connecting the sacred and profane realms of life; and as a reenactment of the primordial creation of the universe, in which the dismembered body of a divinity is transformed into the various elements of our material reality, in order to

A Good Woman Is a Sacrificing One

rejuvenate the world. Sacrificial practices vary so widely, however, that no single theory fits all of them.[2]

Given the many possible meanings of sacrifice, I will focus on those aspects of it in Western culture that have defined and supported women's tendency to be self-sacrificing—especially in relation to the culture's ideas of women's proper place and function. I begin with an analysis of the social function of sacrifice in relation to gender by Nancy Jay, a sociologist of religion.

Looking at the social context in which sacrifices are performed, Jay suggests that one purpose of sacrificial rituals, such as those prescribed in the Old Testament for the ancient Israelites, is to maintain the social structures in agricultural and pastoral societies that ensure the continuity of inheritance of property—land and flocks—through the male line. Sacrifice, she says, is a "remedy for having been born of woman," a way to transcend the break in the direct line of descent from father to son that is caused by the need to rely on childbearing by women who are not part of the patrilineal line. Many societies actually define kinship not according to biological descent but according to which members perform sacrifices together, and women are almost always excluded from these rituals. Sacrifice may also define a purely institutional succession, such as the hierarchy of Roman Catholic priests, who offer the sacrifice of the Mass; correspondingly, the Church excludes women from ordination.

To support the link between sacrifice and social structure, Jay points to the fact that in our industrialized, individualized, democratic society, where property is not held primarily as land and the basic social unit is not the extended kin group but the fragmented nuclear family, sacrifice is generally no longer a central religious practice.[3] I would add that it is instead the province of the same group that was prohibited from sacrificing in preindustrial society: women. Instead of being structural, its social function has become more psychological, while its spiritual purpose remains essentially the same.

In all the theories mentioned above, sacrifice creates some form of connection. "Sacrifice is a celebration of life," says one authority, "a recognition of its divine and imperishable nature.... The consecrated life of an offering is liberated as a sacred potency that establishes a bond between the sacrificer and the sacred power."[4] As a gift to the deity that creates a reciprocal obligation, sacrifice sets "the stream of life flowing" in a circuit between the human and divine realms. A consecrated animal, for example, is an intermediary between human and divine. Sprinkling its blood on the altar or eating its flesh creates a continuity that unites all the participants. The result is "a strengthening of the community's power...binding its members more firmly to each other."[5] Indeed the Kabbalah, or Jewish mystical tradition, interprets the Hebrew term for sacrifice as deriving from a word meaning "to bring together, to unite," and explains sacrifice as a symbolic act that unites not only the believer with God but the male and female divine principles with each other.[6]

This idea of communion, or the creation of unity, provides another way to focus the meaning of sacrifice for women, since both prohibiting them from practicing it and making them largely responsible for it are manifestations of the opposite of unity—of splitting. To understand the meaning of this split for us today, we must trace the history of women's relation to sacrifice in Christian culture.

Women and Sacrifice in Christianity

The ancient Israelites' elaborate system of sacrifice was their predominant mode of worship until the destruction in 70 A.D. of the Second Temple, the only site where the sacrifices could be offered. After that date, prayer took the place of sacrifice. The movement from an external ritual to a more inward form of offering was further emphasized by the new sect of Christians. Although Christians did not sacrifice animals, the pervasiveness of this practice throughout the ancient world made it the dominant metaphor for their worship, which they described as "the offering of spiritual sacrifice," with

A Good Woman Is a Sacrificing One

Jesus' "inner self-offering to the Father" as the model. Christians were to "offer themselves to God as a living sacrifice" in their minds and hearts. In the earlier centuries of Christianity, the "making sacred" aspect of sacrifice was emphasized; later the focus shifted toward the notion of "giving up something."[7]

It was Christianity also that first associated sacrifice as an expiation for sin with suffering, for the Hebrew tradition did not link these ideas. Judaism saw suffering as a punishment for sin or a test of faith (as with Job); an expiatory sacrifice might require many animals and considerable display of repentance, but not pain. In the "suffering servant" of Isaiah 53, and during the Maccabean revolt against the Syrian rulers of Judea in the second century B.C., when some of the rebels voluntarily martyred themselves for their faith, the Jews did develop the idea that suffering could be redemptive and sometimes sacrificial. However, Christianity brought this idea to a new level, and the suffering that Jesus underwent during his sacrifice came itself to be seen as the sacrificial offering. For St. Paul, suffering was an essential aspect of identifying with Christ, and the rest of the New Testament makes it "clear that discipleship involves suffering, particularly in persecution."[8] Thus martyrdom, and later asceticism, came to be seen as forms of expiation.

By the late Middle Ages, suffering as expiation of sin combined with suffering as identification with Christ to produce the "conclusion that an individual's suffering is worth something in itself, that suffering is good in itself." Christianity developed a unique and characteristic emphasis on the possibility of achieving redemption through physical suffering, which in turn evolved into the idea that through mechanisms such as prayer, one person's suffering could be substituted for another's. In this manner, suffering became a form of service—a concept that centuries later continues to resonate particularly for women and, I suggest, lies behind much of the behavior that this book explores.[9] Certainly this concept shaped Sister Elizabeth's automatic response when John asked her to give up sweets for the

sake of the homeless women. Over the centuries this model of suffering and service remained an ideal, and there were many whose desire
for salvation was such that they inflicted extraordinary physical hardships on themselves. They included a remarkable group of female
saints whose extreme ascetic practices—particularly fasting—provide a provocative comparison with modern anorexic girls, as Chapter 6 will show.

During the later Middle Ages, an increase in religious institutions
and movements provided new opportunities for women to express
their piety, and the number of female saints grew. Although the culture told men and women equally that suffering—specifically
"extreme self-mortification"—"was the way to salvation," the differences between women's and men's social circumstances dictated characteristic differences in their religious practices. Women's mysticism
more often involved self-inflicted physical suffering, which was more
likely to center on extreme fasting, sometimes to the point of self-
starvation. The fourteenth-century saint Catherine of Siena, for
example, began to fast as a child and by sixteen was living on raw vegetables, bread, and water. She later became completely unable to eat,
and died in her early thirties of self-starvation. Among her other penitential practices were self-flagellation and sleep deprivation. Other
female saints inflicted equally flamboyant physical disciplines on
themselves, often while struggling against male religious authorities
suspicious of such extremism. Since women were considered morally
weaker than men, it was feared that their austerities might lead to
heresy or be inspired by the devil.[10]

Psychological analyses of the female saints' behavior have focused
on guilt, self-hatred, and family relations, but here it is more useful to
relate their acts to the social context. A central theme of medieval religiosity was the imitation of Christ, whose purpose was a mystical
fusion with his suffering on the cross and the offering of this suffering as a form of service for the salvation of the world.[11] Because of the
nature of their roles in medieval culture, women were particularly

A Good Woman Is a Sacrificing One

drawn to this form of piety, and to expressing it by rejecting food. Unable to control wealth and frequently forced into marriage, medieval women found their sphere of action limited. Their main activities were nurturing and serving; in medieval society, as in many other cultures, they were the preparers and servers of food—though not necessarily its eaters; they were generally expected to eat less than men and to eat lighter food. For them, suffering and fasting were symbolic acts that matched medieval notions ascribing to women a "suffering, giving self." Thus while male saints were seen as "models of action," female saints were "models of suffering and inner spirituality." [12]

Women also chose self-mortification, especially through fasting, at least in part in reaction to a tradition that associated the female with nature and matter—that is, the evils of flesh—and the male with reason and spirit. Woman was "a very weak vessel" who had inherited the failings of Eve and was equally likely to harm man through her voracious sexuality. Fasting was a way to expiate the evils associated with the body and even to punish it. [13] In later ages, women's relationship with food continued to be a significant component of their self-sacrifice. What is more, we can trace the exemplary suffering woman through vast cultural changes, right down to our own culture's fascination with a modern version of the female salvation-seeker: artists like Sylvia Plath and Frida Kahlo.

As the Middle Ages passed, the style of female piety changed: by the end of the sixteenth century, assertive, heroic asceticism like that of Catherine of Siena was frowned upon. The new Catholic model of female piety was a woman "visited by God with strange, painful maladies" that tortured her, deepening her spirituality until she died and could finally embrace the heavenly bridegroom. Unlike the earlier saints, whose self-mortification led them to a mystical wisdom that Church authorities respected, holy women of this period achieved sainthood through suffering only. For example, Mary Magdalen de' Pazzi, daughter of a prominent Florentine family, refused to marry and entered a convent, where she ate very little and mortified her body. "Beginning in 1595 she prayed for…[an] atrocious death from painful illness" and eventually experienced "a three-year terminal illness marked by excruciating toothaches, head and chest pains, fever, and coughing." We will meet the "model of the suffering holy female, immobilized and racked by pain," again in the nineteenth century, in a secular context.[14] Despite its conformance to tradition, however, all this seemingly passive, pious suffering also had an active aspect: it conferred on a woman a kind of autonomy by eliminating the Church and its priests as intermediaries between her and Jesus, while also enabling her to escape traditional roles, particularly that imposed by marriage.

In the seventeenth century, perhaps seeking a more active outlet for their piety, holy women turned to serving the poor and the sick. But meanwhile, suffering took on additional significance for ordinary women, as both Protestant and Catholic authorities became increasingly concerned by the "potentially destructive female nature" and the danger presented by female sexuality unless it was controlled within marriage, where the wife was supposed to be obedient to the husband, serve him, bear children—and suffer in the process. God's judgment on Eve in Genesis—"I will greatly multiply your pain in childbearing; in pain you shall bring forth children"—was taken literally. "Passive suffering and the archetypal female experience of childbirth have been seen as identical. Passive suffering has thus been seen as a universal, 'natural' female destiny, carried into every sphere of our experience," explains Adrienne Rich in her study of motherhood. The sixteenth-century Protestant theologian and reformer John Calvin asserted that woman was saved not by faith but by her suffering in childbirth, which erased the sin she inherited from Eve. So necessary was this suffering considered to be that in 1591 an English midwife was executed for giving pain relievers during labor. Even as late as the mid-nineteenth century, a French bishop, Félix Dupanloup, wrote: "It is quite evident that the mother is destined to an expiatory and holy suffering. She is great because she suffers." In the same period, the British clergy attacked the introduction by a Scottish physician of anesthesia during childbirth as "a decoy of Satan" that would "harden society."[15] The clear implication is that women do the suffering for everyone else; if their pain is taken away, men lose the general redemption it provides. The theological context had changed since the fourteenth century, but the message was the same.

A Shift in Character

Although women's suffering remained necessary in the nineteenth century, the rationale behind it shifted, for the view of woman's nature had undergone a remarkable reversal. The assumption that women were morally inferior to men dated back to Aristotle, who asserted (long before Freud) that they lacked a moral sense. In both the Jewish and Christian traditions, "Eve's disobedience in the Garden of Eden became evidence of all women's inherent weakness and evil."[16] The conviction that women's lustfulness made them unable to be moral unless subject to external restrictions and male control remained firm in Western Christian culture until the beginning of the nineteenth century, when women quite rapidly evolved into pure Angels in the House whose role was to save Adam, rather than ensnare him. What did not change was that, although women's character was now completely opposite from what it had been, they continued to carry out their new role through self-sacrifice. Explaining this will require a short detour through politics and philosophy, for it was the influence of social institutions and intellectual convictions that rooted self-sacrifice so deeply in women's character.

As I said in Chapter 1, what led to this reconceptualization of women's nature was a series of economic changes beginning in the eighteenth century. In newly prosperous middle-class families the women, released from working in family businesses and from heavy household labor, were encouraged to dedicate their free time to their husbands, children, and households. Devotion to domesticity was a new mandate. Previously, wealthy and aristocratic women—the only ones who did not have to work—displayed little interest in their children or homes. They spent their time in society, often involved in cultural and political life and associated sexual intrigues. Late-eighteenth-century political reformers blamed these women and their sexual influence for the corruption and decadence of the European monarchies. The most famous among these reformers, Jean-Jacques Rousseau, glorified virtuous domesticity and contrasted the "'women's world' of the home to a 'man's world' which encompassed the rest of existence." Between 1789 and 1815, the reformers mounted a campaign that successfully excluded women from political life and established instead a "middle-class domesticated ideal" of what Thomas Jefferson, writing from Paris to an American woman friend in 1788, described as "the tender and tranquil amusements of domestic life." In contrast to the influential French "Amazons" who in his view controlled society, Jefferson described American women as "Angels" who had "the good sense to value domestic happiness above all others." The social pressure to conform to this ideal was so great that women's behavior changed radically within a single generation; and one powerful persuasive force was the glorification of the properly domesticated female as a paragon of purity and virtue. So complete was this revolution that by mid-century Patmore was able to contravene nearly two thousand years of theology by asserting that the Angel in the House was "Marr'd less than man by mortal fall."[17]

This cultural pressure toward domesticity was accompanied by economic pressure, since the movement of production into factories meant that women who did have to work could no longer earn an adequate living. Domesticity was therefore equally the goal of working-class women.[18] Most women who could stay home did, and applied themselves to becoming angels.

In this role they could satisfy a new need that industrialization had created. The accompanying expansion of the market economy brought a profound transformation in social relationships, requiring a corresponding restructuring of behavior patterns and even of concepts of human nature.[19] In pre-industrial Europe, people defined themselves in relation to their family group or local community, and their rights and obligations arose from the network of interdependencies inherent in that grouping. These connections regulated political and economic relationships as well as personal ones. Economic transactions were related to an individual's position within the network; a poor person, for example, had a right to alms, and a rich person an obligation to give them. Contracts between individuals could be broken by appealing to a change in circumstances or a higher morality in whose light the terms seemed unfair.

Beginning in the eighteenth century, however, people began to think of individuals as self-contained, independent units who should have equal rights to freely pursue their own self-interest in a competitive market, making decisions based on rational calculations of profit. Each person's economic and political relations with other autonomous individuals were to be based on contractual obligations that bound each side equally. Since the parties were assumed to be equals who had entered into the agreement freely, their social status was not taken into account, and contracts no longer had to be evaluated in terms of fairness or morality. These principles constitute the political philosophy of liberalism, a key aspect of which was that it left women out. By definition the autonomous "person" was male; women were not considered persons. This exclusion of half the population from political citizenship has shaped the development not only of public but of personal relationships in our culture.

The problem was that taking the notion of independence or self-reliance (to use a term that became central to the American self-image) to its limit could lead to an extreme individualism—and an extreme pursuit of self-interest—that left no room for any form of connection, neediness, or dependency, or for considerations of morality. It became necessary to find some area of life in which other values ruled: emotion, compassion, personal obligation, and interdependence. That place, of course, was the home, where the woman, having lost her economic function and being denied a political function, acquired the new one of being everything the man was not. Where he was calculating and ruthlessly egoistic, she was sympathetic, nurturing, and limitlessly altruistic—that is, self-sacrificing.[20]

Indeed men were able to be rational and self-reliant in the public realm only because women were emotional and giving in the personal one. It is, after all, impossible to raise children and live together as a family if every relationship is based on the quid pro quo of the market; someone has to be willing to give based on another person's need, not on her own. But because political thinkers equated the laws of the market with the laws of human nature, to the men who embodied these laws, women appeared mysterious and essentially different. Women represented a dependency—or rather an interdependence and an emotional commitment—that was the antithesis of what the competitive, ambitious, calculating public man strove to be; for "dependency...undermined individualism."[21]

This antithesis reflects a dualism characteristic of our culture. Since the Greeks, Western philosophy has been concerned with separation and distinction. It has distinguished spirit from nature, mind from matter, and man from woman. Our greatest philosophers have seen men as essentially separate and autonomous beings who needed to use their reason to transcend and control the dangers of nature as well as the threat posed by the female's unruly emotions and sexuality. This was the approach of Descartes, for example, who in asserting "I think, therefore I am" staked a claim for reason as the tool that would make such control possible. But the Cartesian method, with its rejection of feelings, intuition, and sensory experience, and its reliance on reason as a form of control, induces a feeling of separation from the entire material world: "the Cartesian method reveals an isolation and an image of autonomy that would become central to the Western image of man in our own century."[22] It is from this dualism that self-defeating sacrifice ultimately derives.

Angel Icons

"Women draw breath only to pay with pain for the honor and glory of motherhood.... Bless the mighty hand which has placed in our sufferings the seeds of virtues to which the world owes its happiness!" exclaimed Mme. Manon Roland, a famous supporter of the French Revolution and admirer of Rousseau, in a book explaining "how the education of women can contribute to making men better." As we saw, the idea that a woman could improve a man was indeed a revolutionary one in the late eighteenth century. But this new notion of woman was so integral to the social reorganization that accompanied the industrial revolution that it soon penetrated everyday life, and the nineteenth century produced endless paeans to the self-sacrificing female savior, in both word and image: "No angel, but a dearer being, all dipt / In angel instincts, breathing Paradise," according to Tennyson.[23]

Popular advice writers and novelists educated the newly domesticated woman on what was expected of her. The Englishwoman Sarah Stickney Ellis's 1839 guide *The Women of England: Their Social Duties and Domestic Habits* became a best-seller both there and in the United States. Ellis admonished women to recognize the predatory nature of the business world with its "strife, which is nothing less than deadly to the highest impulses of the soul." It was the middle-class woman's duty to counteract this negative influence. By "cherishing and protecting the minor morals of life," she could be for her husband "a kind of second conscience," while making the home a place where he might "keep as it were a separate soul for his family, his social duty, and his God."[24]

At mid-century Horace Bushnell, a Congregationalist clergyman in Hartford, Connecticut, "instructed his daughter to have no needs,

Slaying the Mermaid

almost no character of her own: as a woman she should be 'above all…unselfish.'" Others took the ideal beyond angelhood to martyrdom. In 1866 Harriet Beecher Stowe advised the housewife "to look at her domestic trials as her haircloth, her ashes, her scourges—accept them—rejoice in them—smile and be quiet, silent, patient and loving under them." Stowe made this martyrdom literal in her 1862 novel *The Pearl of Orr's Island.* Ethereal, delicate Mara reforms insensitive Moses, who wants to marry her but is contemptuous of her religion, by dying. In effect, she martyrs herself, suffering for his sins. *Lucile,* a vastly popular romance in verse by Owen Meredith (pseudonym of E.R.B. Lytton, first earl of Lytton), tells the story of a young woman's eternal devotion to her true love, who due to a misunderstanding marries another. To ensure that his continuing interest in her will not affect his marriage, Lucile becomes a nun.[25]

The suffering, sacrificing female was not only painted verbally but depicted on canvas by popular artists, whose works, in the last two decades of the century, reached huge international audiences through photographic reproduction in periodicals.[26] The painters portrayed women as nuns; as modern madonnas; crowned by roses as the embodiment of unearthly purity; and as substitute Christ figures, sometimes literally hanging from a cross. More remarkably, artists painted sick women, fragile and feverish, in the last stages of consumption or some other wasting illness; and even, in a remarkable variety of styles, dead women—beautiful pathetic martyrs to unrequited love. Tennyson's two versions of the maiden who expired for love of Sir Lancelot—the Lady of Shalott and Elaine, the lily maid of Astolat—were painted over and over again.

Illness and death were, in fact, no more than the logical extreme of the self-obliteration implied by the injunction to have no needs, and a corollary to the paintings was the veritable "cult of invalidism and death" that developed among middle-class women in the second half of the century. Large numbers suffered from a mysterious malaise whose incapacitating symptoms included weakness, loss of

A Good Woman Is a Sacrificing One

appetite, headaches, insomnia, and obscure aches and pains; mystified physicians gave it such vague labels as "neurasthenia," "nervous prostration," and "hysteria." This syndrome has been interpreted as an effect of the life of dependency and essential idleness that these women were supposed to lead. With no productive work to do and no intellectual stimulation, their only functions the sexual ones of bearing children and looking attractive, they took up being ill as a form of occupation, or even vocation, a way of getting attention and exerting some "psychological and emotional power." Invalidism actually became stylish—not only as a sign of ladylike good breeding and true femininity but as an indication of the wealth and social status of the husband who could afford to maintain a sickly, idle wife.[27]

Accordingly, the image of the suffering, diseased female became an icon of beauty. An astonishing number of paintings—created, remember, for people to buy and hang in their homes—depicted pale young women reclining in limp exhaustion against the raised pillows of a bed or a lounge chair, often with an anxious, sad, or thoughtful parent, husband, or friend looking on. Even healthy young women aspired to the wan, languid aspect of the consumptive. "We thus find the florid and robust assuming ill health when they have it not, and resorting to all kinds of contrivances to give the face a cast of sickliness," chided *The Bazar-Book of Decorum* in 1870. One such "contrivance" was refusing to eat; another was drinking vinegar or arsenic. As Susan Sontag points out, "The tubercular look...became more and more the ideal look for women—while great men of the mid- and late nineteenth century grew fat, founded industrial empires, wrote hundreds of novels, made wars, and plundered continents."[28]

The heavy clothes and tight-laced corset worn throughout this period helped create not only the image of delicacy but also the required invalidism itself. The pressure exerted on the abdomen by the corset in particular caused indigestion and displaced the internal organs, resulting in pelvic disorders which convinced the medical profession that "female functions were inherently pathological," thereby reinforcing the idea that suffering was a natural part of women's lot.[29]

But like medieval women's austerities, this preoccupation with illness can also be interpreted as an attempt, within the context of suffering, to become active instead of remaining passive: taking charge of the self-negation demanded of her, the woman pushes it to its limit—death.[30] In Chapter 6 we will explore this dynamic further, for it is part of the psychology of self-sacrifice. Here I want to stress the cultural context in which it developed: the powerful suggestion that the ultimately pure woman is she whose very life force has drained out of her—and by implication flowed into others—to the point where she ceases to exist as an independent entity. Even though the central image of Western culture is a wounded man on a cross, the icon who mediates our feelings about pain and suffering today is more likely to be a crucified woman: whether figurative or literal, she has made the Christlike redemptive sacrifice.

Non-Angels Still Sacrifice

Although the frail, dependent lady became the model of ideal femininity for women at all levels of society, poorer women were unable to fulfill it, for they had to work; indeed it was their badly paid labor, along with that of working men, which enabled the wives of middle-class and wealthy men to be idle.[31] Considered "coarse," not delicate, and certainly not virtuous, poor women did not become neurasthenics, but they did become ill. An 1889 report described a "working girl" of Boston:

> Constant application to work, often until twelve at night and sometimes on Sundays…affected her health and injured her eyesight. She…was ordered by the doctor to suspend work…but she must earn money, and so she has

A Good Woman Is a Sacrificing One

kept on working. Her eyes weep constantly, she cannot see across the room and "the air seems always in a whirl" before her...[at the time of the interview she] owed... three months' board for self and children.[32]

Like the middle-class woman, the poor one ruined her health and sacrificed whatever potential she had for an active, productive self, but in her case the stake was simply survival. It is the same distinction we saw in Chapter 2 between women like Bernice, who let thirty years go by in a dream of being the perfect mother, and Joyce's mother, who consciously gave up her desire to become a writer to share in the effort to lift her family into the middle class. In both cases, the woman's self-denial greases the wheels that enable the lives around her to run smoothly; but the wealthy white woman has a freedom of choice (which Bernice took advantage of when she left her husband) of which the African-American woman is deprived.

In the nineteenth century, both rich and poor women exhibited the preoccupation with food we saw in the medieval saints. However, whereas rich women abstained from food in order to achieve the status of a lady, poor women went hungry for the sake of their families. Historian Ellen Ross, who studied working-class women in London between 1870 and 1918, describes their "extraordinary tendency...to starve themselves," giving their husbands and children the best food, or all the food. A social worker of the time described one woman who "was in the habit of dining on a 'kettle bender,...a cup of crusts with hot water, pepper and salt, and a knob of margarine,' clearly meant to kill off her hunger while others were eating more appetizing food."[33]

Ross's speculations on the source of these women's "autostarvation" echo familiar themes. Partly, she suggests, this behavior represented the importance of giving the best food to the wage earner in the family, usually the husband. Partly it reflected women's low status and lack of power. "One of the first steps needed to effect the political and social emancipation of woman," asserted a group of activists in 1907, "is a crusade on the part of man calling upon her to eat"—a remarkable statement whose implications Chapter 6 will ponder. Some poor women might have been influenced by the figure of the martyrlike, self-sacrificing mother who appeared in parlor songs and other forms of popular culture. Not eating might also have represented "a struggle for control" in the face of unfulfillable demands from the family to be fed more than the housewife had resources to provide. And finally, not eating was "partly perhaps a statement about being a woman. For women rich and poor as portrayed by nineteenth-century novelists almost never ate....Women's hunger was unmentionable, an indecent subject."[34] We will see these themes again when we consider contemporary girls with eating disorders.

In the late nineteenth century the admiration of self-sacrificing, suffering women acquired new support from scientific opinion claiming that women actually liked to suffer. The German psychologist Richard von Krafft-Ebing, inventor of the term *masochism,* explained that "the wish to suffer pain" was not a perversion in women (as it was in men) but a natural phenomenon, since women's "instinctive inclination" was to subordinate themselves. Other experts discovered that the "normal woman is naturally less sensitive to pain than a man."[35] In the twentieth century, woman's masochism was enshrined into scripture by Freud, whose influence made it the defining characteristic of femininity for much of the century.

Reformed Character of a Mermaid

Enduring silence, mutilation, and suffering for the prince's sake and in the end achieving a saintly purity, Andersen's Little Mermaid exemplifies the Victorian invalid Angel. But she has another aspect that makes her a more apt emblem for us. In order to domesticate her, Andersen had to reimagine her, for originally the mermaid was quite the opposite of angelic.

A Good Woman Is a Sacrificing One

All over the world, legends appear of sea creatures with both life-giving and destructive qualities. The earliest female ancestor of the mermaid was Atargatis, a fertility goddess with a fishtail, who was worshiped by the Syrians and Philistines. The Greek sirens were bird-women whose seductive songs lured men to their deaths; during the Middle Ages they became fish-women whose tails represented sensuality. In the imagery of the medieval Church, the mermaid seduced a man in order to obtain his soul; according to one tradition, she could gain a soul by enticing a mortal man to marry her. Once he listened to her song, he would capitulate to the pleasures of the flesh, which led to moral if not physical death.[36]

In the Elizabethan era, "mermaid" was a synonym for "courtesan." In the nineteenth century, Thackeray presented women like Becky Sharp as mermaids who might "look pretty enough when they sit upon a rock" but were really "fiendish marine cannibals," and in George Eliot's *Middlemarch* the physician Lydgate anticipates his own downfall when he remarks to his wife Rosamond, "Why, what can a man do when he takes to adoring one of you mermaids? He only neglects his work and runs up bills." By the end of the century, the mermaid symbolized a predatory, destructive, sex-crazed, primitive seductress, whose form suggests bestiality; she drags her hapless victims down to the watery depths, where they drown in sensuality.[37]

But meanwhile, Andersen had created a domesticated alternative. "The Little Mermaid" appeared in his first fairy-tale collection, published in 1835; unlike the other stories in the volume, it was original, not a retelling of a tale he had heard, and it converts most of the traditional mermaid's qualities into their opposites.[38] As we saw, though, the longing for a human soul remains. Before ever seeing the prince, the mermaid is obsessed by the human world above the sea, and her love for the prince, whom she saves from drowning in a shipwreck at some risk to herself, is mingled with her feeling that his world is larger and "higher" than her own.

However, this mermaid is sexless. In payment for the magic

potion that endows her with legs, the sea witch demands her voice, "the most beautiful of all those who live in the ocean," with which she had hoped to charm the prince. The witch (whose realm, where ugly, snakelike, slimy polyps grow out of bubbling mud, is clearly the domain of sensuality) tells her to use "your beautiful body…your graceful walk and your lovely eyes" instead.[39]

But although the mermaid's dancing enchants everyone in the prince's castle, she evokes in him no sensual thoughts, for he dresses her in men's clothes, lets her "sleep in front of his door on a velvet pillow," and takes her along on horseback rides like a mascot. "He loved her as he would have loved a good child," Andersen assures us. The only one he can love as a wife is the girl who he thinks saved him from the shipwreck. The mermaid comforts herself with the idea that he is likely never to see this other girl again, since she belongs to a holy temple. "But I am with him and see him every day. I will take care of him, love him, and devote my life to him."[40] Which she does, quite literally, when she chooses to die herself rather than kill him. Plunging a knife into his heart and letting his blood spray on her feet would have made her a mermaid again, with her three hundred years of life to look forward to before becoming foam on the ocean, as all mer-people do at death. But as we saw, her sacrifice and the suffering she has borne entitle her to become a spirit with a chance of obtaining an immortal soul by doing good deeds for three hundred years. Since the soul was the real object of the enterprise, she has triumphed.

In part Andersen's transformation of the traditional mermaid arose from his own character; a neurasthenic obsessive-compulsive who never married, he was terrified of sex, which he believed evil, and seems never to have engaged in the act, even once. Yet he longed to be redeemed from his loneliness by the love of a pure woman, preferably a pure female child (the next best thing to a being with a transparent, ethereal body).[41] Still, the Little Mermaid struck a widely resonant chord in the culture; she became and remains one of his best-loved characters. In the twentieth century she reappeared over and over in numerous variations, always reenacting the very drama this chapter has described: the transformation of a woman into a self-sacrificing angel through amputation of her raw animal energy, as embodied in her tail.

5

The Mermaid's Tail

IN THOMAS MANN'S NOVEL DOCTOR FAUSTUS, THE COMPOSER Adrian Leverkühn, lost in a syphilis-induced delirium, dreams of having the Little Mermaid as his lover. Calling himself "a godlike monster," Leverkühn likens the pains with which he pays for the "towering flights and illuminations" of his art to the pains the "little sea-maid" felt in her legs. Suffering "a raging torment" from headache, he weaves a fantasy of the mermaid as his muse, his "sister and sweet bride" who comes to him sometimes with her fishtail and sometimes with her legs. This fantasy, combining bisexuality (with the fishtail a phallic symbol) and bestiality, expresses Mann's disapproval of the demonic, destructive aspect of artistic genius, as exemplified by his Faust's willingness to abandon himself to the excesses of "artist-nature."[1]

Leverkühn's hybrid Little Mermaid, alternating the depraved sexuality of her mermaid forebears with a more proper womanly aspect, represents a ubiquitous heroine of twentieth-century popular culture. This modern mermaid acts out desires that do not conform to the domestic ideal, but then has to pay the price by submitting to the same mutilation Andersen imposed on his heroine: the amputation of her erotic nature. In its broadest sense, the erotic encompasses not only sexuality but the experience of being in touch with and satisfying one's basic desires. Its loss, therefore, is the essence of destructive self-sacrifice, for (as later chapters will show) what is ultimately lost is the self.

One famous modern-mermaid story, which remained popular for more than a hundred and fifty years, exemplifies the genre. In 1848 Alexandre Dumas the younger published *La Dame aux camélias* ("The Lady of the Camellias," usually titled *Camille* in English translations), a novel that he turned into a play in 1849. The courtesan Marguerite Gautier, known as Camille, falls in love—for the first time in her dishonorable life—with respectable young Armand Duval. For a brief period they live blissfully together, until Armand's father arrives to demand that she give him up in order not to ruin his life and career. Reluctantly Camille agrees, painfully aware that the only way to break off with the impoverished Armand is by pretending that she prefers a luxurious life with the evil but rich Baron de Varville. Having thereby heroically redeemed herself into angelhood, and after a magnificent reconciliation with Armand, she dies of consumption.

Right from the start, this story was immensely popular. "The young Dumas, with his phthisical heroines, as unsound in flesh as in morals, is greatly responsible for the vogue given to the pallid, wan, hectic, and feeble," complained *The Bazar-Book of Decorum.*[2] *Camille* was retold innumerable times, as in Verdi's 1853 opera *La Traviata* ("The Erring Woman"), with its heartrending musical portrayal of Violetta's renunciation of Alfred Germont, which was made into a devastatingly sentimental film by Franco Zeffirelli in 1982. Dumas's original tale was filmed more often than can be listed here, in Danish,

Italian, Spanish, German, Swedish, and French, as well as in six English versions, including the classic 1936 film starring Greta Garbo.

"I don't suppose you can understand," Garbo's Camille protests to Armand's father, "how any woman, unprotected as you say I am, can be lifted above self-interest by sentiments so delicate and pure it would be humiliation to speak of them." He acknowledges that she loves Armand unselfishly, but insists she must give him up. "I want Armand to enjoy life, not be sacrificed to it," he tells her; they seem both to agree that given these facts, it is she who should make the sacrifice. The concluding reconciliation scene reenacts the nineteenth-century dying-invalid paintings as Armand bends over the expiring Marguerite. Nor was Garbo's Camille simply a relic of the past; the story was remade yet again in 1984, as a TV film with a stellar British cast headed by Greta Scacchi and Colin Firth.

Other modern mermaids may not have to die, but still must sacrifice, also usually as expiation for being in a sexually irregular situation. Like *Camille,* their stories were often first best-selling novels that, in two or three film versions, descended through the decades updated but essentially unchanged. They belonged to the Hollywood genre known as the "woman's film," whose audience was middle-class housewives; most of the heroines "embrace the audience as victims, through the common myths of rejection and self-sacrifice and martyrdom."[3]

Stella Dallas, originally a novel by Olive Higgins Prouty published in 1923, was filmed first as a silent in 1925, then in 1937 with Barbara Stanwyck. (For twenty years, it was also a radio soap opera.) Stanwyck's Stella, a working-class girl unwilling to accept her station in life, manages to charm and marry upper-class Stephen Dallas. Before long he is repelled by her vulgarity and refusal to learn refined behavior, while she, the moment her daughter is born, devotes herself entirely to motherhood and loses interest in him or any other man. Eventually they separate and he takes up with a woman of his own class. Their daughter, though she lives with Stella, receives an upper-class upbringing, and Stella comes to realize that her own lower-class appearance and behavior will destroy her daughter's chances with the rich young man who has become enamored of her. Making what is for her the ultimate sacrifice, she sends the girl to live with her father, pretending that she intends to marry her drunken admirer Ed and go with him to South America. In the final scene, a bedraggled, dowdy Stella stands in the rain behind an iron fence, peering in through the window of a grand house at her daughter being married to the rich young man. As a policeman hustles her off, she turns to the camera with a smile in which exultant triumph and searing pain are exquisitely united.

In 1990 this story was again remade as the movie *Stella,* with Bette Midler. Though an attempt was made to modernize it, with Stella a bartender and Stephen Dallas a medical student who have a brief affair but never marry, the movie is unconvincing. Midler plays the magnificent last scene as effectively as Stanwyck—standing in the pouring rain outside the elegant Tavern on the Green restaurant in Manhattan—but the emotional punch is lacking, since there now seems to be no reason why, if someone bought her a decent dress, she couldn't be in there, too. The problem is that the power of the class distinction that was the reason for the sacrifice no longer exists—not that the notion of the mother's heroic sacrifice is outdated.

A particularly prolific source of woman's-movie plots was the novelist Fannie Hurst (1889–1968), known as the "Queen of the Sob Sisters," whose more than thirty books (translated into eighteen languages) were all full of self-sacrificing women—not only mothers, but lovers of weak, narcissistic men to whom they devote their lives. Hurst's two most famous novels were *Imitation of Life* (1933) and *Back Street* (1931), the first filmed twice and the second three times. The changes made between early and later versions demonstrate again that even as the cultural context changed, the core equation woman = sacrifice remained.

Imitation of Life is a rich tissue of themes involving sexuality and self-sacrifice in women's relationships with parents, husbands, daughters, and lovers versus their actions in the public sphere. Its extreme popularity makes it worth discussing in some detail. Widowed Bea Pullman goes into business selling maple syrup to support her daughter and invalid father, aided by her black servant Delilah—an even greater self-sacrificer than Bea who refuses to accept wages and cares for Bea's baby before her own little girl. Eventually Bea turns her business into a chain of wildly successful waffle restaurants and becomes a famous millionaire businesswoman. Yet she remains always alone, without any love or support from a man; her "petty and mundane routine," she realizes, is only "imitation of life."[4] At length she falls in love with one of her employees, a slightly younger man, but loses him to her own daughter and, giving up her dream of selling her business and settling into family life, condemns herself to perpetual traveling all over the world, staying away from her daughter and grandchild in order to spare them the discomfort her son-in-law feels in her presence.

Whereas Bea is in business only to support her daughter, the Bea character in the second *Imitation* film (1959; here called Lora, and played by Lana Turner) is an actress who wants her career for its own sake and insists that she can't give it up to marry Steve (John Gavin), a photographer who loves her. "If you grew up, you could!" he accuses her. Ultimately, of course, Lora finds her success unfulfilling, realizes that she's been neglecting her daughter, and does give up her career to marry him.

In the novel Bea meets Virginia Eden, another successful businesswoman, who unlike her has a rich, crowded life full of ex-lovers and husbands and children. There is a hint that if Bea had not modeled herself from girlhood on her own patient, self-sacrificing mother, she might have been able to create such a life for herself. But in the movie, made at the height of the postwar idealization of domesticity, Lora has only the choice of true love with Steve, or her career and an unsatisfying liaison with the playwright whose comedies she stars in.

The Mermaid's Tail

Both versions have a parallel plot involving the black characters. In the novel Delilah's daughter, light-skinned Peola, refuses to be a "martyr," which her mother insists is the fate of their race, and passes for white. She marries a white man (first having herself sterilized so she will never have black children) and leaves with him for Bolivia, after begging her mother to sever all ties and never see her again. Sarah Jane, the film daughter, also leaves home in order to pass, but here her unwillingness to accept the natural martyrdom deemed appropriate for black people is associated—in accordance with a classic stereotype of African-American women—with a louche sexuality: Sarah Jane tells her mother (here called Annie) that she's a librarian but actually works as a nightclub chorus girl. In both film and novel, Delilah/Annie, having literally worked her life away for other people, dies as a saintly example of black women's true self-sacrificing nature. In the novel Peola vanishes and we never hear what happens to her; her function is to break Delilah's heart—"crucify" her, to use her own word—by refusing to join the "singin', happy, God-lovin', servin' race" who are "filled wid de blessin's of humility."⁵ Sarah Jane, however, shows up at the funeral, agonized at having, she believes, killed her mother. The final scene, where she and Lora reconcile, suggests that remorse has made Sarah Jane willing to accept reality—that is, take up her mother's position as a faithful, sexless servant. Both versions of the story lay down separate sacrifice tracks for black women and white women, based on the stereotypes of the appropriate role of each.

The other Hurst novel, *Back Street,* lays out an equally ambiguous scenario, this time of the woman who sacrifices for a man. Rae is a working-class woman who lives for twenty years as the "back-street girl" of her married lover. Left penniless after he dies, she survives by cadging a few francs at a time from winners at a European casino and finally dies solitary in her room.⁶ In the 1961 film with Susan Hayward, Rae is a glamorous fashion designer who rejects her unsophisticated but decent admirer from Nebraska to set up an illicit household with Paul (John Gavin), whose alcoholic monster wife won't divorce him. But much of Rae's time is spent waiting by the phone; alone in Paris on Thanksgiving, she calls her married sister long-distance and hears in the background the sounds of family togetherness that she cannot have. Finally she tells Paul, "All the old clichés are true. You can't break the rules. You can't live your own life. I'm never going to see you again." But then he and his wife die in a car crash, and his children come to her because "there's nobody left." Now they will be her family. Rae is both admired for the completeness of her devotion and punished for agreeing to an irregular liaison.

For all the modernity of the *mise-en-scène,* the degree of self-sacrifice that movies like this depict is on a par with the most extravagant fantasies of the Victorians. In *Letter from an Unknown Woman* (1948), to take another example, Joan Fontaine gives up her life to Louis Jourdan, an egocentric Don Juan of a pianist, for even less consideration than those nineteenth-century heroines got from the men anxiously bending over their deathbeds. Hearing him play across a courtyard, she falls in love with him while still a teenager, and, refusing a good marriage, continues to haunt his building until he notices her, sleeps with her, then departs for Italy. She has his baby and marries her former suitor, who is willing to accept the child, but leaves him and her son when the pianist crosses her path again, saying, "I've had no will but his, ever…I can't help it." But Jourdan—who has given up his music and spends his time seducing women—doesn't even remember her. Learning that her son is desperately ill—quite as though divine retribution for her desertion of him is being exacted through this innocent—she rushes to him, falls ill herself, and dies after writing Jourdan the letter of the title, proclaiming that she still loves him just as always. The only difference between this modern Lady of Shalott, immolating herself for a love that never even existed, and Tennyson's heroine is that while the latter was stricken by just the sight of Lancelot's flaming manhood—represented by shafts of sunlight reflected off his armor—the Fontaine character dies because she actually gives in to her passion.

The modern mermaid can also take more subtle forms. One fascinating embodiment is Bette Davis, whose varied screen roles sometimes seem to engage in a dialogue with one another about how much a woman is allowed to get away with. Often Davis played a woman whose initial selfishness—manifested as delight in making men fall in love with her without caring about them in return—in films like *Mr. Skeffington* (1944), *Jezebel* (1938), and *Dangerous* (1935), must be redeemed by suffering and sometimes death; even her frivolous rich girl who dies of a brain tumor in *Dark Victory* (1939) seems to be paying for the more sinful Davis personas in other films.

The mermaid's tail is especially explicit in *Dangerous,* where as an actress on the skids, rescued from an alcoholic stupor by Franchot Tone, Davis confesses that she's a jinx—her plays have closed, her leading man and two lovers have died. But, as Tone informs her later, it's really all her fault, because she's a "rotten, selfish…" (he's obviously about to say "bitch") who would "do anything to gain your own desire and go on, leaving somebody else to pay." That is, what's wrong with Bette Davis is that she's not a self-sacrificing woman, but one who wants some gratification herself; and when a woman is like that, somebody else will suffer. As with the Victorian woman whose failure to suffer in childbirth will harm the rest of society, Davis's failure to sacrifice her desires jinxes everyone around her. But it is Tone's housekeeper who cuts to the bone, revealing the deeper source of this selfishness and the jinx it creates: "She's dangerous. A bad woman got something a good woman ain't…she's got it." "It," of course, is the mermaid's tail. By the film's end Davis has renounced "it" and turned herself into a self-sacrificing angel ministering to her handicapped husband.

The amputation of the "dangerous" appendage is performed again in *Now, Voyager* (1942; based on another novel by Olive Higgins Prouty). Early in the film, Charlotte Vale gets caught kissing a handsome officer on a ship; we see she has a strong sexuality. Her domineering mother whisks her off and effectively squashes her, turning her into a dowdy old maid, until on a cruise she falls in love with Jerry (Paul Henreid), whom she can never marry because his wife will not divorce him. As in *Back Street,* the would-be lovers establish an ersatz family in which Jerry's daughter will live with Charlotte and he will visit. The condition is that there can be no actual living together—and no sex. For this arrangement Charlotte gives up a real marriage with a handsome young society man. As in the story of the Giving Tree, the grotesqueness of the situation is eclipsed by a spurious glow that envelops the woman's self-sacrifice, giving it a transcendent quality that appears to justify it.

Discussing all the films that treat versions of this theme would require an entire book in itself; suffice it to say that in the 1990s, new versions of the modern mermaid were still appearing. In *The Spitfire Grill* (1996), a mysterious young woman named Percy arrives in a small Maine town. Just released from prison, she is regarded with suspicion by almost everyone. It turns out that her crime, too, involved sex: she was raped by her stepfather, who then beat her when she was pregnant and killed the baby; trying to fight him off, she killed him. Ultimately Percy is revealed as a saint whose death (she goes over a waterfall trying to save a mentally ill hermit from the police) redeems everyone in the town. At her funeral, although the mourners look sad, there's a curious absence of grief; in fact, Percy's death has the same aesthetic quality as the nineteenth-century paintings of beautiful, expiring invalids. Though Percy's brush with sex involved rape rather than the exercise of her own desires, she is nevertheless stained by this sin and the killings that ensue from it. In the fine tradition of suffering as service, her function is to absorb the sins of others, which she then expiates by her death.

It is much the same with Bess, the heroine of *Breaking the Waves* (1996), yet another angelic young girl initially viewed with suspicion by a narrow-minded community, but finally revealed as a savior; in this case she actually works a miracle. Bess has been in a mental hospital but is really a holy fool who dialogues with God. She develops a wild sexual passion for her husband, Jan, and when a terrible injury makes him a quadriplegic, she sets off on a series of self-sacrificial sexual escapades with other men, for Jan has said that her telling him about these encounters will keep him alive. "I don't make love with them, I make love with Jan and it saves him from dying," she explains. Growing increasingly reckless, she is fatally stabbed by a vicious group of men on a boat. At the inquest her doctor explains that he would describe her not as "neurotic" or "psychotic" but as "good." And Jan, who has been near death, appears at her funeral, much recovered; later, he walks. Like the Little Mermaid, Bess—who in her dialogues tends to confuse Jan with God—seeks transcendence through a man and achieves it by dying in order to save him. But since she is a modern mermaid, her death comes about through sexual transgression.

To these morality plays featuring the sacrifice of sexual desire, the twentieth century added another powerful instrument of mutilation: the psychoanalytic redefinition of woman's nature as masochistic, which effectively excised other forms of desire as well. I will demonstrate how this happened by examining the most important arena for feminine self-sacrifice, the institution of motherhood.

Good Mothers

The question of what it means to be a "good mother" has never been settled, for each age creates its own definition. In Christian legend, the pelican, supposed to love its offspring more than any other creature, was said to pierce its breast to feed them with its own blood. The pelican thus became a symbol of Christ, nourishing humanity with his blood in the Eucharist. The nineteenth century naturally saw the Christlike woman of the domestic ideal as the pelican mother, "feeding her brood with her own vital substance."[7] Yet even the Victorians did not impose quite so heavy a burden on mothers as has the twentieth century.

Nineteenth-century advice to mothers emphasized their responsibility to raise children who would become virtuous citizens, which required vigilance and knowledge of correct child-rearing methods; by the end of the century, this meant submitting to instruction from scientific experts. Progressive-era reforms that prohibited child labor, excluded women from certain occupations, and shortened women's hours where they did work kept more women at home with young children, so that even working-class women absorbed the ideology of domesticity.[8] To these obligations, the twentieth century added a load of guilt.

Previously, the goal of the mother's devoted attention was to raise children whose behavior would conform to the needs of adults. But the 1930s saw the introduction of "child-centered mothering," in which the vigilant mother sought to detect and satisfy the child's every need.[9] The assumption that she would do this happily, even joyfully, was based on Freud's association of femininity with masochism. To successfully mature into a woman, Freud claimed, a girl must learn to renounce self-assertive activity, which he considered "masculine," and accept her passive feminine nature. This process required that she come to terms with masochism. That is, instead of directing what Freud thought of as her aggressive impulses outward by acting on them, she must turn them inward and direct them at her own ego. Two of his disciples, Marie Bonaparte and Helene Deutsch, developed from his work the idea that masochism was innate in women; they "argued that since biology necessitated that women feel pain at various points in their lives (menstruation, the breaking of the hymen, childbirth), the ability to derive pleasure from pain was a mature female adjustment to reality." This adjustment manifested in sex as pleasure in "being masochistically subjugated by the penis" and in maternity as the mother's sacrifice of her own needs for those of her child.[10]

The Mermaid's Tail

Healthy feminine development, furthermore, constituted a series of self-denials: a woman must renounce "all masculine wishes"—such as career ambitions—and transfer these to her child; ultimately, she must give up not only the child himself (having a son was her highest fulfillment) but all expectation that he would fulfill her sublimated ambitions. Women who failed to relinquish their masculine desires would still have too much ego left to be good mothers.[11] When in the 1959 *Imitation of Life,* Steve tells Lora that she would give up her career and marry him if she only "grew up," he is echoing the notion, so pervasive that it infiltrated even this level of culture, that the only truly mature woman is the one who has relinquished her "masculine" ambitions. Lora also must learn that her preoccupation with her career has led her to neglect her daughter, forfeiting the girl's trust.

The theory of feminine masochism justified the requirement for maternal self-sacrifice by asserting that for women, suffering was pleasurable—a notion which, as the French historian of motherhood Elisabeth Badinter remarks, is more punitive than the theological idea that women must suffer to expiate Eve's original sin. That "curse carried a moral justification, and physical pain was the price exacted for her fault. At least she was not asked to like it." But now, as Deutsch warned, mothers in whom feminine masochism with its "readiness for sacrifice does not operate" would suffer "a much crueler aggressive masochism—that stemming from the sense of guilt."[12]

Today experts continue to assure mothers that tender unstinting devotion, critical to the child's mental and physical health, is a natural feminine instinct. Psychiatrist D. W. Winnicott's phrase "ordinary devoted mother" implies that complete preoccupation with the child is the mother's normal state; it leaves no room for maternal love associated with different behavior, like that of Julia in Chapter 3.[13] The importance ascribed to the mother's role also meant that she was blamed for whatever might go wrong with the child, and—because it is always possible to believe that one has not given enough, or experienced enough pleasure in doing so—Deutsch's prediction that she would experience a cruel sense of guilt was often fulfilled.

Not surprisingly, the experts of the 1950s noticed that the middle-class mothers of that era, who were supposedly living out the domestic/Freudian ideal, were not as content as they should have been. Under a seemingly feminine placidity, commented a physician in 1953, one often encountered "an inwardly tense and emotionally unstable individual seething with hidden aggressiveness and resentment."[14] It is out of such feelings that Marilyn French's novel *Her Mother's Daughter* seems to arise. The novel traces the paths by which "the sorrows of the mothers" descend from each generation to the next among four generations of a Polish immigrant family in New York. In each generation, the mother's desire to have her own life in the world is sacrificed to the duty to bear her daughter, who then turns against her in bitterness. French encapsulates her vision of the mother-daughter relationship thus:

> Midge mothers do not lay eggs, they reproduce young from inside their bodies without benefit of clergy, state, or even any informal male assistance. And the baby develops inside the mother's body, not in a uterus, but in her tissues, and eventually, she fills her whole body, devouring it from the inside. When she is ready to be born, she breaks out of her mother/prison, leaving behind only a chitinous shell. They never have mother-daughter squabbles; midge mothers may sacrifice themselves entirely for their young, but the young never have to hear about it.[15]

For French, this gruesome image evidently represents not simply the one family of the novel, but the universal destiny of mothers.

It was this nightmare vision of being totally consumed that led many feminists of the sixties and seventies to vehemently reject motherhood. To writer Alix Kates Shulman, whose first child was born six years before the women's movement began, motherhood meant she must relinquish her previous defiance of convention and her worldly ambitions. "The day I gave birth I surrendered, abandoning my independence, fearing that to fight on would endanger the children. To have done otherwise seemed selfish." From then on, she felt, her life "belonged to others." [16]

Most of the young middle-class women she met in the early feminist groups of the late sixties were not mothers; to them, motherhood was a trap that would isolate them in the home and make them eternally dependent. Looking at their own mothers, the ultradomestic housewives of the 1950s, these women "were left with a deep-seated fear that our lives would be destroyed, we'd be ruined, if we had kids. At some psychic level, we felt it was death," explained (Chude) Pam Allen, cofounder of New York Radical Women, an early feminist group, many years later. "Our mothers told us they loved being a wife and mother, but we felt their anger." [17] For themselves these young women sought "full lives, work that mattered." [18]

"We were trying to assert a basic human right: to act in our own interest and not just sacrifice it for somebody else," explained Shulman.

> To me, the repetitive act of cooking and cleaning, even for someone else, wasn't by itself a sacrifice. What made it a sacrifice was that by dividing things according to gender, women got to do only half of what there was to do, and it was the lousy half. Men got the better half. There's nothing inherently unpleasant about the activities of housework—it was the either/or-ness of it, that meant you couldn't be in the world. Even more—this is so hard to pin down—is what it implies about your desires: whose life counted most. We didn't want to be denied any part of experience just because we were

women. Of course you could do housework and have a
job, and many people did, but still you were not supposed to put your own work first.

Yet unlike many of the childless women, Shulman was not
rebelling against motherhood per se; instead, through feminism she
found a synthesis. "I didn't feel a contradiction between motherhood
and feminism. Other people did, and I had a hard time maintaining
my position, defending and explaining motherhood to the other
women. Feminism showed me I didn't have to choose" between her
children and her ambitions, that "it was okay to act in my own interest. I never questioned that the children's needs came first, but life is
large and there was room for both. I can't say I sacrificed myself for
my children at all, because the minute I realized I could have both, I
started to write. As with housework, it's not motherhood itself but the
heavy burden of guilt and responsibility" that constitutes the sacrifice.[19]

The model these young feminists were opposing was made possible—and even likely—for them by the fact that most were white and
middle-class. But the domestic ideal was not the only model of motherhood that existed. To understand the meaning of sacrifice for
women, it is important to see how women in other social and economic circumstances had quite different experiences of motherhood
and found themselves making different sacrifices. The history of
African-American women offers some revealing distinctions.

The following description is based on what African-American
women have said about their own history and experience. Their tes-
timony differentiates them from stereotyped images of black mothers
created by the larger society, which it uses to define them.
Delilah/Annie in *Imitation of Life,* for example, embodies the faithful
"mammy" who puts her white family ahead of her own (a degree of
sacrifice never asked of any white woman!).[20] This image makes the
black woman an even greater sacrificer than the white woman; while

in many cases this may be true, the image does not depict the true nature of the black woman's sacrifice.

Black women—even those of the middle class—were always unable to live up to the domestic ideal, both because they had to work and because the history of sexual exploitation of slaves by white masters tainted these women with the stereotype of promiscuity, so they could never appear pure. Consequently they created their own definition of moral womanhood; it involved not passivity and withdrawal from the public sphere but activism to promote justice and progress for their race. Frances Ellen Watkins Harper, a nineteenth-century African-American abolitionist, advocate for women, and popular poet and novelist, expressed these values in her 1869 novel *Minnie's Sacrifice*. Minnie is raised as white in the North, but when she discovers she is half black, she chooses to move to the South with her husband Louis and dedicate herself to helping her people rebuild their lives after the Civil War. There she is murdered, apparently by the Ku Klux Klan. "The lesson of Minnie's sacrifice," Watkins concludes, is that "a truly dignified womanhood" consists in dedicating "whatever gifts we possess" to "serve the interests of our race by a generous and loving diffusion, [rather] than by a narrow and selfish isolation."[21]

The tradition Minnie represents continued into the twentieth century. "I think of you and Lucy Laney and myself as being in the most sacrificing class in our group of women," wrote the educator Mary McLeod Bethune in 1927 to a fellow activist. At the time she was president of the National Association of Colored Women; later she became an official in the Roosevelt administration. "I have unselfishly given my best, and I thank God that I have lived long enough to see the fruits for it."[22]

Black women redefined motherhood as well; most saliently, due to poverty and the difficulty black men encountered in finding employment, for these women motherhood included economic independence and the ability to provide for children. Nor did they experience the split between the public world of work and the private sphere of family posited by the domestic ideal. Since they had to work, they created communal child-care networks in which a group of women shared responsibility for all the children in the community, and they adapted African traditions of extended family units into a concept of family that included the entire black community.[23]

In one way, then, black women's experience of sacrifice inverted that of white women. As Antonia Cottrell Martin explained, for black women, staying at home to raise children "is a real luxury. Sacrifice in the black community is that mothers cannot be at home with their children because they have to work. When a black woman goes out to work, she sacrifices her children so they can all eat. The children have to learn to become independent very early." African-American mothers had no opportunity to practice child-centered mothering; indeed, according to their daughters, the demands of providing for and raising children amid poverty and the need to mount psychic defenses against the effects of racism were so great that these mothers tended not to be demonstratively affectionate. "Survival is the greatest gift of love," wrote poet Audre Lorde. "Sometimes, for Black mothers, it is the only gift possible, and tenderness gets lost." In Toni Morrison's *Sula,* Hannah asks her mother, Eva, who raised three children alone, "Mamma, did you ever love us?" "No," Eva responds. "I don't reckon I did. Not the way you thinkin'." Life was too hard for her to cuddle and play with them: "They wasn't no time" when they weren't sick, when she didn't have to worry about what to feed them: "...did I love you girl I stayed alive for you can't you get that through your thick head...?"[24]

In such a context, staying home as a housewife was not a defeat. Being able to decline the poorly paid jobs that were available meant that the black mother could give her labor to her family, bolstering its social and economic position. Historian Elsa Barkley Brown, describing how her college-educated mother turned down work as a maid—the only job she could get—calls this "decision to be a wife and mother first in a world which defined Black women in so many other ways…an act of resistance."[25]

Joyce described to me a still deeper level of self-sacrifice:

> a sacrifice of self indoctrinated in women—I certainly received it, I know my mother received it. The things they don't say even though you know there are opinions and ideas and a spirit, and all kinds of stuff locked up in there. It was like the good girl kind of thing. Not making waves, the smile on the face. I think that's a legacy of Jim Crow in the South. It's the same with black men, though you have a whole history of women being the recipients of the rage that they felt. There was a lot of that swallowing down of feelings—you had to or else I think you'd die.

At another level, African-American women have felt a duty to subordinate their desire for individual development to the needs of black people as a whole, putting their energy into holding families together and supporting men under assault. "For years in this country there was no one for black men to vent their rage on except black women," wrote Toni Morrison. "And for years black women accepted that rage, even regarded that acceptance as their unpleasant duty. But in so doing they frequently kicked back, and they seem never to have become the true slaves that white women see in their own history."[26]

There was therefore quite a gap between the view of motherhood held by the young white feminists described above and that of a group of young black feminists of the same period in the New York City suburbs of Mount Vernon and New Rochelle. Where the middle-class white women saw motherhood as a form of oppression, the black women, who were mostly working class or on welfare, saw it as a source of power, emotional satisfaction, and positive identity; it represented far more meaningful labor than the low-level jobs they could get. And since being a mother meant becoming a part of a community network, it was not isolating.[27]

More profoundly, for these black women the concept of motherhood encompassed working for the good of the entire community. In their writings they contrasted "dick-happy sisters," for whom the most important thing was having a man, with those who "put their children first." Unlike the white women, they did not express a need to put themselves first. Yet for them putting children first had a larger meaning than it did for the more individualistically-oriented white women: it meant working to uplift the entire community—becoming active in schooling, getting landlords to make repairs, working for welfare rights.[28] Later I will analyze more deeply how poverty and political oppression further redefine sacrifice; here I just note that while the white women's more advantaged social position allowed them the opportunity to think in terms of self-development, the black women's community orientation could equally build up and develop the self.

In any case, neither the feminists' rejection of self-sacrificing motherhood nor the black women's style of mothering born of necessity entered the mainstream. It is still true that, as Julia put it, "Everything you read tells you that loving your children as a good mother, by its very definition, means sacrifice." The massive acceptance of this model was evident in the reactions she and her husband encountered when they reversed conventional child-rearing roles. In fact, according to research by scholar Sharon Hays, poor, working-class, middle-class, and upper-middle-class women all share the assumption that mother love means sacrifice. Jacqueline, a highly paid scientist, scaled back her hours when she had children, since "her children's needs come before her own.... 'I work my day around their needs and not mine.'" Eva, a working-class Chicana, said, "I think I'm a good mother because I sacrifice a lot for my daughter." Most likely her feeling was also shaped by the traditional Latino image of mothers as "self-sacrificing and saintly," patient and enduring.[29]

The Mermaid's Tail

Many women saw motherhood as a lesson in becoming unselfish. "I think we all have a tendency to get really selfish," said one, "and children come along, and you can't be selfish because they demand so much nurturing. It helps *you* to give more to them." The women Hays quotes sound proud and even joyous in their child-centered mothering, and as she points out, while they may never put their own needs before their children's, most do at least take those needs into account. Yet it seems extreme to associate working just for personal gratification with selfishness, as they tended to do, echoing the magazine articles that exhort women not to sacrifice themselves too much for their families yet never acknowledge that they might have other compelling interests. "Make sure you're reassuring the kids that what Mommy's doing…is not for herself, but for all of them," advised one mother. "You should work to get money not for material things but for family togetherness."[30] No doubt she would disapprove of Julia's explanation to her daughter: "I do love to be with you, but I also love to go to my work."

Accordingly *The Good Mother,* a film that came out in 1988, when large numbers of white middle-class mothers had entered the labor force, presents a mother who has no interest at all in a career. In this film, based on the 1981 novel by Sue Miller, the eternal question of what constitutes a good mother receives an ironic twist, since the heroine Anna actually is what all those eighties career women were running away from being: a mother whose child is her entire life. When her lover Leo objects that she has no passionate commitment, Anna retorts that her commitment is to her daughter Molly and that she hates hearing someone say there's no honor in that.

Anna still has not given up enough, however, for she retains her mermaid's tail, and when it gives a flick, it must be cut off. With Leo her sexuality has flowered, and the openness she permits in front of Molly leads him to think it's all right to allow the little girl to touch his penis. When Anna's ex-husband finds out, he takes her to court, and she loses custody. Devastated, she screams at Leo that her life is ruined and throws him out. At the film's end she is living a passive half-life with no apparent content—except, perhaps, waiting for a new lover to manifest and give her a new baby.

Although the film portrays Anna sympathetically, there is also a hint that by introducing her to sexual passion, Leo destroyed the garden of innocence she and Molly inhabited before he showed up. Anna was complicit in this fall because instead of maintaining her pure Victorian state of chastity, she tasted the fruit he offered. She winds up as the obverse of Bette Davis at the end of *Now, Voyager:* whereas Charlotte Vale could have the man's child but no sex life, Anna has the sex life but loses the child, even though the child is her own. In this definition, being a good mother means radical self-mutilation.

A Real-Life Siren's Song

Popular fictions of feminine self-sacrifice are paralleled by opinions circulating through other media, from the lowbrow to the high. Therapist John Gray, for example, has published a series of best-selling books and videos based on the notion that since "men are from Mars, women are from Venus," they can improve their relationships through a better understanding of their differences. Whereas, says Gray, "men are wired to give their all to work, then come home and receive…women are built to give and receive simultaneously"; women have a "natural inclination to give unconditionally." In the old days, when "men were still the providers and women the nurturers," full-time housewives received support from other women during the day and were therefore able to be "pleasing and accommodating to a man when he came home" without feeling stressed. But now that women too work outside the home, their load is doubled, because "when they get home, instinct takes over and they continue giving." They wind up "feeling like martyrs who sacrifice their own needs to ensure harmony in the relationship."[31]

An "important difference between men and women," Gray maintains, is that if a man doesn't get support, he'll "stop giving more"; "men give only what their fathers gave and expect to receive the same measure of support." But "when a woman feels unsupported, she feels responsible for doing more"; she will "give too much and feel overworked." To remedy this situation, men must learn how to listen to women and make them feel emotionally supported. Women will then "appreciate" men more. And once men feel appreciated, they will naturally start helping women more in the home.[32]

Gray puts his finger on a real problem in people's experience, and his explanation of it has the considerable virtue of avoiding blame, allowing women and men to impute only positive motives to themselves and each other. But his solution does not address the actual physical burden of women's double load (since men at best are just "helping" them do the job that is still defined as theirs). In fact, his hodgepodge of half-baked assertions about "innate" human nature that hopelessly mix biology, prehistory, and evolution (man the hunter, woman the nurturing homemaker) only perpetuates the notion that selfless, unconditional giving is inherent in femininity. And he casts it as the same type of glowing tribute to "the loving female nature" that the advice-givers of the nineteenth century used to domesticate women in the first place.[33] Once men learn the rhetoric, the problem is solved; the only difference is that now, instead of having servants, she gets a little help around the house and a lot more appreciation.

Considerably farther toward the highbrow end of the intellectual spectrum, we find conservative computer scientist David Gelernter writing an article for *Commentary* on "Why Mothers Should Stay Home" that drew some thoughtful objections from equally conservative readers. Several describe the tedium and isolation of full-time child care and the depression it engenders in many women. One correspondent objects that while no one questions a man's desire to exercise his talents and gain professional prestige, "in women [these feelings] are regarded as selfish and antisocial." She wants to know "why the call for self-abnegation goes out to women only...why must women sacrifice everything for family and society, when men need not?"[34]

Gelernter's defense of his position is about as scientific as John Gray's: "Here are the facts: women and men are different; the differences are such as to make women better than men, on the whole, at caring for children....Every sensible person knows this to be true.... If you don't know the difference between mothers and fathers, any two-year-old will explain it to you." He adds that his own children prefer to be comforted when unhappy and sung to sleep when sick by his wife, who doesn't find mothering "a miserable occupation." And he chooses to believe her, not anybody else.[35]

To their very different audiences, Gray and Gelernter—the one encouraging, tolerant, and gently humorous, the other supercilious and dogmatic—preach the same message. Multiplied by hundreds, they turn into a rousing chorus still singing a real-life siren's song that casts a spell on women. Denise, for example, sounded almost as though she had spent her childhood and young womanhood in a trance. She "never questioned" her choices to get married and to become a hygienist instead of a dentist, because all she wanted was "to please everyone, to live up to the expectations of my family. Nothing I did was for what I wanted. Everything was either for Bill, or my children, or my mom, or my dad. I never even knew I had the choice to do what I wanted."

This absence of any desire other than "to please" is precisely the consequence of amputating the mermaid's tail. Writer Dalma Heyn, who intervewed married women who had had adulterous affairs, concluded that this amputation—that is, the loss of the erotic in both its narrow and its widest senses—was the underlying motive for their infidelity. Under the influence of the icon Heyn calls the "Perfect Wife," whose "virtue exists in direct proportion to how much of her self is whittled away," these wives—without even being asked to— had sacrificed vital elements of themselves when they got married. The parts of the self that they buried for the sake of marriage contained their deepest feelings—in particular, intense sexual feelings. One of the "love lessons for girls" that teach them to become Perfect Wives, says Heyn, is the story of the Little Mermaid, from which they learn that in addition to being selfless and forgiving, to win the prince they must give up their sexuality—that is, accept silence and mutilation.[36]

The women Heyn spoke to had fully intended to continue their own self-development during marriage, but no matter what their age, they all came up against a conflict between "the old selfless model" of the wife and "the new, more self-fulfilling one." She quotes "forty-nine-year-old Hope, married twenty-three years and with three teenage boys": "My marriage works best when I genuinely care more for us as a family than for myself—which most of the time is how I really feel. I feel best then…and everyone else is of course happiest. But the truth? It leaves no room for me at all. It's full-time. And the setup simply works best that way."[37]

These women had affairs, says Heyn, in order to regenerate their mermaid's tail. In her affair, confides Clara, "I got my brain back." Now she "can think straight again" and make choices "for me only"—like refusing to go along on the family fishing trips that made her seasick and sunsick.[38] It took a reconnection with her deepest physical desires to make her realize that she was allowed not to suffer.

Among the women I interviewed, Sharon incarnates the mermaid's mutilation in a startlingly literal way. "I got married knowing it was wrong," Sharon recalled. "I did not love him."

> I was eighteen and very beautiful; I looked like Elizabeth Taylor. My parents were very concerned about my safety: the sooner they got me settled…They thought this was a good match, I would be taken care of. Jack was a very rich boy, and it was really almost like a corporate takeover—I was just the prop. Jack proposed to me, but

Slaying the Mermaid

I didn't want to get married and I said to my mother, "Don't you think I'm too young?" She said I was mature. I was really a prop. I understood what they were doing and yet I was helpless to change it.

The takeover was executed by Jack's parents, determined to obtain this desirable commodity for their son and install her in her position with appropriate fanfare. They overpowered her father's attempts to hold the wedding in Sharon's hometown and organized a magnificent ceremony on their own turf.

It was at a beautiful home. I was dressed in my dress, standing on top of these stone steps you had to walk down and around to the other side of the house, where they had all the chairs. I had no one there. They were playing "Here Comes the Bride," and I said to myself, "I wonder how many times they would play 'Here Comes the Bride' if I fell. I could be lying in a pool of blood, and they'd keep playing the music." There didn't seem to be anyone wondering if I could get down. I remember looking up at the sky and saying, "God, you wouldn't let me make a mistake, would you?" Then I looked at the parking lot and said, "I wonder if I have the nerve to see if there's a key in the car, and play a Holly Golightly thing?" And I said no. I had all these doubts. But I felt this was the picture I was in, so I might as well go finish it out.

I just didn't know how to rock the boat and jump out, or think I had the right to say, "I don't want to get married." When he proposed to me, I didn't want to hurt his feelings and say no. I was totally geared for pleasing someone else and being very concerned about another's feelings.

"Sharon," I exclaimed, "you were like a virgin sacrifice."

"I never told anybody this," she responded, "but my mother sent me to a doctor to have my hymen broken, so it wouldn't hurt."

> But the invasive thing done by the doctor, who was not a gentleman, was worse. It was almost as though she sent me to be raped, and that accompanied me into marriage, which was detestable. So when you said "sacrificial virgin," you really hit a nerve.

Sacrifice stops being metaphoric here; it acquires a fleshly reality substantiated in blood—transporting us back to ancient rituals that put a live creature to the knife so that the gods would bless the plans of the sacrificers. Chapter 6 will take up this motif of the sacrifice of a virgin daughter; Sharon's story serves to ground us in its basis in reality.

Suffering Artists

Some women aim at salvation not through a man but by and for themselves, as artists. But creativity is a potent form of the erotic, so they must pay for this refusal to give up their mermaid's tail. The notion that the artist must sacrifice for art is a cliché, but when the artist is female, the cliché is inverted. In an essay on women writers, Ursula Le Guin asserts that women who combine household work with writing have been judged "unnatural" because of the tenet that the artist must sacrifice "all 'lesser' obligations and affections to a 'higher' cause, embracing the moral responsibility of the soldier or the saint." She terms "this heroic stance, the *Gauguin Pose,*" noting that what the heroic artist really sacrifices is all the people around him, as Gauguin did when he deserted his family to pursue his higher cause in Tahiti.[39]

By contrast, says Le Guin, women artists are expected to sacrifice *themselves*—that is, forgo children and a normal domestic life. The "artist-housewife" who sticks by her "lesser" obligations is not considered a real artist; for, as Freud said, since a true woman cannot be "active," to be an artist "a woman must unwoman herself."[40] Whereas Heyn's wives had to sacrifice those parts of their selves that did not fit into domesticity, female artists must give up domesticity in order to truly create.

This was another lesson taught by the "woman's film." In *Morning Glory* (1933), for example, when fledgling actress Katharine Hepburn debuts with stunning success on Broadway, she sends away her suitor Douglas Fairbanks, Jr., telling him she cannot be married and have her career. Still, the film warns, her success may fade like a morning glory and she'll be left alone—like the old wardrobe mistress, whose own head was turned by a momentary success when she was young; now, she sighs, she wishes she had listened when someone told her he loved her. Even as Hepburn stoutly affirms, "I'm not afraid!" the film ends on a disconcerting note of ambiguity and threat.

Certainly many women artists have managed to live more positive versions of the creative life, especially since the 1970s, but the old mandate still exerts its influence; Moira, as we saw, was convinced that maintaining her commitment to her art meant she could not have a husband and children. And despite much revision of Freud, the association between women and masochism remains compelling, so that women who achieve recognition as artists without "unwomaning" themselves often do so by virtue of association with the cardinal female virtue of suffering. In 1977 the main character of Marilyn French's first novel, *The Women's Room,* despite her feminist awakening, is left embittered and alone at the end; this essentially despairing, defeatist outlook was what made the novel so popular among mainstream critics and the public as a representative of the early women's movement. In 1994 an exemplary book was *Prozac Nation,* twenty-six-year-old Elizabeth Wurtzel's memoir of suicidal depression.[41] It is not that cultural arbiters consciously try to enforce an ideology of women as sufferers, but that most people are so steeped in this association that images which match it feel comfortable and familiar. This is why the iconic equivalent of the heroic male artist is the suffering female artist. Two in particular have attained that status: Frida Kahlo and Sylvia Plath.

When in 1996 *The New York Times Magazine* devoted an entire issue to female icons of our century, Kahlo made the cut. Her "worldwide constituency" included "art students, leftists, feminists, the genuinely ill, the merely miserable—anyone who can identify with her tale of grief and grit," asserted the profile of her.[42] As a child Kahlo contracted polio; then at eighteen she sustained devastating injuries in a bus accident that left her in constant pain for the rest of her life. The work that made her famous consists of a series of self-portraits representing the suffering resulting from both the injury to her body and the emotional wounds inflicted by her unfaithful husband, the renowned muralist Diego Rivera.

According to her biographer Hayden Herrera,

> the role of the heroic sufferer became an integral part of Frida: the mask became the face. And as the dramatization of pain became ever more central to her self-image, she exaggerated the painful facts of her past....She created a self that would be strong enough to withstand the blows life dealt her....Both the strength and the emphasis on suffering pervade Frida's paintings.

And, adds Herrera, "Almost everyone in Mexico who speaks of Frida's accident says that it was fated: she did not die because it was her destiny to survive, to live out a calvary of pain."[43]

This potently romantic vision appealed to many people: Herrera's book became a best-seller, and fascination with Kahlo led "a million people" to initiate "Frida projects," according to Madonna, who

Slaying the Mermaid

herself hoped to make a film of Kahlo's life.[44] Following several large exhibitions, Kahlo self-portraits began to appear on T-shirts, calendars, posters, aprons, and other items. Her paintings now sell for millions.

Some people hated this vicarious "wallowing" in Kahlo's suffering. Critic Deborah Solomon found the paintings' "victimized, over-intimate point of view" tiresome, noting crankily that Kahlo's work confirmed "the notion that art is the product of suffering and the dearly held belief that no one suffers more than women. Her paintings seize on illness as an appropriate metaphor for her gender." Solomon blamed "Kahlo's feminist admirers" for making her into "a saint with a paintbrush"; but as we know, it was not twentieth-century feminists who first made saints out of suffering women. If to her admirers Kahlo made martyrdom and womanhood seem twinned conditions—to paraphrase one of them—they had plenty of precedent for this reading of her work.[45]

Kahlo, remarked one observer of her "huge cult," is "the art world's version of Sylvia Plath"; and *Newsweek*'s reviewer of a cookbook containing Kahlo's Mexican fiesta recipes jocularly anticipated that the next volume in the series would be *"In the Kitchen with Sylvia Plath"*—also calculated to appeal to the "legions of fans who can't resist a suffering artist." And indeed much the same "glamour of fatality" surrounds this other "feminist martyr," the poet who at thirty-two committed suicide by putting her head in an oven while her two small children slept. "The details of Plath's suicide have assumed totemic significance for a cult of followers who regard her as St. Sylvia, the high priestess of suffering," wrote a reviewer of two of the many books about her that continued to be written despite the opposition of the Plath estate.[46]

Whereas Kahlo painted her tortured, bleeding body with a stoic, masklike face, Plath was the opposite of stoic: she cried out in her poetry all "the horrible things that we don't dare say out loud, the crazy, violent, self-loathing things we all secretly feel sometimes," as a reviewer for *Mademoiselle* put it. To women who themselves felt too fearful to express "prohibited, ugly, dangerous emotion," seeing this truth expressed in public was "a wonderful gift."[47] But what made Plath a totemic poet, instead of just an angry one, was her suicide.

When she first read Plath's book *Ariel,* written just before she killed herself, poet Alicia Ostriker was also a mother of two babies, as well as a teacher of college freshmen. "Either set of duties was inherently infinite, infinitely guilt-producing," and she had to steal time late at night to read. "Often it seemed I never slept." Reading Plath's poems one such night, she reacted with "stunned amazement"—first, because "she had dared to kill herself.... This made her somehow an aristocrat and me a peasant gasping at her nobility.... Second: she had permitted herself emotions which for me were forbidden, and which I spent a considerable amount of effort attempting to repress. Self-loathing, that drug. Loathing of others, especially my near and dear." To Ostriker then, Plath's self-destructiveness was "seductive."

Writing about this reaction fifteen years later, however, Ostriker knows that "in middle age I am a peasant...concerned with survival.... But to my first encounter with Plath I date the initial stirrings of a realization...that to accomplish this intention will require...reconciliation with a self that wants to kill or die." While she honors Plath for casting light into the murky cave of female fear and hatred, she and "many other women...are pulling ourselves from martyrdom's shadows to some sort of daylight."[48] In the following chapters, I will try to do that too. But first we need to poke around a bit more inside the cave.

6

Disappearing Acts

BROWSING THROUGH A STREET FAIR ONE DAY IN OCTOBER, CLARA came upon a local political group asking for volunteers. According to their fliers, the group addressed women's economic issues in a way Clara liked, focusing on financially struggling working-class and poor women. Immediately she thought of her daughter Vera, who was due to graduate high school that January and had a case of senioritis. "She was bored with everything," Clara explained. "I wanted her to be exposed to something socially active, and this was up her alley because it would give her a chance to write, which she likes to do." So she put Vera's name and phone number on a list.

Right away, the group made contact. Prodded by several phone calls, Vera visited their office and did some typing for them, but came home distinctly unimpressed; they had made her sit near a window that leaked freezing-cold air, and nobody talked to her. They continued to call, however, and she went back, telling Clara she was working on their newspaper. She brought home copies of the paper, which Clara thought "bland and boring, not very political"—strange for such a group. But Clara, overworked at her job and with younger children to care for, did not pay too much attention to Vera's new interest.

Soon Vera started talking about other organizations, apparently linked to the original one—all far-left political groups—and particularly about one man whom she described as a well-known leftist leader. She was surprised that Clara, who came from a left-wing background and was familiar with the entire spectrum of leftist politics, had never heard of him. Then one day Vera let drop that about forty members of this group, including some of the leaders, lived together in a few apartments in the same building. In response to Clara's questioning, she said that only one of them held an outside job. Pressed further, she revealed that a couple of times when she had stayed there overnight—telling her mother that all the teenage volunteers had stayed in order to meet the newspaper deadline—after finishing their work they had gone to classes that started at two A.M.

"Then I freaked," Clara recalled. "I told her it was a cult, and she clammed up. I hadn't known the names of any of the organizations she had mentioned. Now I couldn't remember them, and she hid all the newspapers. That's when I actively started finding out more information."

Meanwhile Vera was spending more and more time with the group. It turned out that after her first visit she had never been back to the local group at all, but had gone instead to the nearby headquarters of the national organization it was connected to. By early December she was going there several afternoons a week after school and staying over one night each weekend. The changes in her during this period frightened her mother.

She was so completely wasted, I thought she was being drugged. She would come home Sunday morning and sleep all day. Even Monday she had a hard time getting up for school, which she had never had before. There was a rapid change in her body. Her stomach popped out like she was bloated, and I wondered whether she was pregnant. Her voice changed—she started talking in a high, cheery, chipper voice, especially on the phone. Her eyes got shinier. Her whole train of thought was different, like connections had been snipped. The papers she wrote for school were half-baked, not logical. It was the same when she talked about the organization—I had a hard time understanding what she was saying. Instead of talking about a subject, she'd tell anecdotes that didn't hang together.

By the time Vera graduated in January, she was coming home only twice a week; then once a week. After her eighteenth birthday in February, she moved out.

By now Clara had discovered the name of the organization and confirmed that it was indeed a cult. She learned that members had been beaten in the past; that new recruits were cut off from their families and friends and physically punished for attempting to leave. Longtime members couldn't leave even if they wanted to, because they had no money and no place to go. To ensure that Vera always knew she had a home to return to, for three years Clara managed to maintain tenuous contact with her daughter. She was allowed occasionally to speak to Vera by phone; and, playing on her leftist credentials, she volunteered at the headquarters, where it became clear that this organization was unlike any leftist group she had ever known.

Supposedly, they were revolutionaries: a small dedicated band, preparing themselves to take over the government and transform society so there would no longer be rich and poor. At least half of the members, in Clara's opinion, were sincerely dedicated to equality and social justice. But she saw that their many hours of intensive work served simply to maintain the organization rather than help people; although the group did distribute some food, its claim to be doing vital political work for low-paid, nonunionized workers was a sham.

The members put in prodigious amounts of labor under harsh living conditions. Forty-five people shared three bathrooms. Converting their offices to bedrooms each night by pushing back the furniture and laying down pieces of foam rubber, they slept shoulder to shoulder. Officially they were allowed five hours of sleep a night, but when something special was happening—as it often was—they had to stay up longer. They were not free to walk out the door; people wanting to go even next door to the group's other apartment had to report their movements to three different functionaries. Music—very important to Vera and many of the others—was allowed only via headphones and only after the eighteen-hour workday was over. Phone calls were not allowed until after work either, which meant they couldn't be made, since work did not end until two A.M.

Clara met the charismatic leader, whose gift was for manipulating people and who lived off the kicks he got from wielding power. Maintaining contact with Vera, who never came home and hardly ever even left the headquarters, required shrewd strategy, for despite her volunteer work and her leftist background, as a parent Clara was never trusted. Then suddenly the leader died, and Clara felt a surge of hope, for although the group managed to hold together, she knew her daughter was increasingly dissatisfied under the new leadership. Six months later Vera, who had been sent to another city and was not under the same close supervision as at the headquarters, walked out.

Several factors had contributed to her departure, Clara learned later. For one, the new leaders found her hard to handle, decided she was more trouble than she was worth, and deliberately made her life miserable. But more important were her own conclusions about what social action should be like.

"It's the politics that confuse me now, not the actions," Vera reflected some months later.

I still— If somebody said to me today, "Would you give your life so that a hundred people could be happy?"—whatever—there'd be no *question*. That just wouldn't be.

It's not true that only idiots join cults, that you would have to be stupid to do it. It's all based on underlying belief. You don't get into it because you think, "Oh, I just don't want to be me anymore." Or that might be a factor, but you do it because you think, "Oh, that's a good idea."

In her case the idea resonated with an intense but undirected altruism that ran like a clear stream under Vera's adolescent contrariness. "In the household I grew up in, I spent a lot of time around adults who were very frank about the human condition, why people were starving, that things weren't okay." As a child she cried for hours over TV commercials asking viewers to sponsor children in Ethiopia, demanding to know why they couldn't come here.

I would fantasize that the entire country was surrounded by barbed wire. I would cut all the barbed wire and let all the children of Ethiopia onto a big boat. And if they needed me to, I would stay behind and take anybody's place. I don't know where that came from, that idea that it was better for me to suffer than anybody else.

So when she met a group of people who were saying "something I had always thought—you can accomplish things, you can make a difference if you try hard enough," this young woman, a member of a generation identified by its nihilistic slacker mentality, flung herself into fulfilling a vision of self-sacrifice certainly as pure as—if philosophically remote from—that of St. Catherine:

Hey: this is the whole answer to the ills of the world lying in your hands. What else are you going to do to put food on people's tables, what other way is there to get medical care to people? Can you really just give up on everybody?

In this country you see a lot of liberalism. Liberals think helping people is fine till it encroaches on their own life. But our mentality was not that everybody's going to be happy. We're saying that everybody's going to have a plate of food on their table. The most important thing is to keep people alive. If you have the answer to the entire problems of humankind in your hand and all you had to do was try real hard, of course a person would do it. Most people would, I think.

What drove her out out of the organization was fundamentally its failure to live up to its own ideals. The leadership's method of controlling its workers, she explained, was to "tear people down" by telling them they were stupid and incompetent, "slam" them, "lambaste" them. She wrote endless "polemics" objecting to this, all of which were ignored.

What are you sacrificing yourself for? Are you going to push to protect the people you work alongside and who are ostensibly your friends, or are you going to knock over your friends for the greater good? My conclusion was: an organization who can't treat people that they're close with, and live and work with, with respect is not going to do much good for the people of this country or for the world.

Vera's family background led her to answer the siren call of self-sacrifice in the arena of far-left politics (or at least what she thought was far-left politics), but images of dedication entice many young girls, and the same extremism can be played out in other arenas. "I think the image of the nun is something that every Catholic girl works against or with or plays off in some way," novelist Mary Gordon told an interviewer in 1981 when her novel *The Company of Women* was published. "Which is very different from other religious traditions. You do have the notion of a woman, without men, living a very pure centered life which has nothing to do with the domestic." She herself had felt the pull of the "notion of an unencumbered, devoted, directed singular life," which "came out of those images of the virgin martyrs." Knowing that she could not live that way herself, she chose to experience it vicariously by creating a heroine who tries to do so. Her character Felicitas is damaged by the attempt, however; she becomes "unfit for ordinary life," which seems a "definite comedown from the exalted ideal that she grew up with."[1]

And of course I myself encountered the same unquestioning assumption of the necessity for self-sacrifice among the nuns at the homeless women's shelter. In fact, in terms of devotion to dogma, authoritarian structure, and general absolutism, the Roman Catholic sect and the average far-left sect exhibit a certain resemblance. But women don't need an education in extremism to become virgin martyrs, as we saw with Sharon in the previous chapter; they learn to give up their lives in other ways.

A Sentimental Education

Even girls formed only by the most middle-of-the-road culture feel the force of one ideal of perfection: the selfless "perfect girl" I spoke of in Chapter 1. When they reach early adolescence, "girls are expected to sacrifice the parts of themselves that our culture considers masculine on the altar of social acceptability and to shrink their souls down to a petite size," says psychologist Mary Pipher. What is left once all the "masculine" parts are excised is the "perfect girl," who "in white middle-class America…is the girl who has no bad thoughts or feelings" and therefore is "worthy of inclusion and love," according to

Disappearing Acts

Lyn Mikel Brown and Carol Gilligan, reporting on a five-year study. Each year they interviewed about a hundred girls between eight and seventeen at a private school in Cleveland, observing how they changed.[2] The result is a step-by-step account of how girls lose their mermaid's tail.

The hallmark of the perfect girl is "niceness," a concept that begins to terrorize girls as early as age eight as they absorb images from television, magazines, movies, and books, in addition to parents' and teachers' reactions to their behavior. Being angry or aggressive; expressing feelings that conflict with someone else's; acting bossy; being loud; and making trouble are all not nice—or, to use Pipher's term, "masculine." One seventh-grader announced proudly that she had changed in the past year: "I think of, more of what to do to be nice than…what I want to do." "Doing what she wants to do," Brown and Gilligan point out, "is…not nice."[3]

Over the five years, the researchers saw the younger girls' quickness to perceive and express anger or disagreement, to distinguish between sincerity and insincerity—that is, to be fully aware of the emotional reality of relationships—give way to the imperatives of "niceness" as they lost the ability to voice their own experience. In the quest to become nice, the girls began to stifle anger or dissatisfaction they felt in response to family, friends, and teachers, and they became unwilling to disagree with other people's opinions. Brown and Gilligan equate having a voice with having an "experience of self," so that losing voice also meant becoming self-less. Accordingly, the girls lost awareness of their own emotions and desires, even of whether they liked or disliked those they considered their friends. "Many girls are 'empathy sick,'" explains Pipher. "They know more about others' feelings than their own.…Girls are uncomfortable identifying and stating their needs, especially with boys and adults. They worry about not being nice or appearing selfish" and instead focus on the needs of others. Girls and women behave this way, Brown and Gilligan believe, because "an inner sense of connection with others" is so important to them that they will "silence themselves in relationships rather than risk open conflict or disagreement that might lead to isolation or to violence."[4]

Among the images that teach girls niceness, one that is particularly appropriate to consider here is Ariel, the Disney Little Mermaid, who was "shown all over the world—a gruesome role model for five-year-old girls," as Julia exclaimed indignantly. "The whole thing is that love equals sacrifice!" Ariel, cast as a rebellious teenager preparing to grow up and leave home, literally enacts the loss of voice that Brown and Gilligan describe, as she agrees to give the villainess Ursula her voice in payment for acquiring legs. (She does get it back in the end, but—as Julia pointed out—she didn't *know* she would; she was willing to sacrifice it.) Ariel's rebellion, of course, only extends as far as wanting to leave her father for the prince, and the film ends like Denise's bedtime fantasy, as she prepares to begin her adult life with him.

Julia was not particularly concerned about Ariel's effect on her daughter because she believed that such images only affect children powerfully if they are also getting the same message from their parents. Many do, however. Denise did, to disastrous effect; and Laura described how she struggled to derail her daughter's education in niceness—or to use her word, "enabling."

> If you hear children in dramatic play, when the little girls play the mommy, they imitate, of course, what they hear their own mamas doing, and they have their dolls enable the boy dolls. If you ever hear kids playing with Barbie and Ken, as my own daughter did—of course I interceded—but they *do,* I mean Barbie will say to Ken, "What can I get you to eat?" Ken will *never* say, "What can I get you to eat?"
>
> If they were the mommy, they dressed the boy. If they were the sister, they were happy passengers in the

car—the boy was driving. If they had the Barbie town
house, which came with all this paraphernalia, they got
everything ready for Ken when he got home—it seemed
so natural. I would get on the floor and play with them,
and say, "Now, Ken is going to make dinner. And Barbie is going to be coming home from work." They were
fine—kids are fine with that. But how many times do
people intercede?

Evidently Julia did: "We have Barbies in my house, but my son has as
many Barbies as my daughter, and they play with them together.
They go food shopping a lot. He loves Barbies." But as we know, that
was a topsy-turvy household to begin with.

The paradox is that once girls—and women—have sacrificed self
for relationship, relationship becomes inauthentic, since no true feelings are left in it—not their own, which were stifled, and not the
other person's, since not enough of the woman is left for the other person to make a genuine connection to. As Brown and Gilligan put it,
"The hallmark of this loss in women's lives and also in men's is the
move from authentic into idealized relationships." During their
transformation into young women, girls move "from flesh to image"
as the sensuous reality of emotions rooted in the physical body is
replaced by the idealized image of the perfect woman.[5] The effect of
this disconnection from reality is paralysis, as we saw with Sharon,
whose hold on her own feelings was so tenuous that, when sought by
a rich man purely for her beauty, she could not say, "I don't want to
get married."

Brown and Gilligan further lament the dominance of "niceness"
because they fear that losing "their ability to name relational viola-
tions" will make girls "vulnerable to abuse," a danger exemplified by
an incident unearthed in another researcher's survey of college students. A student named Lisa was in the shower when a man walked
into the dormitory bathroom and peeked at her over the shower cur-

tain. When she demanded, "What's wrong with you?" he apologized fulsomely, so she began to worry whether he was all right. "Are you on anything?" she asked. "What is your name?" She hadn't screamed, she explained to the interviewer, because he "looked so helpless, and so lost." When asked why she cared, Lisa responded, "I care about people, and I'm always trying to help out wherever I can…especially if it's like a call for help, and that's what I thought it was." Later she learned that this man had been going around the campus that evening peeping at a number of women. Instead of reacting with indignation to what was essentially sexual harassment, she had allowed herself to be victimized in order to act out her self-image that her caring was limitless.[6]

Take such caring to the point of victimization to an extreme, and you wind up with the ideology of Vera's group—the great majority of which, not coincidentally, consisted of women:

> So if you're not going to be happy in that communal society where everybody is provided for at least economically, we're going to make you. Because your desires can't come in the way of other people's needs. How dare you think that you're so much better than the majority of the world that you can go off and do whatever the hell you want?

The answer to this question is not simple, nor can the question itself be disregarded just because it is posed by an organization that uses it as an excuse for abusing people. It brings up a critical issue that goes back to "Am I my brother's keeper?"—a question many have struggled with over the ages. Because of their history of excessive self-sacrifice, however, women need to think differently about it than men.

Niceness, as Brown and Gilligan emphasize, is an ideal particularly of middle-class white girls; they found that working-class scholarship students and middle-class girls of color at the Cleveland school did not aspire to be perfect in the same way. Nor did the twenty-six girls "at risk" of dropping out of high school and/or getting pregnant, whom Gilligan studied with other colleagues at a high school in the Boston area, for these poor and working-class girls—from a variety of ethnic and racial backgrounds—were by definition so remote from "the dominant models of female beauty and perfection" as to make such aspiration impossible.[7]

Most of these girls did not shrink from acknowledging unpleasant feelings or behavior, or from being loud. The white and African-American girls in the Boston study were more like each other in this respect than either group was like the middle-class white girls at the Cleveland school, suggesting that traits that on first glance seem to reflect personal character are actually shaped by economic level. The Latina and Portuguese girls in the Boston study, however, came from a culture that set its own exacting standards of virtue and obedience, based on the tradition that "women are morally and spiritually superior to men." This tradition and the dominant American culture seemed to "amplify each other—both embrace similar ideals of femininity and self-sacrifice from women and girls." Consequently the researchers saw in these girls, as in the white middle-class ones, "signs of depression or self-silencing."[8]

Though the black and white working-class girls did not absorb the standard image of the devoted mother—since their own mothers filled far more roles than that ideal allowed—some did see themselves in the future in terms of a "Super Woman." But no less than the devoted mother, the researchers comment, the Super Woman is an image of "sacrificial isolation": "The ideal mother, although involved in relationships, is portrayed in selfless separation from her voice, without a sense of self; the 'Super Woman' is independent, self-sufficient, able to manage everything by herself."[9]

There are, then, a variety of paths to selflessness; as we saw in Chapter 5, women from non-mainstream groups, though they may not buy into the prevailing image of female perfection, can be forced into other kinds of sacrifices. But I am after more here than a personal or even a sociological explanation, for a pattern of behavior that is so widespread also has a symbolic or mythic meaning reflecting a deep psychic or cognitive structure in the culture. To find this meaning, it is useful to examine extreme experiences, because these magnify tendencies that are present to some degree within everyone. Therefore we begin excavating down to the deepest impulses that turn selfless girls into self-sacrificing women by examining a particularly feminine form of sacrifice, not only of psychological self but of body: the eating disorder anorexia nervosa.

"Disappearing Sounded Good"

Anorexia nervosa is characterized by a pathological fear of gaining weight that leads to refusal, then inability, to eat, to the point of self-starvation. Unlike disorders such as infectious disease or migraine, anorexia nervosa has not been around for thousands of years. It was born, so to speak, in the nineteenth century, along with the Angel in the House, as a concomitant of the same economic changes that created the middle class; in fact, anorexia was a condition specifically of girls who knew that the Angel was what they were supposed to become. Today, the vast majority of anorexics are still adolescent girls from affluent white families. But although this specific affliction is modern, it represents only the most recent phase in the long history of women's special involvement with food.

For the medieval female saints described in Chapter 4, control of appetite was a way to achieve salvation in the form of union with Christ through suffering. Their fasting behavior has been called "anorexia mirabilis," or "miraculously inspired loss of appetite." In later centuries, "fasting girls"—seemingly ordinary middle-class or working-class young women, such as Mollie Fancher (1848–1916), the celebrated "Brooklyn Enigma," a merchant's daughter who combined food abstinence with clairvoyance—claimed to be able, through divine empowerment, to live without eating. Fasting girls continued to appear as late as 1900; but by then they were rare holdouts against the rationalist, materialist spirit of the time, for during the nineteenth century "food refusal was transformed from a legitimate act of personal piety into a symptom of disease."[10]

The term *anorexia nervosa* was invented by Sir William Withey Gull, one of the physicians who treated this disorder. Also known as "hysterical anorexia," it appeared almost entirely in young girls from middle-class families. This new type of family, a product of industrial development, bred "greater emotional intensity between parents and children" and consequently provided new ground for conflict. Adolescent daughters felt pressure to conform to the prevailing feminine ideal—marked, as we saw, by admiration of thinness and frailty—in order to make a desirable marriage. In such a setting, a girl's refusal to eat was a power play that could disrupt her parents' plans for her and throw the family into turmoil. Anorexia was rare if not nonexistent among working-class girls, who lacked these motivations for refusing food.[11]

The anorexic's power play was couched in the symbolic vocabulary of her time and place. The Victorians associated a hearty appetite in women with "dangerous sexuality," gluttony, and ugliness; animal flesh in particular was thought to stimulate sexuality. This meant that the middle-class female, in order to incarnate moral purity and spirituality, had to deny any interest in food. "One of the most convincing demonstrations of a spiritual orientation was a thin body—that is, a physique that symbolized rejection of all carnal appetites...," explains historian Joan Jacobs Brumberg. "Denial became a form of moral certitude." Many young women intensely concerned with controlling their appetites took inspiration from "the spiritual intensity" of Catherine of Siena, whose biography was used by Victorian writers "to demonstrate how selfhood could be lost to a higher moral or spiritual purpose. This message was considered particularly relevant to

girls, in that self-love was supposed to be a distinguishing characteristic of the female adolescent." For middle-class girls as for the
medieval saints, food became a language to express their adherence to
their own "ideal of female perfection."[12]

By the end of the nineteenth century, thinness was a mark not
only of moral virtue but of social status, signifying gentility as well as
wealth. In the twentieth century, although sexiness replaced spirituality as women's highest virtue, thinness remained paramount. Overweight became a character flaw, signaling lack of self-control, and the
modern woman's struggle with dieting took on the same overtones of
renunciation and pain, sin and redemption, as the austerities of
Catherine of Siena. (Think of Nicole Hollander's cartoon character
Sylvia, who tapes to her refrigerator door a series of edifying messages
warning of the calamities that will afflict the pathetic, weak-willed
creature who opens it.) In this "new secular credo of physical
denial...women suffered to be beautiful," as "an external body con-
figuration rather than an internal spiritual state" became the mark of
salvation.[13]

In the twentieth century, then, as earlier, the ability to deny
hunger and control appetite became central to women's identity. But
doing so in a modern context did not confer the social and spiritual
rewards afforded a fasting saint of the Middle Ages. "Hunger makes
women feel poor and think poor," asserts social commentator Naomi
Wolf. "A wealthy woman on a diet feels physically at the mercy of a
scarcity economy.... Hunger...undermines each experience of control, economic security, and leadership that women have had only a
generation to learn to enjoy."[14] No wonder the activists seeking to
emancipate working-class London women, quoted in Chapter 4,
called for them to begin to acquire political power by learning to eat.
For the question of power underlies not only anorexia but also other
forms of self-sacrifice.

Nineteenth-century physicians considered anorexia in middle-
class girls a nervous disease, and the most prevalent explanation was

Disappearing Acts

that they refused to eat in order to attract attention. Around the turn of the century, Freud and the French neurologist Pierre Janet both suggested that anorexia was "a form of symbolic behavior" expressing fear and disgust toward sexuality and shame about the body. By the 1970s, psychiatrists had concluded that anorexia was essentially an attempt to control appetite and deny hunger despite intense preoccupation with food.[15]

Today it seems that several factors interact in the genesis of anorexia. A girl might begin to eat less for any of a variety of reasons: distress over family problems, wanting to be thin and beautiful, or hoping to remain childlike so as to avoid confronting adult sexuality. Eventually her dieting becomes obsessive, perhaps because it makes her the center of attention, or because she sees it effectively punishing her parents. Meanwhile her mind and body become accustomed "to both the feeling of hunger and nutritional deprivation." At this point, physiological mechanisms can kick in, which make her actually unable to eat.[16]

"What causes an eating disorder is so individual," said Heidi Dalzell, a therapeutic educator who worked on the eating disorders unit of a psychiatric hospital. "Some people are always talking about body image, looking gorgeous like the models, and all that. In others you just see anger; the eating disorder is a way they can express their anger safely." Sometimes, she explained, an eating disorder is a protest—for example, against parental expectations.

Jennifer was a twenty-three-year-old anorexic who was near death when she was admitted to Dalzell's unit. From an early age she had been treated as a mediator by her battling parents and made to listen to extremely inappropriate information, such as her mother's complaints about her father's impotence. "She developed the expectation that she had to handle this and be the perfect child, which meant living up to her parents' expectations in every way," said Dalzell. In college Jennifer had taken a double major—one her parents wanted her to take—even though she hated it. "She told me she felt unreal, like everyone around her didn't know who she was because she was playing a role. I think that's what precipitated her eating disorder."

As part of counseling, Dalzell administered a test intended to elicit personality styles or preferences, such as introversion versus extroversion.

> She had described herself [in the test] as an introvert, very quiet, as someone who liked very detailed work, liked to do things in a very established way, was very time-oriented, focused on meeting deadlines, people-oriented. But when we started talking about [these results], she broke down and said, "This isn't me!" It turned out she wasn't an introvert, she was an extrovert. But her parents liked her to be quiet and obedient, that perfect child. I said, "Why did you answer the questions this way?" She looked at the description of this particular type that she came up as, and said, "This is what my parents always wanted me to be." Then we redid it and she was able to make choices based on who she felt she was. She had originally been enrolled in school in the same city as her parents, living at home. She decided she needed to go away, and she enrolled in a completely different major.

In Jennifer's case, anorexia was partly a protest against the position her parents had put her into; "she had a lot of repressed anger at her family, for the role that she had assumed." But most often, Dalzell believed,

> anorexia is a way to hold a family together, to get that caring, to develop relationships with other people, in a strange kind of way. Especially in mother-daughter relationships, I see the mother has an agenda of what she

needs to do as a mother. She has a list; it's very task-ori-
ented—doing things but not really connecting. I see in
the daughter that overwhelming need to connect, and
sometimes that plays out in an eating disorder. It's the
only way to connect, to be recognized, try to say "I need
you."

In Dalzell's experience, many different women's issues are
expressed through eating disorders. "Another one is sexual abuse. We
see it an awful lot in anorexics and bulimics. The eating disorder is a
way of punishing themselves. It's just the only way that people can
express their pain."

Pain and anorexia are common among female athletes, between
15 and 62 percent of whom are afflicted by eating disorders. (By contrast, these conditions "are virtually unknown" among male athletes.)[17] Gymnasts and figure skaters in particular try to shape
themselves into the fairy-tale image of the little-girl princess that the
public, judges, and their own parents hold up to them. These "little
girls in pretty boxes," as sportswriter Joan Ryan calls them, starve
themselves to stave off puberty and retain the child's body that the
sport demands. They will do anything to please their parents and
coaches—suffer abusive criticism and numb themselves so they can
train and compete through pain in order to get that approval. "I felt
like I was worthless unless I was running," confessed Kate Landau, a
top-rated high-school distance runner who spent five years struggling
with anorexia, which she attributed to "a fear of growing up, a lack
of self-esteem and a sibling rivalry with her older sister."[18]

For a gymnast, growing up means the end of a career. But for
other girls who still inhabit a free and easy child's body, the prospect
of sexual development terrifies because it means confronting the con-
straints and expectations inflicted on women. "Adolescent starvation
was, for me, a prolonged reluctance to be born into woman if that
meant assuming a station of beauty," is how Naomi Wolf explains her

Slaying the Mermaid

year of self-starvation at the age of twelve. "Anorexia was the only way I could see to keep the dignity in my body that I had had as a kid, and that I would lose as a woman.... I knew my parents wanted me not to starve because they loved me; but their love contradicted the message of the larger world, which wanted me to starve in order to love me." Looking at little girls who are already dieting in the fourth and fifth grades, she sees them learning to "associate femaleness with deprivation," so that by the time they actually have sex, "they will have spent over half their lives learning masochism in preparation for sexual gratification."[19]

The fact that anorexia is in large measure a cultural construction emerges clearly when different population groups are compared. In males the syndrome is not only rare but different: male anorexics are likely to be extremely obese before becoming thin and not as likely to be affluent; they also show greater psychopathology.[20] African-American and Latina girls are unlikely to become anorexic. A study in Arizona found that 90 percent of white junior-high and high-school girls were dissatisfied with their bodies and wanted to be thin, and 62 percent had dieted in the past year. By contrast 70 percent of black girls said they were *satisfied* with their bodies—although half of them had also dieted.[21] These differences reflect the fact that African-American girls can never meet a standard of beauty based on white skin and straight hair simply because they are black. They thus escape the pressure white girls feel to meet it, though at the same time, as sociologist Patricia Hill Collins notes, "the pain of never being able to live up to externally defined standards of beauty" exacts its own emotional costs.[22]

In a sense, then, anorexia becomes the final common path for a variety of issues white middle-class girls encounter; it is a mode of expression linked to their cultural identity. (Boys facing equivalent issues generally "act out" instead.) This cultural identity defines the path as one of self-denial, and what is denied—or sacrificed—is the self. "They sacrifice themselves, some of these poor women, from the time they're young," Dalzell remarked sadly. "Jennifer was one. It was almost as if she was born to play that parent role. That was her sacrifice."

When we look at anorexia as a form of self-denial, thinness takes on an additional meaning, for the ultimate thinness is to disappear. Dalzell saw this on her unit:

> With a lot of women, we see that they want to disappear. It's not only their thinness—it's their overall manner. One patient wears her hair over her face, to cover it up. We see that a lot—you can't see their face because their hair flops forward over it. I rarely see our women with their hair pulled back. They also camouflage their bodies with clothing. Some don't want people to see how thin they are, but it's also a way of disappearing.

"Disappearing sounded good," Wendy, the caretaker of her mentally ill sister, recalled of her own episode of anorexia when she was seventeen. Drowning in her family problems, she was "desperately hanging on" to a boyfriend while trying to suppress her real sexual feelings toward women. When the boy broke up with her, she began to starve herself, and got down to eighty-seven pounds. "I think the last thing I wanted to be was a seventeen-year-old girl with the body of a seventeen-year-old girl. I wanted to be a boy or I wanted to be dead or I wanted to be gone." And (like Vera, also precipitated into self-sacrifice at this time of transition), "I had no direction, no idea what I was going to do with myself in a year when I graduated high school." Fortunately she got a summer job at a camp in the country, and being away from home in a healthy environment enabled her to eat again.

Another type of disappearing act was performed by Liza, an anorexic in the Cleveland study who was unable to speak her own thoughts and feelings using the word "I." The main phrase she could say with "I" was "I don't know." She phrased her other responses to the interviewer's questions in terms of "you": e.g., "You just can't do whatever you want." As the researchers put it, "Liza's first person slips into a second person and she disappears."[23] As with other anorexic girls, sacrificing her body on the altar of the feminine ideal means sacrificing her self.

Blood Sacrifice

Girls trained in niceness are still prone to sacrificial disappearing acts as women. "The risk of being left alone is very great in women's psychologies, so they cut off pieces of themselves to stay connected," said Helen Wintrob, Ph.D., a clinical psychologist. "It's become a cliché to talk about women needing to be in relationships and characterizing them in terms of a sense of relatedness and connectedness, but I think it's true. Women can be successful nowadays, but they're afraid of success because they fear the loss of family or friends" who will be envious and desert them. "In order not to outshine friends," they downplay or even denigrate their achievements. "Look at Kathie Lee Gifford, who always tells stories in which she was ill at ease: she got a run in her stocking, she got a pimple just before a performance—something to show she's just a regular girl and you can identify with her."

For someone like Gifford, Wintrob believed, this is a conscious, deliberate effort to forestall envy. Gifford can separate the external persona who had a bad-hair day from her inner reality of being a tremendous success. But most women can't maintain this distinction between an inner and outer self, and begin to believe the negative ways they present themselves. Thus, said Wintrob, they "sacrifice a part of themselves"—the part that can both feel and be successful—"to stay connected."

A woman risks loss of connection when she "moves out of the cultural definition of who she should be." Men, by contrast, "don't have to worry about loss in the same way," since "a man's cultural definition allows for greater upward mobility. Men are thought of as providers for their family, and if they don't have a family now, the expectation is that in the future they will. Becoming very successful isn't something they're doing just for themselves but for their family, so it's not as distancing a mechanism as it is for women"—since for a woman, success "implies that she's left the family."

To show how women hide and deny their true intelligence and competence, Wintrob described Linda, a thirty-year-old African-American woman who found herself

> frequently in academic and professional situations where she was the only black person or one of a small minority. Although there was always evidence that she had met the same standards as had the white people, she always thought she was there as the token black person and never felt she deserved what she had. In high school, when she was recruited by several Ivy League schools, she believed it was only because she was African American; she thought her SAT scores were mediocre.

When Wintrob had her send away for them, they turned out to be in the ninety-ninth percentile.

Linda's belief that she was only a token was aggravated by the fact that she was outshining her two brothers. "Success is even more of a problem for African Americans than for white women, because they feel they're deserting their men, and because the image of the black man is such a fragile one. They feel they're consorting with the white establishment and have abandoned their people," Wintrob explained. Looking at the concrete evidence of her abilities, such as the SAT scores, enabled Linda to perceive the reality of her life, so she could let go of her distorted image of herself. She could then find ways to stay connected to her family other than by denying who she was.

Self-diminishment of this sort is so routine for so many women that we don't even notice we do it. But the significance of such willingness to slice off part of our being emerges if we return for a moment to the more flagrant disappearing act of the anorexic. When you are really successful in the quest to disappear, you stop feeling real. Heidi Dalzell noted that the patients on her unit "often come to treatment feeling so 'unreal' we see almost a blank slate. They have permanent smiles plastered on their faces, agreeably acquiesce to our suggestions but make few gains. Or like chameleons they 'become' the other patients, adopting their behaviors in a desperate effort to connect and feel."

In a phone call a few weeks after her discharge from the unit, an anorexic named Sarah told Dalzell that she had not only lost ten pounds but had "started cutting her arms in an effort to 'feel something.'" "Her eating disorder was her identity, the first thing she really owned; it had both become her reality and allowed her to feel 'real,'" Dalzell commented. "In helping her gain weight, we had quite possibly saved her life, but had taken away who she was."[24]

Cutting helped Sarah feel real because of its indubitable material effect on the flesh, the ground of our awareness of both physical and emotional reality. From groundedness arises, in turn, the capacity to act. In *Prozac Nation,* her chronicle of suicidal depression, Elizabeth Wurtzel describes her panic in high school when she realized she had metamorphosed into a "monster"—a "nihilistic, unhappy girl" driven to hide in the locker room to prevent people from seeing her. It was there one day that she got out a nail file, rolled down her socks,

> and looked at my bare white legs.... A perfect, clean canvas. So I took the nail file, found its sharp edge, and ran it across my lower leg, watching a red line of blood appear across my skin. I was surprised...at how easy it was for me to hurt myself this way.... I wanted to know that if...the desperation got so terribly bad, I could inflict harm on my body....Knowing this gave me a

Disappearing Acts

sense of peace and power, so I started cutting up my legs all the time.[25]

"Girls deal with their internal pain by picking at their skin, burning themselves or cutting themselves with razors or knives," explains Mary Pipher, who frequently sees such girls in her practice. "Self-mutilation can be seen as a concrete interpretation of our culture's injunction to young women to carve themselves into culturally acceptable pieces." The practice may be a protest, an attempt at control, or "a cry for help." As for Wurtzel, it has a calming effect.[26]

But why pick this way to feel calm and effective? There are, of course, psychodynamic explanations: "Most of them can't project aggression outward. When they get angry, the anger goes inward. They punish themselves instead of punishing other people," suggests Dalzell. On the level of myth, however, the psychological amputation and the physical cutting are related as forms of blood sacrifice.

The basis of blood sacrifice is the association between blood and the sacred life force; because it embodies this elemental power, blood is an immensely potent agent.[27] Shedding blood liberates the life force, whether for regeneration, binding a covenant, or eliciting a return gift from the power being sacrificed to. In most cases, naturally, sacrificers shed not their own blood but that of a designated victim.

We have already seen that women acquired the function of doing the suffering, and thereby supplying the soul, for men who had become distant from their own spiritual nature. I suggest that the image of blood sacrifice is appropriate to describe this substitution since what the women are sacrificing is their own vital force. Adult women who cut off the pieces of themselves that would allow them to experience and savor success are sacrificing their drive and their will for the sake of maintaining connection. The girls who cut their bodies are carving into their flesh a literal sign of this mutilation.

In the past, women's sacrifice has indeed been understood as supplying the spiritual glue that holds the works of man together. A 1912 essay by the philosopher and critic Georg Lukács recounts an old Hungarian legend about the building of a castle. "Every night the wall, which the masons have built during the day, crumbles. Finally, the masons decide that the first wife to arrive, bringing dinner to her husband, will be sacrificed and embalmed in the wall." When this was done, the victim provided the "cement" that kept the wall standing.[28] The tale itself reflects a practice widespread in many cultures of making animal and human sacrifices during the construction of temples, houses, and other buildings, as well as in laying out towns. The purpose was both to ensure the beneficent presence of the sacred power in the building and to drive away any malevolent forces.[29] In this essay, however, the legend serves Lukács's attempt to come to terms with the suicide of a woman he had loved, although refusing either to marry her or make her his mistress. "She had to die so that my work could be completed," concludes his alter ego in the essay. With the temptation she represented removed, he can move beyond ordinary life into the pure realm of his work, which he likens to the castle built on the blood sacrifice of the mason's wife.

Such thinking may sound archaic, but echoes of it resonate today. In *The Shadow Man,* a memoir of her quest to understand her father, David, who died when she was seven, the novelist Mary Gordon describes her youthful fascination with a children's magazine he wrote and edited, full of descriptions of his version of the perfect daughter. One issue included a story by the nineteenth-century writer Lafcadio Hearn titled "The Soul of the Bell." Kuan-Yo, a Chinese mandarin, must supervise the casting of "the most perfect bell ever yet constructed." Gold, silver, and brass are heated together, but they will not blend. Under pain of death if the bell is not cast, Kuan-Yo consults a wise man,

who declares that only the body of a beautiful and spot-
less virgin will allow the metal to blend. Ku-Ngui,

Kuan-Yo's beautiful daughter, hears this. Immediately, she knows what she must do. She goes to the vat where the molten metals will not blend. She stands at the side, and crying out, "For thy sake, O father," she jumps into the vat.... The metals blend.[30]

The reason the castle construction can be undone and the bell refuses to blend is that—as Hearn's title indicates—they are missing a soul: the insubstantial but vivifying spirit that was lost from men's works when the distinction between male and female hardened into opposition. The fantasy of the perfect girl—and of the Angel in the House, and the devoted mother—are all versions of this missing "soul."

David Gordon's magazine featured other daughters, too: the pliant, innocent Miranda of *The Tempest* and "Rip Van Winkle's Daughter," a "perfect housewife, meeting her resurrected father's every need."[31] In these images the child Mary was confronting her father's fantasy of the perfect girl. Fortunately, even at four or five she was aware that she was not this kind of daughter. But girls who lack her sense of self—of reality—may disappear into such images, to the point where the blood sacrifice becomes literal.

Images are not the only source of blood sacrifice, however. Here is another twelve-year-old making one:

Four white boys in their early teens...occasionally entertained themselves in the afternoon by harassing black schoolchildren....[Nel and Sula] walked up the street until they got to the bend of Carpenter's Road where the boys lounged....When the girls were three feet in front of the boys, Sula reached into her coat pocket and pulled out Eva's paring knife....Holding the knife in her right hand, she pulled [her] slate toward her and pressed her left forefinger down hard on its edge. Her aim was determined but inaccurate. She slashed off only the tip of her finger....Her voice was quiet. "If I can do that to myself, what you suppose I'll do to you?"[32]

Compare that to this act, performed by a Crow Indian vision seeker:

As soon as the sun rose, he laid his left forefinger on a stick and chopped off a joint. This he put on a buffalo chip and held it out to the Sun, whom he addressed as follows: "Uncle, you see me. I am pitiable. Here is a part of my body. I give it to you, eat it. Give me something good."[33]

The Crow man gives up this piece of himself as part of a well-defined transaction from which he will derive a vision to guide him, but the girl in Toni Morrison's novel *Sula* is only warding off harm. Years later, the grown-up Nel concludes that an irrational fear had made Sula try to protect herself: "Whatever those hunkies did, it wouldn't have been as bad as what she did to herself." Sula herself recalls that she was trying to protect Nel. Either way, her extravagantly self-destructive gesture does not resonate with her environment as does the Crow man's sacrifice, directed toward a specific divinity to obtain a specific gift—the vision—as part of a coherent religious system. Sula does scare the boys off, but one might agree with Nel that the cost was too great, for nothing has happened to prevent the need for chopping off another finger should a new set of boys come along. What is more, the finger is only one in a chain of blood sacrifices made by the women in Sula's family. Her grandmother Eva, for example—the same Eva who told Sula's mother Hannah that she didn't "love" her but stayed alive for her—was left by her husband with two children and no money. Eva disappeared for eighteen months, then returned with only one leg. To get money to survive,

Sula realizes, Eva had stuck her leg "under a train to collect insurance." [34]

The ultimate determinant of these sacrifices, as the scene of the girl driven to hurt herself by the white "hunkies" suggests, is the brutal segregated society in which these women live. As I noted in Chapter 1, the basic issue underlying self-defeating sacrifice, both in society at large and in individual relationships, is a power imbalance. Chapter 9 will investigate its broader social implications, but first we must consider its psychological effects. For where power is unequal, sacrifice is debased into suffering.

7

Victimhood and Identity

IN COLLEGE I HAD A ROOMMATE WHO NEEDED TO FEEL POOR. HER father deposited a certain sum in her checking account each month, and since our other roommate and I did not have checks, Evelyn was supposed to pay the rent and the phone bill. But having money made her so uncomfortable that to avoid acknowledging its existence, she never balanced her checkbook. For a couple of weeks after the money came, she wrote checks without filling in the stubs. Then, with no record of how much she had withdrawn, she began to worry about being overdrawn and would not write any more (banks did not then have service lines you could call to learn your account balance). This stratagem enabled her to feel poor for the rest of the month. If the phone bill came then, she didn't pay it, since she "had no money"; if we needed to put cash into the kitty for groceries, she "couldn't" contribute her share; and of course she never paid the rent on time.

Evelyn's father was a doctor and quite well off, but she felt compelled to construct around herself a generalized feeling of deprivation that she inhabited like a tent. Not coincidentally she was a sucker for needy boyfriends who immersed themselves in the stream of selfless caring she emanated and made unreasonable demands to which she could barely even contemplate saying no, even when she really wanted them to leave her alone. Her behavior exemplifies a link between self-sacrifice and a generalized victim mentality that is central to the psychology of sacrifice.

Anne Wilson Schaef makes the same connection in her best-selling *Meditations for Women Who Do Too Much,* which she wrote for those of us "who do too much, keep too busy, spend all our time taking care of others and, in general do not take care of ourselves. Many of us have crossed over the line to compulsive, addictive, self-defeating behavior and need to make some major changes in our lives." The March 31 meditation, for "pain/suffering," is intended to assist the letting-go process for women who are "attached to our suffering": "Contrary to much religious belief," Schaef asserts, "suffering is not noble. It is often just plain stupid and comes out of our stubbornness and need to control."[1]

While this analysis strikes me as glib and too narrowly personal, I agree that there is a powerful tendency in our culture to value suffering for its own sake, which encourages people to grow "attached" to it. Historian Joseph Amato, author of *Victims and Values: A History of Suffering,* told a reporter that "people who are cast as victims carry a lot of power in our culture, especially if they can claim suffering.... 'Saints and gods undergo great suffering. We often attribute wisdom or virtue to those who have suffered, or we argue that it is a way to cross a threshold so the good is purchased by blood, tears and sacrifice.'"[2]

Catholics in particular seem to understand this in their bones. Among the women I interviewed, those who had been brought up Catholic spoke in the same voice, across all divisions of age, race, and ethnicity. Their understanding of the concept of sacrifice was so specific and consistent that it helped focus the more muddled reactions of Protestants and even Jews, for almost everyone is affected to some degree by the ramifications of that central image of Christ on the cross.

"We're raised on this idea that to sacrifice is the greatest thing we can do. Actually practicing sacrifice is one of the noblest paths one can go on," explained Irish Catholic Moira. "We do small sacrifices to be Christlike, in our own pitiful, very human way," elaborated Caribbean Catholic Christine.

> I remember as a young girl in Catholic school reading or hearing about saints who have the stigmata, and I thought, Oh my God, that has to be the most wonderful thing in the world! That you were so blessed that there's an actual physical outward manifestation of how Christlike you are. And since Christ dying for us is the ultimate sacrifice of God and Christ, you can't get any better than stigmata. Sacrifice is expected—you should be guilty if you never sacrifice something. And this whole Catholic notion of the more sacrifice, the better—call it the quest for stigmata. The more things I'm involved in, the more things I'm giving up, whether it's money or time, really means I'm a better person.

"After my mother died I liked going to church frequently because I felt a connection to her," explained Eastern European Catholic Diane.

> The solemn atmosphere, the incense, the pictures of Christ with the stigmata, these glorious saints with auras—bright lights around their heads—but they'd have arrows in their side, in the case of St. Sebastian, or the stigmata on the hands. There was a sense of suffer-

ing but it was a glorious kind of suffering. If you suffered for Christ, you would enjoy everlasting happiness—that was the story. There's a whole notion of sacrifice, giving up: What are you going to give up in imitation of Christ?

Diane then recounted the tale of Christ's suffering during the Passion, using her actress's skill so affectingly that even I, with no relationship to the story as a believer, was moved. And despite the skepticism she now professed, I could tell she still felt its power herself:

> That's how suffering and sacrifice are linked. It's the sacrifice of his life, but it's not an easy, painless sacrifice. It's humiliation, it's extreme physical pain. Lent is supposed to be a period of sacrifice, where you stop eating meat certain days of the week—particularly devout people perhaps fast certain days. As a child—let's say—I'm going to give up watching TV on Wednesday, I'm going to give up eating candy bars the whole season of Lent.

And Christine:

> I looked forward to Lent because I got to give up something. I usually gave up candy. As much as you missed the candy, you always got this surge of joy knowing that you were giving it up—*and* people knew about it.

After having been lapsed from Catholicism for many years, Christine became a Baptist, and soon discovered a culture gap. She was on a committee formed to plan an anniversary celebration at her church, for which a special offering of $150 was being asked from members.

At a meeting last week a decision was made that members who donated the $150 would be given, as a kind of thank-you, the journal that's being printed—the journal that we expect to sell for $40. I was the only person out of about six people who objected to this. My thoughts were: Why do you have to give them anything? You asked for a sacrifice. Period. And people make a sacrifice. Giving them something for their sacrifice wipes out the whole reason for the sacrifice. And I argued this, I thought, so eloquently, and no one understood me. I remember sitting there thinking, Damn Baptists, they don't understand the whole notion of sacrifice!

No doubt Annette would have understood; for her, the whole notion of sin and sacrifice provided a conceptual framework for understanding her eating disorder. Now thirty-two and married, she had "been battling obesity since I was seven years old. Eating disorders and weight control have a very *powerful* moral thread behind them," she explained. "It's often a hidden belief that many of us unconsciously have. After all, isn't *gluttony* one of the seven mortal sins?"

Like anorexics, Annette saw control of appetite as a path to salvation.

I have internalized the sacrifice of food to being closer to God...during Lent, when I have fatty or sweet foods...I feel guilty and like I have "sinned" since I have eaten foods I'm supposed to have given up in remembrance of the sacrifices Jesus made for humanity...So...by giving up my favorite foods...and by dieting...I'm in a sense acting piously...at least that's how it feels to me...it gives me a sense of purpose besides the desire to be healthier...

Victimhood and Identity

In the past, Annette said, she

> fell into the trap of believing that if I were to lose my
> excess weight, then all of my problems would be solved
> and in a sense I'd be saved. I felt like a glutton, and being
> a glutton was sinful in my mind. So, if I lost the weight
> and conquered my gluttony, then the good within me
> would have overcome the bad within me...so I would
> have been "saved" from the evil part of myself...

In other words, she saw her struggle in terms of the characteristic
Western dualism discussed in Chapter 4: "Another layer of this 'being
saved' debate is the Cartesian one...mind over matter...My mind
would have saved me from my excess matter." But this salvation
required amputating the mermaid's tail—here, Annette's intense sensory enjoyment of food. And like all dreams of salvation based on
some form of self-mutilation, this one proved false, for when Annette
did lose the weight, she found that being a normal size "didn't save
me"; excess weight was only "something to take my mind off what
my *real* problems were." Ultimately she decided not to deprive herself
of the "very high level of comfort" she derived "from cooking and
eating" and was now "not interested in trying to get to 145 again...I'll
be content at 250."

Many women, however, find the experience of "giving up" more
difficult to let go of, for over time it can acquire a certain gratifying
emotional charge that may then become associated with whatever
feeling of deprivation the sacrifice engenders. Mary Gilligan Wong,
who grew up in an Irish Catholic family in the Midwest and became
a nun when she graduated high school in 1961, describes how this
works:

> I knew from religion class that Jesus...wanted us to pray
> and sacrifice in order to make reparation for all the pain

His heart had suffered because of people's sins. It was the sacrifice part that confused me at first…I sure couldn't figure out how my giving up chocolate bars would make Him feel better.

Eventually I learned, however, that suffering and self-sacrifice were valuable currencies, as valuable as prayer, and that by subjecting *myself* to suffering I could somehow make *His* load lighter.… The value of sacrifice and of self-denial: it was a lesson that, once learned, would seep into countless corners of my psyche until I, too, would learn to cherish my suffering like so many badges of honor.[3]

In this manner the imperative to sacrifice can turn into a glorification of suffering.

But although Catholics have a particularly well-defined relationship to the concept of sacrifice, it isn't an exclusive relationship. Suffering and self-sacrifice are valuable currencies for many people, and it is what they can buy that make them, and martyrdom in general, so attractive.

Glorious Martyrs

"We're living in an age dominated by the Judeo-Christian perspective, which involves sacrifice—that's the very nature of it," said Vivian Goldstein, a psychotherapist whose long-term study of Buddhism gives her a wider perspective on our own culture. "Even though we talk about autonomy, equality, and independence, suffering and sacrifice are still legitimated, not only in the church but in the culture at large: no pain, no gain." Certainly this assumption underlies many of the stories our culture tells. But there is a difference between "You must go through pain in order to get anything" and "Since you can't avoid some degree of pain in life, you might as well make the best use of it." Too often, this distinction is blurred into a sentimental mishmash proclaiming that suffering is noble—period.

In John Sayles's film *Passion Fish,* an auto accident leaves soap-opera actress May-Alice paraplegic, bitter, and unspeakably bitchy. The film traces the stages of suffering through which she finds her true self and becomes a better person, ready to start a new life with a new lover. My friend Phyllis, who had a disabled sister and knew what life is like with a person in a wheelchair, objected that the presentation of May-Alice and her caretaker Chantelle (who also bears a load of tragedy) as the only good, true, noble characters because of their suffering was a kind of lie. Phyllis disliked the notion of self-transformation via disability not only because disability doesn't necessarily improve people's character but because the film portrays the crippled woman as the real one: "She only becomes her true self when she can no longer walk."

This lie, however, has a lot of currency. The hero of Dick Francis's novel *Longshot* is a young writer about to publish a novel about survival and "the spiritual consequences of deprivation and fear." He meets a famous older woman novelist who informs him that he is too young to know anything about such a topic, for "intensity of understanding...comes only through deep adversity." Contentment, she proclaims, has no insights, for "Insight grows best on stony ground. Unless you have suffered or are poor or can tap into melancholy, you have defective perception."

When the young man objects that he is "poor enough to perceive that poverty is the enemy of moral strength," she dismisses him as "a lightweight person" with "no conception of the moral strength of redemption and atonement in penury."

> I swallowed. "I don't seek sainthood. I seek insight through a combination of imagination and common sense."
>
> "You are not a serious writer."...

Slaying the Mermaid

"I write to entertain," I said.

"I," she said simply, "write to enlighten."[4]

Here, in Dick Francis's gentle (though rather anti-intellectual) satire, is the whole gender split brought up to date and out into mass culture. Certainly it isn't only women who think suffering ennobles: "In the past, I thought that to be creative you had to suffer somehow," Sting reflected in a 1996 interview. Now, at forty-four, he said, "I don't subscribe to that thing anymore of being traumatized or living in the gutter to produce decent work."[5] But, as Schaef's comments indicate, and for the reasons previous chapters have explored, it is women who most easily fall into that assumption, and for whom glorifying suffering leads to self-identification as a victim.

In her book *On Boxing,* Joyce Carol Oates remarks, "Women, watching a boxing match, are likely to identify with the losing, or hurt, boxer; men are likely to identify with the winning boxer," to the point where if the boxer they initially favored begins to lose, their loyalty shifts unconsciously to the winner.[6] This observation evoked my own childhood reasons for rooting for the Brooklyn Dodgers against the Yankees when both were in the World Series: not only did it feel more comfortable being associated with the underdogs (for the Dodgers were always expected to lose), but I disliked the preening of Yankee fans.

"For a woman, a conscious autobiography means facing not only her past as a 'female impersonator'—the realization that every accoutrement of her sex has been culturally determined—but the ways in which she has been and continues to be victimized in that role, even when she no longer looks or acts or dresses or for that matter feels the part," wrote art critic and author Jill Johnston in 1993, in a breathtaking dismissal of the possibility that any woman could ever not be a victim. Johnston was contemplating a new style of autobiography written by victims instead of, as previously, by winners.[7] The increasing popularity of this genre was emphasized by a "hot young literary agent" who three years later told a meeting of professional writers that the new big trend, memoirs, was dominated by "pain and suffering" books; as an example he cited *Prozac Nation*.

A good popular-culture example of the creation of a sufferer identity is Sara Paretsky's series of detective novels featuring the female PI V.I. Warshawski. The atmosphere of these books is compounded of physical discomfort and existential nightmare: Vic drives recklessly through a Chicago that is either searingly hot or bone-chillingly cold, either dismal, decaying working-class or smug, heartless, glossy yuppie. Usually in considerable physical pain from the injuries she incurs in trying to take on powerful evildoers single-handedly, Vic is also burdened by tormented memories of her tragic mother, Gabriella, as well as by agonizing guilt; she lashes herself nonstop for failing to save and/or solve the problems of every helpless victim who crosses her path.

Among the traits that make Vic an interesting character are the fierce intensity with which she feels other people's pain and her outrage over injustice, especially when the strong take advantage of the weak. But Vic's rage goes beyond her progressive politics; she identifies with the victimized, who in these books are always being sacrificed to the greed of the rich and powerful.

> "Do you know what my middle name is, Lotty?" I burst out. "Do you know the myth of Iphigenia? How Agamemnon sacrificed her to get a fair wind to sail for Troy?...I can't stop dreaming about it. Only in my dreams it's Gabriella. She keeps laying me on the pyre and setting the torch to it and weeping for me."[8]

In addition to intricate plots and exciting action, the appeal of this best-selling series lies, I think, in the operatic intensity of Vic's nearly constant anguish; even when she has a brief moment of sunshine, the clouds soon gather.

Slaying the Mermaid

More pervasive than the image of Iphigenia is that of the Christian martyr, and real-life women often use it to make sense of their experience. In her book *Trauma and Recovery,* describing the psychological effects of severe trauma such as domestic violence and sexual abuse, Judith Lewis Herman explains that abused children may

> embrace the identity of the saint chosen for martyrdom as a way of preserving a sense of value. Eleanore Hill, an incest survivor, describes her stereotypical role as the virgin chosen for sacrifice.... "In the family myth I am the one to play the 'beauty and the sympathetic one.' The one who had to hold [my father] together. In primitive tribes, young virgins are sacrificed to angry male gods. In families it is the same."[9]

My interviewee Wendy, who felt that she was expected to give all her blood so her sister could get well, also experienced herself in this role.

Nor is serious trauma required to evoke the martyr image; women embrace it in the most mundane contexts. *The Wendy Dilemma,* by Dr. Dan Kiley, offers advice to women who sacrifice their own needs in order to over-mother men, as J. M. Barrie's Wendy mothered the eternal boy Peter Pan. Kiley describes a woman who was disappointed by her life as a housewife but afraid of rejection if she complained. "Her only solace was that offered by the identity of self-sacrifice. She wore her martyrdom as a badge of honor." Martyrdom, Kiley explains, is "the hallmark of the Wendy responses.... Symbolically, the martyr believes that, if she wears sackcloth and ashes, sacrificing her happiness for others, she will find some sort of emotional resurrection. When she doesn't, she rededicates herself to the cause of martyrdom, comforting herself with pity."[10]

"To choose to be a victim and wear that as a badge is so backward," forty-two-year-old Frances exclaimed to me.

My mother is a wonderful example. She can't even give a gift anymore without the price tag being on it, so that I know how much I owe her that she has sacrificed to give this wonderful thing to me. For my birthday she gave me a jar—clear full, bless her heart—five hundred little slips of paper with an uplifting thought or a Scripture on each one. She doesn't have a word processor or a computer—they were individually typed or written, and then copied, because my sister got one and my aunt got one. She must have made these for everybody. And then they're all cut up and folded and put in this thing. And she told me to be sure not to throw these away—I could give them to another friend or something—because it was so difficult for her to do this and it took so much time. They were not for me at all—they were for her to spend all this time, and suffer and sacrifice. So every day when I looked at one of these I would feel guilty.

Fortunately, a week of guilt was enough to make Frances give up on them.

Frances's mother fits a pattern described by educator Carol Pearson, who explains that martyrs "believe that salvation must be earned by suffering and hard work." They "work very hard to please God, their employers, their mates....It never occurs to them that they may deserve to have love and respect simply by the fact of their being alive, so they bargain."

Martyrs not only feel deprived most of the time because they are sacrificing parts of themselves in an effort to get validation from God or from other people, but...they often also are angry. It is essential to them that other people follow the same rules they have bought into because they cannot fully believe their sacrifices will work for them unless the same system works for other people. They need the unmarried pregnant woman to suffer... or their chastity will seem less virtuous; they need welfare chiselers to be punished or their hard work seems meaningless.[11]

This model of martyrdom as a kind of manipulation was also described by psychologist Helen Wintrob, who maintained that much self-sacrifice occurs not in the quest to be perfect, but because women are afraid that if they don't do it, either they won't get what they want or something bad will happen. "They might be really thinking, 'If I don't make this sacrifice, he's going to leave me, my mother will be angry at me, no one will talk to me.'"

In her memoir *Leaving a Doll's House,* actress Claire Bloom, narrating the extremely ugly ending of her eighteen-year relationship with the writer Philip Roth, paints a portrait of herself as an eternally self-sacrificing victim who agreed to any demand he made in order not to lose him. Two years into the relationship, when Roth refused to live in the same house with her daughter—Bloom's own house in London—she asked eighteen-year-old Anna to leave. "I know I was diminishing my own character [i.e., cutting off pieces of herself] with each successive act of capitulation," Bloom acknowledges. "These confrontations left me debilitated and unsure, and were to shape many of my future decisions." Indeed, fifteen years later, with Roth in the midst of a mental breakdown, snarling accusations at her, she was simply "paralyzed in the face of this hatred."[12] But he was only the latest of the many men she seems to have allowed to seduce her (most notably Anthony Quinn, even though he had been hostile to her for weeks during play rehearsals, and she despised him), as though her romantic life consisted of nothing but passive waiting for the next man to make a move on her. Having signed an outrageous prenuptial agreement with Roth that gave her absolutely no bargaining power during the divorce, she had no alternative except simply to wait to see what he would do next. "She seems virtually paralyzed by loving him," commented one reviewer, "as if she believed her strength as a woman was best expressed by giving herself away."[13] Nor, apparently, did her considerable success as an actress, from a very young age—and despite the fact that her career was the one thing she never gave up—endow Bloom with enough sense of a self that belonged only to her to protect herself.

Some women realize early how easy it is to lapse into a victim identity. Forty-six-year-old Renee told interviewer Dalma Heyn, "Nobody even questioned why my mother didn't have a life outside of us, except I remember thinking that she wasn't happy, and that she might get very sick some day, and that if she did, no matter what anyone said, I would know why. It would be *Victim's Disease.*" Not catching the disease then becomes vital. Heyn reports that Vickie, when she thought she was beginning to sound like her mother—"talking in that good-woman way about my kids and my recipes"—told herself, "Get *over* that victim crap!"[14] And in her song "Haven't Got Time for the Pain" Carly Simon triumphantly renounces "victim crap," rejecting the belief that existence itself depends upon suffering.

The victim/martyr image is not only for the weak, the soft, the submissive. Erica Jong, in a polemic defending Hillary Rodham Clinton after the 1996 election, lists the sacrifices Clinton had to make "for the greater glory of Bill Clinton and the pillow power he bestowed," the most telling one being "the surrender of her maiden name," which signified the total submergence of "her identity in her husband's ambitions." Jong paints Hillary Clinton as a female Christ, crucified daily in the media:

A woman is sacrificed to her husband's ambitions. Her personality is deformed. She takes almost all the flak in the press while he gets away with murder. You might almost say she is taking the punishment for him, and for all women who step outside the lines prescribed for paper-doll political wives—in fact, for all contemporary women. Hillary Rodham Clinton looks more to me like Joan of Arc every day. She is burned as a witch week in and week out so that her husband can rise in the polls. She is the scapegoat half of the Clinton duo, the rear end that gets whipped so the smiling Clinton head can triumph. She is Agamemnon's Iphigenia sacrificed for a propitious wind, Euripides' Alcestis going across the Styx instead of her husband.[15]

Whether or not it is justifiable to view Hillary Clinton as a modern-day Iphigenia—or whether she ever perceived herself as a scapegoat—the point is the way Jong's climactic drumroll of images of Hillary-as-sacrificial-victim fits the First Lady so naturally into the procession of women who suffer to save others, investing even this powerful, assertive, and self-aware woman with the glory of martyrdom.

Developing the Victim Identity

Psychiatrist Natalie Shainess opens the first chapter of a book titled *Sweet Suffering: Woman as Victim* with the story of the Little Mermaid, which she presents as "a nearly perfect parable of masochism, for it expresses the self-punishment, the submission to another, and the sense of suffering as a way of life that lie at the heart of masochistic behavior." Countless women, says Shainess, "like the mermaid, believe that life and love are hinged on suffering." She notes that masochists—who include some men, but many more women—do not take pleasure in suffering, as Freud claimed, but simply "do not know any other way to live" and so perpetuate their suffering through subtle ways of communicating submissiveness to others.[16] The title of her book, however, contradicts this assurance: the phrase "sweet suffering," with its suggestion of pleasure, is evidently calculated to attract female readers by playing on their identification with the idea that women love to suffer.

But do they really? So far I have traced social, economic, and cultural sources of women's self-sacrifice, and have shown how sacrifice is linked to suffering. I want now to examine the internal psychological dynamic that turns these influences into self-sacrificing behavior by individual women. For a long time this dynamic was called "masochism" and was not even connected to external causes since, as we saw in Chapter 5, psychotherapists considered masochism innate in women. As a result, according to psychologist Paula Caplan, many therapists treated men and women differently; therapists tended to focus "on discovering how women supposedly bring suffering on themselves but on encouraging males to be 'real men' and to refuse to put up with whatever gets in the way of their happiness."[17] Telling unhappy women that they have brought their problems on themselves (the implication being that they want to be in pain) is one way to get them to define themselves as self-sacrificing victims. Still, this analysis does not get at the psychological mechanism that underlies the victim mentality.

"When people are victimized early in life, what they do to take care of themselves is develop a self around being a victim," explained William F. Weber, M.D., a psychoanalyst and director of the Individual Psychotherapy Clinic at the Stanford University Department of Psychiatry. By "victimization" he meant not only severe abuse such as incest or beating but also any "criticism, pain, denial of the right to grow" that stunts a child's development. When parents scold or punish a child who disagrees with them or who plays in an adventurous way that makes them uncomfortable, they inhibit the child's self-expression and make the child "a victim who draws back" from experience. By approving this withdrawal from life because it relieves their own anxiety, they reinforce it as a style of behavior.

At the same time, the parents let the child know what behavior is acceptable, such as "being mother's helper. So there's a gain in the family for aborting a child's development, since she becomes the help-meet for one or more of the family members. Later on in adulthood, that child may say, 'Well, this was approved-of behavior, to be this terribly conscientious houseperson,' but of course it isn't fulfilling, because it interferes with other needs and forms of expression."

The victim identity, Weber continued, develops when people who have had this experience "create an affirmation for themselves by saying, 'Well, this is who I am—this is even a good thing. It's what I have dealt with in the past, what I know how to do. I can evoke in others the behaviors I'm familiar with. And then I can accuse them: it's not my fault that my capacities are limited—other people have caused me to be limited.'" A person who is "masochistically organized" in this way assumes a victim stance, accusing others of mistreating her while she sacrifices herself for everyone else.

In our culture this dynamic occurs more in women because, said Weber, "the culture doesn't permit men to behave as victims." Boys learn that they can't cry, can't have hurt feelings, can't "retreat from encountering the world so easily" as girls. "You can't be a victim without a victimizer, and so the men in our culture tend to be trained to be victimizers more; the women are trained more to be victims." Weber gave the example of a man who says to his wife, "I don't want you going out to work!" Following the pattern she developed with her parents, she takes up the role of compulsive housekeeper while blaming him because her life is so limited. But the underlying mechanism is that she chose him initially because he reinforced the withdrawal from life that was acceptable when she was a child.

For many women, this analysis is dead accurate; in fact, in it I recognize my own mother. But any psychological mechanism operates within a multilayered context where external forces also shape people's options. A woman may choose a husband who limits her as her parents did, but if, when she wakes up and realizes this twenty years later, she has no independent financial resources, she may still be unable to leave him or to live the kind of life she wants.

Furthermore, victimization such as Weber described can result not simply from the individual insecurities of parents but from generalized social conditions that stifle children's natural expansiveness. When she was five, writer Audre Lorde sat down innocently in a subway seat next to a white woman who with a grimace of disgust pulled her fur coat away. The black child could only conclude that "there must be something terribly wrong with me that inspired such contempt." This experience of "growing up, metabolizing hatred like a daily bread" is also a form of victimization in Weber's sense.[18] A less extreme example is the well-documented tendency of teachers to call mostly on boys, disregarding girls with their hands up.

Once the victim identity is well established, it is difficult to relinquish, for doing so means "giving up a whole way of life, way of being, and who you are," explained Weber. "In order to get past the experience of being a victim, people have to be able to look at who they were in that experience." That is, they need to go beyond an exclusive focus on blaming the victimizer—whether family, employer, or culture—and examine the complexity of their own feelings and reactions while the victimization was occurring. Once they do this, they "begin to feel less like a victim," for they are no longer defined purely by passivity or helplessness. Judith Herman, discussing people who have been severely traumatized, adds that the "remedy for injustice also requires action"—which means assuming some measure of power.[19]

But the ability to assume power and the form the action can take also depend on social factors. It seems, for example, that both gender and socioeconomic level influence the outcome of victimization: "Men with histories of childhood abuse are more likely to take out their aggressions on others, while women are more likely to be victimized by others or to injure themselves." Among survivors of abuse, middle-class women "tend to become successful overachievers, whereas poorer women tend to become drug and alcohol abusers."[20] In Chapter 9 we will see more of how power and social class interact with self-sacrifice.

Often self-sacrificers develop an identity as caretakers instead of victims, which puts a different spin on the question of power. Weber speculates that the caretaking identity may grow out of the child's sacrifice of her "own growth and autonomy" to keep her parents comfortable. She becomes "very sensitive to others' anxiety," he noted, and as she sacrifices herself to relieve it, "what does get reinforced, instead of caring for herself, is caring for others."

Thus Heidi Dalzell's patient Jennifer, as we saw, turned her entire personality inside out for her parents. Such caretaking, Dalzell noted, is typical of anorexics: "We have a whole unit of caretakers. The women are always so concerned about where other patients are, what they're doing, why they're not with the group. They just want to make sure that they're okay. A lot of them get that way just from playing that role in the family. That role as the caretaker, being the feeling person—you see it to the extreme." The physicians trying to treat nineteenth-century anorexic girls portrayed them too as

> caught up in a frenzied pattern of good works: "A young woman thus afflicted, her clothes scarcely hanging together on her anatomy...this wan creature, whose daily food might lie on a crown piece, will be busy with mother's meetings, with little sister's frocks, with university extension, and with what else of unselfish effort, yet on what funds God only knows."[21]

Such caretaking is often "a form of control," asserted Helen Wintrob. "It's a way that people who feel they don't have much power try to control somebody else." Or, as my friend Nancy, an inveterate caretaker, put it with remarkable self-insight:

It feels very satisfying. It creates a dependency, but you feel like you're doing something good. You can talk yourself into believing this. It creates a veneer of goodness while actually you're masking the fact that you enjoy having someone dependent on you. It's power without having to look directly at things. You feel powerful, and that you're helping the other person. It's destructive to the other, but unlike screaming or abusing, you can gloss it over by saying, "I was helping!"

Or as Vivian Goldstein put it, "It's more palatable to see yourself as helping other people than being harmed by other people." But the power the caretaker experiences, she added, is "not real power."

Underneath we may be burning out and depleting ourselves, or not recognizing that we're really dependent on people we think we're taking care of. If your identity is focused on this role of taking care of other people, you can be giving it all away, and masking a wish to get something in return that's impossible to get: love or some kind of gratification that goes beyond the limits of what's really possible. There's a fantasy that in some way you'll be taken care of in return. It can even be extended to tie in with religious concepts of good works—that if you sacrifice yourself, you will be taken care of by an even higher power. Anybody who's in a helping profession has that somewhere in their character—even in myself I can recognize it.

Chapter 8 will take up the complex question of the higher reward for sacrifice. Now we must delve further into the relationship between self-sacrifice and power, by investigating whether self-sacrificers really should be called masochists.

Masochism and Power

Masochist is a word that many people, like Natalie Shainess, would apply to those who adopt the victim identity. Although "a masochist is a victim," Weber agreed, he avoided this term because of its problematic history. It is true that professional definitions of masochism have evolved from the original notion of pleasure in pain. Richard C. Simons, president of the American Psychoanalytic Association during a fierce debate over this question in the mid-1980s, claimed that "the word's clinical definition has evolved from a desire for suffering to simply a proclivity toward self-defeating behavior and is no longer overtly linked with femininity." Feminist psychoanalyst Jessica Benjamin notes that many psychoanalysts now "see masochism as a desire for submission to an idealized other in order to protect against overwhelming feelings of psychic pain," loss of connection to others, and fragmentation of the self.[22] Although neither of these definitions specifies women, it is women whose character and fate they are most likely to affect.

For this reason the definition of masochism has political implications, a fact that became evident in 1985, when a panel made up mostly of male psychoanalysts proposed adding a new category called "masochistic personality disorder" to a revision of the American Psychiatric Association's *Diagnostic and Statistical Manual of Mental Disorders*. Two of the traits that defined this disorder were "rejects help, gifts, or favors so as not to be a burden on others" and "remains in relationships in which others exploit, abuse or take advantage of him or her, despite opportunities to alter the situation."[23]

Since the manual is used by all types of therapists, as well as by insurance companies and judges, to define, categorize, determine treatment for, and pass judgment on the mentally ill, its contents have significant consequences in people's lives. Accordingly, women members of the association protested that the proposed diagnosis not only raised echoes of the original Freudian concept of masochism, but labeled as a mental disorder that same self-abnegation that for a hundred and fifty years women had been urged to emulate as the ideal of femininity. Under threat of a lawsuit, the panel agreed to hold a hearing at which the women therapists could present their arguments: first, that the diagnosis blamed women for their problems without taking their social conditioning into account; and second, that it could be used specifically to label battered women as mentally ill, whereas research indicated that their behavior resulted from the violence they experienced and was not inherent in their characters. On the basis of such a diagnosis, the critics feared, not only would battered women receive inappropriate treatment but they could lose custody of their children. The panel refused, however, to look at the research supporting these claims, and the chairman cut the hearing short.

Later, in response to letters, petitions, and a formal protest by the American Psychological Association, the panel very reluctantly agreed to change the disorder's name to "self-defeating personality disorder." The final definition consisted of eight traits—a person would have to manifest six of them to receive the diagnosis—including "fails to accomplish tasks crucial to his or her personal objectives despite demonstrated ability to do so (e.g., helps fellow students write papers but is unable to write his or her own)" and "engages in excessive self-sacrifice that is unsolicited and discouraged by the intended recipients of the sacrifice." Clearly the new version was not much of an improvement. After another hearing and further protests, the APA agreed to place the diagnosis in an appendix, signaling that it was controversial.[24]

In 1994 still another revision of the manual was published, and "self-defeating personality disorder" was at last nowhere to be found in it. But the intensity of the battle is telling. Female participants reported "unbelievable" anger on the part of the men on the panel when the women challenged the diagnosis.[25] Why should a group of men holding magisterial power to define the nature of woman be outraged enough to mount a year-long resistance to a group of female colleagues who wanted to participate in the defining process? To me their reaction indicates that women's self-sacrifice is not a question merely of individual personality, nor even just of women's socialization, but has implications for the balance of power in society as a whole.

In fact, according to Jessica Benjamin, the ultimate source of women's excessive self-sacrifice is a power imbalance. Her analysis suggests how psychological processes and cultural attitudes interact to create a bedrock of psychic structures in both men and women that pattern our feelings even when our conscious intentions contradict them. In Benjamin's view, the basic dualism of Western thought is grounded in a polarity between female and male in which the male is usually dominant. Why, she asks, does male dominance persist throughout our society despite our "formal commitment to equality"?[26] Or to put it in our terms, why are women still self-sacrificers?

The answer, Benjamin suggests, lies in the way Westerners learn to experience individuality. For two people to meet as equals in a relationship, they must maintain a "tension between self-assertion and mutual recognition"; each must be able to assert his or her own separate, autonomous individuality while also acknowledging the other's autonomy. To put it another way, they recognize each other as subjects—beings who possess both sovereignty over themselves and agency (the ability to act, to exert power on one's own behalf)—yet are still able to feel connected.[27] The problem is that this recognition is extremely difficult to achieve. A central tradition in Western culture assumes that each human naturally seeks to be the sole, omnipotent subject and dominate all others, reducing them to objects—less-than-human instruments of the subject's will and desires. Freud, for example, believed that the urge to dominate was inevitable in human nature, and civilization was necessary to control it. This focus on the separateness of self and other is the essence of the dualism I have spoken of. What is significant for the question of women's self-sacrifice is that this pattern of domination shapes the relation between the sexes, making man the subject and woman the object.

Following other theorists, Benjamin traces this polarity back to differences in the male and female experience of differentiation—the process by which an infant develops a sense of its own distinct self. She locates the source of the polarity in the devoted mother described in Chapter 5, who by renouncing her own will and needs in favor of her child becomes simply an extension of it, an object of its needs. "The view of mother as object resounds throughout our culture," with "disastrous results for women," Benjamin asserts. "The possibility of balancing the recognition of the child's needs with the assertion of one's own has scarcely been put forward as an ideal." She reports the reaction of a "mother who, when asked what care and support *mothers* need, could not understand the question and finally replied, 'Someone taking care of *me?*...*I'm* the mother, *I'm* the one, I take care of *him!*'" Thus, while the infant first develops a sense of its self through the mother's recognition of its own feelings and acts, it never learns to recognize her as an independent self since she never "feels entitled to be a person in her own right." [28]

To assume a male identity, the boy must give up his identification with his mother, his infantile sense of oneness with her. If she is a typical devoted mother, he will be unable to recognize her as a separate subject, and this will shape how he relates to others—especially women—in the future. Preserving that male identity will depend on a total repudiation not only of his mother but of connection and dependency in general, since the only alternative to autonomy will appear to be dissolving back into oneness. And this "male experience of differentiation," Benjamin asserts, "has stamped the image of individuality" in Western culture as a whole so that "the other, especially the female other, is related to as an object" and individuality has come to mean absolute separateness, self-sufficiency, and independence. [29]

While producing males who deny the self of the other, the differentiation process creates females who deny their own self in favor of the other. Since girls establish their gender identity by identifying with their mother, they tend to grow up with a fear of separation, "emphasizing merging and continuity at the expense of individuality and independence"—that is, experiencing themselves as objects, not as subjects. This "'fault line' in female development…leads to masochism," as girls, fearing separateness, use the kind of self-denial that Wintrob described to sustain their sense of connection. Whereas the boy rejects his self-sacrificing mother, for the girl the mother becomes a model for submitting to the desires of others and deriving vicarious pleasure from fulfilling their needs.[30]

Even though current concepts of masochism do not associate it specifically with women, "the mother's lack of subjectivity," as Benjamin puts it, "creates an internal propensity toward feminine masochism and male sadism," or domination. The value our culture places on the masculine ideal of autonomous individuality and self-reliance "is the chief manifestation of male hegemony, far more pervasive than overtly authoritarian forms of male domination." Another manifestation is "the banishment of nurturance to the private sphere."[31] That is, Benjamin identifies the split between male domination and female submission as the *psychological* underpinning of the split in gender roles that I identified in Chapter 4 as the *historical* root of women's self-sacrifice. As we excavate downward, at each level we find parallel versions of this split.

To give these ideas concrete form, I will illustrate the actual process by which this split between subject and object, self-sufficiency and dependence "gets into women's heads" (as Benjamin puts it) and produces self-sacrifice by taking as example that most exalting and cataclysmic state of mind: romance.[32]

The Idealized Life

"I think romance believed too strongly too early is damaging," remarked Mary Gordon in the interview already quoted, for it causes "women who are very powerful" to enthusiastically hand their power over to some authoritative male. "Whether it's the romance of sexual love or the romance of religion or the romance of political purity, it is damaging." By "romance" Gordon meant the "compelling sense of the ideal," of pure, absolute, passionate commitment.[33] Certainly this was the engine driving both the nuns at the shelter and the political activist Vera. But for most women romance means love, and their ideal is not a grand vision of ministry to the poor or social justice; they long simply—to use Benjamin's terms—for subjectivity, for connection to a self that possesses will and agency.

Claire Bloom's account of sexual passivity incarnates this yearning, and for her the ideal very early assumed a shape that is familiar to us. Her strongest memory from childhood, she writes,

> is the sound of Mother's voice as she read to me from Hans Christian Andersen's *The Little Mermaid* and *The Snow Queen*. These emotionally wrenching tales, to which I raptly listened and to which I was powerfully drawn, instilled in me a longing to be overwhelmed by romantic passion and led me in my teens and early twenties to attempt to emulate these self-sacrificing heroines, at least on the stage.

Charles Chaplin chose her to play the dancer in *Limelight,* "a young girl who is ready to sacrifice her life for a much older man," because he sensed in her "an instinctive romantic sensibility" nurtured by those fairy tales.[34]

Women at every point along the social spectrum nurture some version of this longing to sacrifice their very being to a male into whose potency they can dissolve. Sarah, the anorexic who cut herself in order to feel real, confided to Heidi Dalzell after gaining some weight that she no longer felt "'special.' She liked feeling fragile; having her bones show; boys feeling they needed to protect her. This made her feel beautiful."[35] "When they're thin they feel protected," Dalzell explained, "like someone's going to take care of them—they can get their needs met."

Working with homeless women, I was continually astonished to find that even after being repeatedly tricked, betrayed, robbed, or worse by men, so many lapsed into virtual unconsciousness the minute a new one came along, and simply followed wherever he led. I once taught a writing class at a shelter for unmarried homeless mothers. Though some had developed a measure of skepticism toward men, a surprising number were still waiting for the prince to ride in on his horse. Two of them, asked to imagine what they saw themselves doing in five years, responded that their boyfriends would go to college, get good jobs, and marry them (although they also expected to work themselves). The boyfriends in question (the fathers of their children) were around nineteen and had not finished high school. These young women were so segregated from middle-class culture that much of it was incomprehensible to them, yet they had absorbed the romantic ideal.

Women, says Jessica Benjamin, "seem to have a propensity for... 'ideal love'—a love in which the woman submits to and adores an other who is what she cannot be." Lacking agency of her own, she turns to this other—usually a man—and accepts his agency as hers; "from there it is just a step to surrender to the other's will." The hope is that by thus submitting she can vicariously experience his "glory and power." Benjamin traces this "masochism" of women back to the conventional gender split in the family, where the mother is a passive object and the father an active subject whom the boy can identify with but the girl cannot. Despite today's more flexible gender roles, with parents like Julia breaking down these old patterns, the larger cultural dualism that associates the female with dependence and objectivity and the male with independence and subjectivity remains in place, Benjamin believes, continually re-creating this polarity at the deepest cognitive levels, so that the pattern of the split reappears at many levels of experience.[36] "This is why there are so many stories of woman's love being directed toward a hero such as she herself would be—the wish for disciplehood, serving an idol, submission to an ideal....The belief that the man will provide access to a world that is otherwise closed to her is one of the great motives in ideal love."[37] We are back with the Little Mermaid and her longing for the larger world above the sea—a longing still reflected in women's lives.

"It was maybe easier to assume somebody else's identity—that's the way I was conditioned, or what was expected of me," said Charlotte, who was fifty-eight. She had dropped out of college to get married at twenty and worked to put her husband through medical school and a Ph.D. program. Raised in a rigid German family, she was taught "to be subservient to the man, who takes care of the family." Charlotte worked on her husband's thesis, then took care of his house and children, even helped with his work, all the while waiting for "everything to get settled" so she could begin a career "with some identity of my own." She "felt left behind, in terms of intellectual expansion or development—since I basically lived through another person. And that I certainly didn't want." It took her twenty years to acknowledge that her husband did not, in fact, match her ideal. "In the beginning I respected his intelligence, but you see I had such little confidence in myself, and I had such a miserable opinion about myself, that anything that smelled of somewhat more—far more—than I had was God to me." A long, hellish separation and divorce left her bitter over the sacrifice of her education and development and without enough money to go back to school. For Charlotte her husband had been the image of the drive and ambition she lacked. By giving herself over to his career, she could participate in these qualities vicariously. But since he turned out to be a false god, she never enjoyed even that substitute satisfaction.

More generally, women sacrifice to a god-image to participate in his power. "I always used to try to please my older brother, he is like my god," twelve-year-old Victoria told her interviewer in the Cleveland study, discussed in Chapter 6. This was a cruel, vicious brother who hit her with a Reebok, read her diary, and walked into her room without knocking—for which he was not disciplined by their alcoholic father, who (the interviewer suspected) beat Victoria. Seeing clearly her mother's feelings of betrayal and disappointment over the discovery that he was nothing like the man she thought he was when she married him, Victoria still shaped her own hopes in terms of "the romance stuff," an extension of her childhood belief in "the fairy princess and happily ever afters." She described "the perfect prince" she would love: tall, gentle, and rich. As the researchers point out, maintaining this ideal required disregarding her knowledge of her mother's real situation. "Victoria, like her mother…longs to disconnect from this reality and take in the possibility of romance, crafted with the help of her mother and the novels they read."[38] Her intense belief in romance signals her own feeling of powerlessness, and it is her longing for power that leads her to idealize her brother's brutality as godly.

If, as Benjamin asserts, ideal love is a form of masochism, what of political and spiritual ideals?[39] Vera explained the ideal that had motivated her work for her organization:

> If we do it, if we do take over the country, we'll be heros for having done this kind of work for this long under these conditions, and still going, not giving up. That's a lot of what a hero is, isn't it? Somebody who pushes himself further than the average person would or can. A lot of the whole thing was how hard you could push yourself, how far you could go without breaking. That nobody could beat you, you were being steeled and hardened, that was the term. If you could push yourself this hard, the bourgeoisie couldn't beat you.

Vera said she derived a sense of "empowerment" from being able to "work and work and not stop working. 'I can handle this responsibility.' After that almost everything seemed easy. Like in comparison, the idea of going to college seemed easy, a waste of time." But this frenetic activity, shaped by the dictates of a power-mad leader, rested on the condition of Vera's total submission. She acted not as a sovereign being but as an extension of his will, and her actions served only to maintain his power; they did not extend out into the world to create the beneficent effects she intended. She too was worshiping a false god.

The fact is that for a woman conditioned by the idealism of the fairy tale and the saint's tale, the only possible form of heroism is the sacrifice of the self. And this indeed was the heroic ideal that had inspired Sister Elizabeth at the shelter. Thinking back on what induced her to accept John's judgment and thus come under his influence, she concluded that what he had done was reinforce her own idealism:

> He was the first person who did not tell me I was doing too much, living too radically. People all my life had told me, "You're too good." He was the first one telling me not to compromise what I was really believing. I liked his values.…I think it was basically because he wasn't asking me to compromise. He was the one person who agreed with me.

Now for Elizabeth the heroism of the saint was not an inappropriate ideal. She had a strong spiritual life and was truly a saintlike woman. Focused quite purely on her intention "to live the Gospel without compromise," she more than anyone at the shelter could penetrate the homeless women's fears, delusions, and lies and connect to them at some deep spiritual level that enabled them to overcome their distrust and accept help. But she was also the one who completely disregarded her own needs, even the most basic—who expected herself to work a sixteen-hour day at an outside job and then in the shelter, to support the work of others while getting no support herself, to sacrifice even minor pleasures, like dried fruit, for the sake of others. As she herself acknowledged, "When you've worked twenty-two hours a day, and you've been eating just high-carbohydrate food [she meant their all-fruit diet], it was all distorted"—that is, in a frenzy of submission to a false ideal, she completely lost the capacity to draw that line I spoke of in Chapter 1, beyond which you stop giving.

Elizabeth's idealism was grounded in a spirituality which taught that "if you die to self, then you live for the Christ in others." This is the essence of sainthood in many religions; but saints need to have strong selves before they can give them up. Otherwise they will wind up like the nuns, sacrificing to a false god. For when John walked in and assumed the power to pass judgment and make decisions, Elizabeth and the others felt the relief of the female aware of no such power within herself, and made John into their ideal—not into God, but into someone who knew better than they what God wanted.

In all these cases of idealism, where the sacrifice is literally of the self, the salvation being sought is ultimately a form of transcendence—being elevated, as the Little Mermaid dreamed, to a higher world. No one can quarrel with the desire to transcend the boundaries of the separate self through love, or to be a conduit for God's love to the poor, or to eradicate poverty altogether. The problem arises when the self-sacrifice required to attain these ends entails powerlessness and submission, for it seems then that the only route to accomplishing them lies through pain.

8

Pain: False Transcendence

LEAVING THE DENTIST'S...AND GETTING ON THE W bus, strange reaction. How is it that I, a slave, can get on this bus and ride on it for my 12 sous just like anyone else? What an extraordinary favor! If someone brutally ordered me to get off, telling me that such comfortable forms of transportation are not for me, that I have to go on foot, I think that would seem completely natural to me. Slavery has made me entirely lose the feeling of having any rights. It appears to me to be a favor when I have a few moments in which I have nothing to bear in the way of human brutality.[1]

To the eye of any objective observer, the author of this statement was no slave. Simone Weil, who made this note in her journal on June 26, 1935, was a brilliant twenty-six-year-old French philosophy professor who at the time of that bus ride was laboring, by choice, as an unskilled milling machine operator in a Renault factory outside Paris. Factory work, she later wrote, "implanted so deep in my heart the affliction of social degradation that I have felt a slave ever since."[2]

The daughter of an assimilated, nonobservant middle-class Jewish family (her father was a doctor), Weil, a contemporary of Simone de Beauvoir, had graduated in 1931 from the elite École Normale, certified to teach philosophy in lycées and universities. From adolescence, however, she had not merely sympathized but identified with the exploited French working class—as well as the poor and oppressed everywhere—and vowed to dedicate her life to relieving their suffering. As a student and then a philosophy teacher she was active in left-wing politics, but eventually lost hope in the prospect for revolutionary change and decided to experience working life herself in an attempt to understand more clearly how society needed to be reorganized to remedy the misery in which workers existed.[3]

Even as a child Weil had been unusual; at three, she responded to the gift of an expensive ring by saying, "I do not like luxury." Throughout her life people remarked on her saintliness. Hating her own privilege, she imposed upon herself the privations of those at the bottom of the social hierarchy. She refused to heat her room since she thought the unemployed could not afford coal. Often she forgot to eat, and when she did, ate badly (meals of boiled potatoes and tea), driving her Jewish mother to all sorts of stratagems to preserve her health. Instead of using the entire professor's salary to which her Normale diploma entitled her, she lived on the much lower rate paid to less qualified teachers and gave the rest away to various workers' causes. During her period of working in factories (three in all, since due to clumsiness and lack of strength she was unable to make the minimum piecework rate and kept getting fired), she insisted on living on the inadequate sum she earned, even paying her parents for meals she ate at their house.[4]

The numbing, degrading, dehumanizing factory system converted Weil's previous intellectual identification with workers into an experience of real suffering that stayed with her for the rest of her life. "The affliction of others entered into my flesh and my soul," she wrote to a friend. "There I received forever the mark of slavery.... Since then I have always regarded myself as a slave."[5]

In August 1935 Weil quit the job at Renault, and to recover from the immense exhaustion her nine months of factory work had induced, went on vacation with her parents. In a small Portuguese coastal town, watching a procession of fishermen's wives singing hymns, she was suddenly seized by the conviction quoted in Chapter 1: that "Christianity is pre-eminently the religion of slaves, that slaves cannot help belonging to it, and I among others." All her future thinking was colored by this belief, including her theological speculations on how people who lived lives of perpetual pain could achieve transcendence—or, as she put it, come to love God.

From this point on Weil's thinking turned increasingly toward Christianity; she had mystical experiences of Christ's love, and by the time she died, she considered herself a Catholic, although her version of Catholicism was somewhat eccentric, and she never joined the Church. To her, Christianity was the religion of slaves because, founded on Christ's suffering, it offered the suffering masses of humanity the route to salvation through suffering itself. Weil's factory experience, which combined physical pain with the degrading feeling of belonging to "the class of those who *do not count,*" led her to develop a concept she called "affliction" (*malheur* in French), which combined "physical pain, distress of soul, and social degradation." The real horror of affliction was that the individual became complicit in it and was unable to seek any form of deliverance; thus the factory worker came "to acquiesce down deep that he counts for nothing" and consequently never thought of political resistance.[6]

To Weil (writing as the Nazis occupied more and more of Europe) affliction "contains the truth about our condition"—that truth being the brutal nature of the material reality we live in—and so through affliction humans could achieve transcendence. To convey how this might happen, she used the image of a nail. "The point of the nail is applied to the very centre of the soul," and its shaft traverses "the infinite distance which separates God from the creature." The physical pain and mental anguish of affliction, applied like a series of hammer blows to the head of the nail, enter via its point into the soul of the "creature," who remains "like a butterfly pinned alive to a tray." Yet at the same time, "the nail has pierced...through the dense screen which separates the soul from God," so that the soul which is "oriented towards God" will be able to "traverse the whole of space and time and come into the actual presence of God." Weil's ultimate goal was a form of self-annihilation: "Our sin consists in wanting to be....Expiation consists in desiring to cease to be; and salvation consists for us in perceiving that we are not."[7]

Although Weil believed that one should not seek out suffering, she also felt she had "a special vocation" that obliged her to encounter it, and she did so in ways that still disturb the many people, like me, who are fascinated by her. When Paris was captured by the Germans in 1940, she and her parents fled to Marseille, in the south of France, where she worked for the Resistance. In 1942 they left for New York, where she pulled all the strings she could to get herself to London. There she hoped to join de Gaulle's Free French forces, to which she proposed a plan for a virtual suicide mission of nurses (including herself) to tend the wounded on the front lines in the midst of combat. Alternatively, she asked to be sent into occupied France on a dangerous sabotage mission—something every official whom she tried to convince that she could withstand torture considered impossible, if not completely crazy. "The suffering all over the world obsesses me and overwhelms me to the point of annihilating my faculties," she wrote to an old classmate who was a Free French officer, "and the only way I can...release myself from the obsession is by getting for myself a large share of danger and hardship."[8]

Although she did prevail upon the Free French to bring her to

Pain: False Transcendence

London, they rejected both her schemes and gave her an office job evaluating proposals for reorganizing France after the war. Meanwhile she refused to eat more than the official rations permitted the French people, while working night and day on her own plans for postwar France, and grew increasingly exhausted. In April 1943 she was found unconscious in her room, hospitalized, and diagnosed with tuberculosis. The doctors expected to cure her, but she did not get better because she would not eat, "overfeeding" being essential to the cure. That August she died, of starvation as much as tuberculosis: the coroner's verdict was suicide.

Whether Weil's death was truly self-willed, or whether, as with anorexics, years of restricted intake had simply made her physiologically unable to eat, is unclear. Certainly her attitude toward food was problematic; one acquaintance reported that she considered eating "a base and disgusting function." At the same time food and hunger were central metaphors in her writings. "If [Eve] caused humanity to be lost by eating the fruit," she wrote, "the opposite attitude, looking at the fruit without eating it, should be what is required to save it." She also depicted spiritual longing as hunger, and religion as "a form of nourishment." Weil had other body-related peculiarities as well, especially an intense distaste for physical contact and a determined sexlessness or, as some have called it, repression of her femininity.[9]

To discuss Weil in terms of psychopathology alone, however, is equivalent to dismissing Catherine of Siena as an anorexic—it wipes out the meaning of her acts. Comparing Weil with Catherine and other medieval mystics, historian Caroline Walker Bynum comments, "The notion of substituting one's own suffering through illness and starvation for the guilt and destitution of others is not 'symptom'—it is theology."[10] Weil was in fact a modern mystic for whom, as one of her biographers says, "the attainment of truth through total sacrifice [was] no less than a command of God."[11]

Like Mary Gordon, who was powerfully drawn to the idealist's life but knew she could not live it, I was fascinated by Weil's self-sacrificing extremism, which I could never match, in pursuit of a social vision that I shared. The closeness of her ethnic background to my own reinforced my sense of affinity with her; but the strongest draw was the fact that everything she did was achieved through pain. Simone Weil suffered from almost constant severe migraine headaches that began in 1930, when she was twenty-one. She had worse periods and better periods, but no doctor could ever discover the cause, and the headaches continued for the rest of her life. She did much of her work—teaching classes, voluminous reading, and writing her many articles and essays—through a screen of terrible pain. Her headaches contributed largely to the excruciating quality of her factory experience: "I thought I was going to faint," she notes of one particularly hot Tuesday in her factory journal, "when the weather was so humid, when my whole body felt on fire, when I had such a headache." In a letter to a friend in 1936, she explained that any "ineptness in speaking or acting" or "thoughtlessness" that he noticed in her could be the result of physical suffering that she was trying to hide. Of the period from 1938 to 1940, when the headaches were at their worst, she wrote another friend that "my existence seemed to be blotted out by physical pain." "No doubt because of this her life was secretly darkened by a sense of misfortune," writes her biographer Simone Pétrement, who was also her close friend.[12]

I too have suffered from headaches and know what it is to lie in bed, watching many hours of life pass by filled with nothing but pain, or, when there is no alternative, to spend the day working despite it, concealing it from others. When it becomes that large a presence, pain demands a response, practical, emotional, and philosophical. Weil wrote of "the terrible temptation I feel when my courage gives out, to use my headaches as an alibi, an excuse for my idleness and all my failings."[13] Rather than succumbing to that temptation, she built an entire philosophy on the experience of pain, which she broadened into her concept of affliction to encompass the mental and spiritual anguish caused by social misery. While I feel no affinity for her theology, her transformation of pain into an instrument of salvation strikes home: it is a danger zone that women in particular should be wary of entering.

Although Weil also wrote of other links to God, such as beauty, the power of her vision of pain—combined with the events of her life—tends to dominate. Certainly the image of living with the point of a cosmic nail embedded in one's heart (or so I visualize it), with God tapping on the other end to make one aware, through excruciating pain, of the overwhelming brutal force that rules the created universe, is a gruesomely vivid rendering of a state of being in which pain outbalances pleasure, or joy, in one's perception of the nature of existence. And a remarkable number of women apparently perceive life through such a lens. "We have been ordered—organized—by pain," writes Margaret R. Miles, in a contribution to a 1982 book titled *The Feminist Mystic.*

> Several years ago I was trying to explain to a close friend who'd asked why I always wore a cross. The cross, I said, is the basic symbol of my psyche, meaning for me productive pain, pain that moves one to a new and more fruitful orientation....She said, "Yes, well, but...what about learning through joy?"
>
> It had not occurred to me to collect joyous experiences as learning and energy....Since we expect and even trust pain, we begin to look for it, maybe even to put ourselves in situations in which it's inevitable. And then we don't take the next step...of learning by the careful observation of one's own delight.[14]

Trust pain? What makes it so reliable? My own experience is that by making me feel like a victim, it distorts my perception of reality. But the pervasive influence of this aspect of Christianity in Western culture combines with habits of mind and feeling derived from our history and our training as women to persuade us that pain leads to salvation.

Pain Is Power

Searching for someone to compare with Simone Weil, you might not think automatically of Emily Dickinson. But the very differences between these two women only make more striking their common use of certain themes in tackling similar issues.

Whereas Weil, brought up by agnostic parents, was drawn by a destiny she had not anticipated to Christianity, Dickinson was born into a world of New England Congregationalism whose fundamental premises she rejected. Whereas Weil sought to lose her individual self and become nothing so she could become everything with God, Dickinson chose to present herself as nothing in order to challenge God and become completely independent of him. And whereas Weil welcomed affliction for its ability to pulverize the self that resisted God, Dickinson refused her faith to a God who sent afflictions upon humanity.[15] To carry out these opposing programs, however, both used two compelling images, hunger and pain; and both sought, in some sense, to disappear.

To read through the bulk of Dickinson's collected poems—not just those commonly anthologized—is to be left breathless by a mind so powerful, so audacious, so sure of its artistic vocation that it wipes out for good the conventional image of the demure recluse hiding in her room and writing poetry because she was too timid and/or sexually repressed to encounter the world. Instead, given the choices available to an unmarried woman in mid-nineteenth-century New England, as Adrienne Rich says, "Dickinson chose her seclusion, knowing she was exceptional and knowing what she needed." She was then free to proceed with her grand enterprise, the development of a poetic voice that could take on the fundamental issues of life and death while mounting an attack

Pain: False Transcendence

upon a God who, in her view, plagued humans with undeserved adversities while hiding his own face from them and remaining inscrutable.[16] One component of this project was the transmutation of pain into power.

In "I can wade Grief—" (#252), speaking as poet, Dickinson chooses to experience "Grief" over "Joy," for Joy "Breaks up my feet—," the meter of her verse, her own means of salvation; "Power is only Pain—," she concludes. In Cynthia Griffin Wolff's interpretation, "In order to win 'Power,' an individual must accept 'Pain.'... The poem addresses human response to adversity and suffering" by rejecting Christ's sacrifice, his suffering for humanity's sake. "Permit no one to suffer in your behalf, the poem entreats, for when you seek to evade sorrow, you only relinquish the means to strength." Dickinson's own art, the formal structuring of verse, is a model for various other possible ways to "discipline the suffering of life" and thus "acquire the 'Power' that includes both 'Kingdom' and 'Glory.'"[17]

One of Dickinson's many poems concerned with the use of pain begins, "It might be lonelier / Without the Loneliness—." She clings to her "Loneliness," for "I am not used to Hope—," and she fears that "Hope" might "blaspheme the place— / Ordained to Suffering—" (#405). Another poem states that "Delight—becomes pictorial— / When viewed through Pain—" (#572); that is, pain is a lens or, perhaps, a frame through which beauty acquires the formal harmony and the immortality—the transcendence—of art. To take one more example, the poem below, in conveying the relationship between God and human, sketches an imaginative structure astonishingly similar to Weil's:

> You left me—Sire—two Legacies—
> A Legacy of Love
> A Heavenly Father would suffice
> Had He the offer of—

Slaying the Mermaid

You left me Boundaries of Pain—
Capacious as the Sea—
Between Eternity and Time—
Your Consciousness—and Me—
                    (#644)

Like Weil, Dickinson imagines the distance between God ("Eternity," "Your Consciousness") and human ("Time," "Me") as defined by "Boundaries of Pain." Only instead of gratefully accepting the pain as God's way of teaching her to love him more fully, Dickinson announces that she intends to remain on her side of the divide, within "Time" and "Pain," in order to retain the autonomy of her own consciousness—while rather scornfully dismissing the "Legacy of Love" as good enough for a "Heavenly Father," but not for her.

Many poems characterize this autonomous consciousness of hers as infinitely small—part of a strategy in which "assertions of self-abasement and apparent humility become affirmations of power and worth."[18] The most well-known example is "I'm Nobody! Who are You?" (#288), but there are many others, including a series of poems in which she portrays herself as a gnat. One poem remarks, "It would have starved a Gnat / To live so small as I—" (#612). Another poem, "Who Giants know, with lesser Men / Are incomplete, and shy—" (#796), informs us that while "Greatness" is "ill at ease" in "minor Company," the reverse is not true, for the tiny gnat is sublimely unaware that larger creatures even exist, and so its smallness renders it invulnerable.

In the same vein, Dickinson's poetic voice speaks of hunger and deprivation that paradoxically make her rich and powerful. "It was given to me by the Gods—," she says of her poetic gift; "I did not dare to eat—or sleep— / For fear it would be gone—." That is, she nurtured her gift through deprivation. Hearing other people referred to as "Rich" makes her "smile," for "'Twas Myself—was rich—" (#454).[19] Again, she notes, "God gave a Loaf to every Bird— / But just a

Pain: False Transcendence

Crumb—to Me— / I dare not eat it—tho' I starve— / My poignant luxury—." Yet possessing just this "Crumb," she is richer than "An Indiaman—An Earl—" and "Sovereign of them all—" (#791). In yet another poem, "I had been hungry, all the Years—" (#579), she is invited to a great banquet of a type she has seen before only by looking in through windows at other people's tables. Yet once there herself, "the Plenty hurt me—," and she finds herself not hungry. Hunger, it seems, is only "a way / Of Persons outside Windows— / The Entering—takes away—"; the implication is that she prefers the "Crumb" she has shared with the "Birds" in "Nature's— Dining Room—."

In Dickinson, according to Wolff, images of banquets and food refer to the Last Supper and Christ's promise of a new dispensation; her food imagery therefore parallels Weil's references to religion as nourishment. Even though Dickinson is discovering that she is not hungry and rejecting this sacrament, while Weil is convinced that even a soul that thinks it is not hungry is deluding itself and really does long to "eat" religion, it is clear that hunger and deprivation loom large in both imaginations; and the same goes for pain.[20]

On one hand, to see these two women single-handedly taking on God (in their different ways) is thrilling. But there is also something chilling in the fact that to do it they had to resort to a vision of solitary pain and deprivation. And from another point of view, without the grandeur of their conceptions and the elevation of their spirits, some of their assertions would resemble those of a sulky (Dickinson) or romantic (Weil) adolescent engaged in what my mother used to call "cutting off your nose to spite your face." The impulse to nurture a sense of superiority or specialness by clinging to some form of pain, physical or spiritual—deprivation, loneliness, or (as we will see) headaches and depression—is also shared by ordinary people. I don't wish to pass judgment on saints or geniuses, but simply to use their large, brilliant conceptions to illuminate our own more muddled thinking, and to suggest that for most women, involvement with pain is often a tempting lure that should be resisted.

Pain Is a Mystery

Although everyone (with certain quite rare exceptions) has felt physical pain, it is not at all clear what pain is. Medical researchers have found that describing pain simply in physiological terms as the transmission of nerve impulses does not adequately explain the perplexing, contradictory ways people actually experience it. Even the seemingly natural distinction we make between physical pain and mental or emotional pain is not actually natural, but belongs specifically to our modern mode of perception.

For most of history, pain was considered an emotion, not a physical sensation; in fact, before the dualism of mind and body was invented, there was no reason to distinguish between pain that afflicted the one as opposed to the other. To the ancient Greeks, for example, pain was not something to get rid of, as it is for us, but a necessary component of experience, the inevitable counterpart of pleasure, a signal of a cosmic flaw in the universe. Consequently it had metaphysical meaning, and learning to live with it was simply part of life. It was not until Descartes split mind from body in the seventeenth century, conceiving the body as a mechanism separate from but managed by the mind, that pain was reduced to a sensation notifying the mind that something was wrong with the machine.[21]

The definition of pain as a sensation is the foundation of the contemporary medical approach to it, although by the end of the twentieth century researchers increasingly recognized that emotions and thoughts are integral to the way pain is experienced.[22] Nevertheless there is still a gulf between the modern approach to pain and the older understanding, which becomes evident when neurologist Oliver Sacks contemplates the eleventh-century abbess Hildegard of Bingen, a remarkable literary, scientific, and musical genius widely respected

Pain: False Transcendence

in her time. Throughout her life Hildegard had mystical visions, which she depicted in both words and pictures. She saw these visions not in sleep or madness, she says, but "wakeful, alert, and with the eyes of the spirit and the inward ears." In one vision, which she called "The Fall of the Angels," "I saw a great star most splendid and beautiful, and with it an exceeding multitude of falling stars, which with the star followed southwards."[23]

Sacks quotes this description in his book *Migraine,* after having minutely detailed the various forms of the "aura," visual hallucinations experienced by people with classical migraines: brilliant flashes of light or geometric patterns sweeping across the visual field. The close correspondence of Hildegard's visions to the characteristic figures of the migraine aura leads Sacks to conclude that the visions were "indisputably migrainous." In contrast to "Hildegard's allegorical interpretation," he offers his own "literal interpretation...that she experienced a shower of phosphenes [radiant lights or sparks] in transit across the visual field, their passage being succeeded by a negative scotoma [absence of vision]." He remarks further on how "a physiological event, banal, hateful, or meaningless to the vast majority of people, can become, in a privileged consciousness, the substrate of a supreme ecstatic inspiration." For him, the migraine is fundamentally a physiological event with no intrinsic meaning; the inspiration Hildegard drew from it was a function of her genius. But to medieval people pain was as much an attribute of the body as pleasure, and equally meaningful.[24] Thus for Hildegard, the fact that these visual manifestations may have been accompanied by pain was not their primary meaning; rather, they were a gift of grace from God. The use of her physiology as a medium of transmission would not detract in the slightest from their significance; nor would she feel, as we do, that the first imperative was to get rid of them.

In examining women's relationship to pain, then, it is important to cast our imagination beyond the limits of the categories imposed by our culture and to look at pain as a plastic phenomenon that flows into varying configurations depending on place, time, and circumstance. For even in this post-Descartes age, pain acquires meaning beyond physiology.

Pain Is Female

We have already encountered women's duty to suffer pain that followed from Eve's curse, as well as the nineteenth-century cult of invalidism and female suffering. But beyond invalid women's own adoption of sickliness as virtue, the physicians who treated them believed that suffering was physiologically inherent in femininity, because the very functioning of the female reproductive system necessarily entailed pain: "Woman's reproductive organs...exercise a controlling influence upon her entire system, and entail upon her many painful and dangerous diseases," wrote one medical reformer.[25] Thus when Freud's disciples elaborated the theory of masochism based on the pain women experience in relation to their sexual functions, they were following a well-established medical tradition. And although today women's nature is not overtly entwined with pain in this manner, there still exists what might be called a pain differential between them and men.

Epidemiological surveys find more pain among women than among men. Not counting disorders affecting women's reproductive system, "there is a marked preponderance of women over men in a surprising number of specific conditions," including migraine, facial pain, temporomandibular joint syndrome, irritable bowel syndrome, multiple sclerosis, and rheumatoid arthritis, according to the prominent pain expert Patrick D. Wall. Pain that has a psychological (as opposed to physical) origin also occurs more frequently in women than in men. Wall remarks that instead of serious study of this phenomenon, "there is a subculture of flippant and sexist pseudo explanations" focused on the myths "that women have lower pain thresholds and a high tendency to complain" and that "the difference is explained by hormones."[26]

Pain: False Transcendence

The fact that most chronic-pain patients are women does suggest that in some way experiencing pain is related to gender.[27] In some studies women report feeling greater pain than men in response to the same stimulus. Already in adolescence girls are more likely to seek medical care than boys, and women generally report pain in more body parts than men. Possibly women, being more able to express emotions than men, are also quicker to translate discomfort into a statement to a physician that they need pain relief. However, there are no consistent research results that explain women's greater involvement with pain. One problem is that studies measure pain reported to physicians by people seeking help, so that the results may be affected by different attitudes toward pain between men and women. Men perhaps feel obliged to live up to a cultural image of being tough and thus don't admit to pain, while the regular experience of menstrual pain that many women have may shape the ideas that females develop of "what pain is and how best to cope with it."[28] How much the sex differential has to do with differences in physiology between men and women, and how much it is shaped by social expectations of how women and men should behave, is therefore unknown.

It seems clear, however, that pain is a large issue for women that must have some effect on their thinking and feeling, such as the "sense of misfortune" that Simone Pétrement attributes to Simone Weil. Here there is a great deal of research, which unfortunately does not tell us much beyond what common sense would suggest. "Persistence of pain," writes one expert, "can have a profoundly debilitating effect....Despondency and a sense of hopelessness become likely outcomes."[29] People with chronic pain often develop what is called "learned helplessness," a sense of having lost control not only over their pain but over life in general. Depression, low self-esteem, passivity, sadness, loss of appetite, aggression, and self-blame promote a vicious cycle in which negative thoughts and feelings generate more pain. Thoughts about pain may come to dominate people's thinking, so that they "label all sensations as 'pain,'" rather than discriminating among them, or they tend toward "catastrophizing," generating negative thoughts about themselves and their future.[30]

Not surprisingly, people in chronic pain are often clinically depressed, although different researchers have come up with widely varying estimates of what the proportion is.[31] The question of whether depression causes pain or vice versa has been much studied, with no definitive conclusion. One theory proposed that both chronic-pain patients and depressed patients are unable to "modulate or express intense, unacceptable feelings"; the pain (or depression) then becomes the path through which these feelings manifest. But many other people remain stoic in the face of pain; they seem either to have "strong personal or social resources" or to use their pain as "a focus in life that enables them to ignore" stressful events that would otherwise elicit depression. "In this paradoxical manner, pain can provide a means of coping with an unsatisfactory existence."[32]

In the previous two paragraphs I have duplicated the gender-neutral language of the medical texts from which I drew this information. But bear in mind that the pain patients being described are largely female. This fact is especially germane to one particularly influential hypothesis, which claimed that "many patients could adapt themselves to life only by...having a traumatic social or personal relationship, such as a bad marriage in which they played a masochistic role, or by suffering from chronic pain." Attempts to confirm this theory were not very successful; one study, however, found that "female pain patients experienced more brutality, sexual abuse, punishment and guilt feelings in childhood than three other types of patient," although these results "could be related to social class differences and differences in employment." Because of this childhood experience, another researcher suggested, the women could only relate to other people through pain and suffering; pain served the same function as masochistic relationships, "enabling them to feel that they could be loved."[33] Such notions bring us right back to the

Pain: False Transcendence

belief in women's masochism. But while it is true that people often use pain this way, we must always put their behavior in context.

Many studies have found that beliefs influence how people interpret painful sensations; in experiments, subjects perceived the same stimulus as more or less painful (or even painful or not painful) depending on what the instructions they received beforehand led them to expect. In particular, a belief that one has some control over pain can diminish its intensity—even, in one experiment, among a group of patients who thought they were giving themselves doses of analgesia but in fact were getting nothing. When people feel competent and able to exercise some control over their pain, they cope better with it, need less medication, and are less dependent on doctors.[34]

If this is true of beliefs about control, how much more effective must be the objective reality of control; and so perhaps the question of why women experience more pain than men is related to how much control (or perception of control) they have over their lives in general as compared with men. One large epidemiological study found that chronic pain was more likely to lead to depression than vice versa, and that this was particularly true among poorly educated, unemployed rural women, a group who certainly have little control over their lives.[35] When people lack an income, the question of whether their depression or their chronic pain came first becomes academic; the "meaning" of the pain is more likely to reside in unemployment and the dismal prospects it entails.

Perhaps this is why studies of pain that focus on physiology or on individual psychopathology come to such inconsistent conclusions. As medical anthropologist Arthur Kleinman asserts, evaluating anyone's experience of pain requires taking into account what Kleinman calls the "local moral world" the pain sufferer inhabits, a world where pain occurs within a network of interpersonal relationships and is interpreted through a set of specific cultural meanings.[36] My previous chapters have in fact constructed such a "moral world" for women, except that instead of occurring at a particular geographic locality, it exists as a set of meanings that continue over time. For despite their differences, most Western women do share the tradition I have described, which tells them suffering is good, true womanhood means self-sacrifice, and so on. Within this world, what set of meanings do everyday women, our contemporaries, give to pain? It is impossible, as I said, to live through a lot of pain without developing some type of interpretation, and that interpretation will be tinted with the colors of our history.

Pain Is Muddy

My friend Marsha—whom we saw in Chapter 2 feeling unworthy of telling me she was upset by my breaking a date when I had a headache—as it happens, gets migraines herself. But when she's in pain, she feels unworthy of doing what I did.

> Sometimes I'll push myself, even when I have a headache. Sometimes a job has to get done, sometimes I don't want to disappoint people because I've made plans. But it's easier for me to stop when I'm in terrible pain than just because I need to rest. The headache makes it legitimate. One day my husband's cousins came to visit, and we barbecued. I had a horrible, horrible headache and I just stopped and said, "Look, I have this horrible headache and I'm going to go lie down." And it was fine. The world didn't stop, and they didn't run off home, and they didn't think I was an awful person. That's what makes me think that I need the headache to take care of myself. Still it was really hard for me to do that.

Migraines, says Oliver Sacks, are multidimensional events that serve a function for the organism. This function may be simply physiological—a "retreat" or withdrawal, as Sacks puts it, that protects

Pain: False Transcendence

the organism from some kind of harm, such as overexertion. And Marsha's migraines do "take care" of her in that way when she ignores her need for rest and keeps "pushing" beyond her limits. But the physiological event may also "be pressed into service as a symbolic event" and assume an emotional function as well.[37] Thus Marsha's feeling of being unworthy to take time off—from work or from obligations to family and friends—just because she needs it is transformed by the migraines into a kind of specialness: "It's mine—*my* headache! It makes me a person. It puts you in a club. So many people have headaches. Even if I don't have a headache at the moment, I'm a person who gets migraine headaches. It's almost—a sexy thing to have. It's almost like being a martyr, in a way..." But only if she really acts like a martyr, and keeps working. "I can tell people I have headaches as long as they don't stop me from doing what I'm supposed to be doing. If I'm at work and I say, 'I have a headache and I have to go home,' that's letting people down and being weak." Marsha's headaches seem to be tangled up with her sense of identity: who she is, at least in part, is a person in pain, a martyr.

For Alicia, who had migraines at least once a week, pain "screws around a lot with my sense of reality." Trying to pin down its elusiveness, she mused, "Because it's so hard to put a label on pain, the migraine feels so mysterious. There's all that—kind of—damp, dark world where you don't know whether it's you, or it's something external—it's really a very muddy area. Is something chemical happening that makes it hard for me to do these things that are objectively out there that I could do, or is it my out when the going gets tough?" Alicia saw pain as a large obstacle blocking her path. "I think of pain less as 'my suffering' than as this really tangible thing that's like a block. I need to get around it, I need to climb over it, I need to slide under it, but there it is."

Alicia had to give her pain "a lot of space," which meant paring down her life and working freelance so she did not have to show up someplace at a certain time every day. But this brought on frustration that she was not accomplishing what she wanted to. "And I do some-times think, when I'm very depressed, and I'm lying in bed with all the lights off, and the blackout curtains that I made, that maybe my pain is the big thing I've stuck in the middle of my life because there are empty spaces and this takes up a lot of space, like a big coffee table."

Mary Ellen listened to her with some surprise. "I drag mine behind me," she said. The three of us were sharing our secret life of migraine—for we each had mostly kept it secret. "*I'm* not willing to make room for it in my life," Mary Ellen went on.

> I'm not willing to give up as big a part of me as it wants to take. That inner turmoil and struggle has caused a part of it, I'm sure. I just try to hold them down some way, keep 'em in the back till nighttime. If your head always hurts, you just learn to deal with it. It's amazing what you can do if you have to do it.
>
> It's been—what—twenty years that I've struggled with migraines. And the last two years they've gotten really, really bad. In July and August I was averaging two three-day migraines a week. But the first of September I started using a new drug, and I took a thousand dollars' worth since then…which is insane, because [she hesitated] I don't feel I'm worth it [she gave a nervous laugh]. But that's what it has taken to keep me a functioning person.

As for me, I sometimes found myself feeling that the world was painful, and I was simply reduced to a person in pain—a victim. This feeling seemed so inevitable that I was repeatedly surprised when no one else I spoke to about migraine shared it—at least in so many words. But having migraines did shape everyone's feeling of who she was and, to some extent, how she perceived reality.

Pain: False Transcendence

"One of the reasons I'm willing to talk about this," Alicia remarked, "is that it's really important to me to hear that other people have pain and know what this is. And I think, Oh, okay, so it's something that's tangible—it's not me, or my disappointment in myself, or that I'm making excuses because I'd thought I'd be someplace now that I'm not."

I don't know whether or not Alicia's pain is some form of "excuse" for a disappointing career; however, her account does show clearly how pain constricts people's lives by absorbing a great deal of time and energy that could be devoted to something else. This leads us back to the question of cultural meanings. Just as more men sustain traumatic injuries in accidents involving cars and motorcycles, more women suffer behind blackout curtains with headaches. And just as maleness has a set of meanings that leads men to recklessness or drunk driving, the meanings of femaleness that I have traced lead women to feel a certain affinity for pain. And—not to point the finger just at those afflicted by physical pain—the affinity appears to extend to emotional pain as well.

The research team that carried out the study of adolescent girls in the Boston area, described in Chapter 6, consisted of women from various ethnic and racial backgrounds. During the study they held a series of retreats to discuss issues of "women and race" that came up in the research. Out of these discussions came the observation that "women seem more able to support one another's painful experiences than to join one another in pleasure: being able to support a full range of feelings, including honesty, passion, creativity, joy, jealousy, and anger, is much more difficult." They could express the negative emotions, but felt that "energy and joy" were "somehow too threatening" for other women to hear about. This is the same phenomenon Helen Wintrob described as women's fear of being deserted by others envious of their success; but whichever way you look at it, the result is a withdrawal into the painful feelings for the sake of safety. Later in the retreat, a white woman's expression of exuberance about an experience she and a black woman had shared was checked by the black woman's lack of a similar feeling. Another black woman "pointed out that 'pain is the ticket that gets us through race,' but to experience... joy is much harder."[38]

Because women's history has trained them to take on pain, many are too prompt to do so, out of an assumption that it somehow belongs to them. I imagine this is why studies of the effect of chronic pain on patients' spouses have found differences between wives and husbands. Wives of male pain sufferers are more likely to develop disturbed sleep, digestive disorders, anxiety, and depression than are husbands of female pain patients. The wives' satisfaction with their marriages was also diminished, while the husbands' satisfaction was not diminished.[39] I think pain feels safe because there is a certain resonance between pain and goodness, arising from the valuation of suffering and women's experience of embodying it. Pain lets you off the hook: it gives you the excuse to remain constricted and still be good. Pain offers a letting-go experience; it takes over, you can just fall into it. Not only is the identity of the sufferer, complete, there for you, but so many powerful imaginations have embellished it over time that it has acquired a factitious romantic glow.

In 1846 Emily Brontë published a poem called "The Prisoner," which describes a female captive in a dungeon—a metaphoric expression of the middle-class woman's imprisonment in the domestic ideal. Anticipating no release in this life, the prisoner dreams every night of deliverance through death. Critic Bram Dijkstra connects this poem to nineteenth-century women's preoccupation with invalidism: "Immersion in illness and even the escape into death came to be seen as creative options," he says, alternatives to "the psychological obliteration they were being asked to undergo." The "masochistic ecstasy" of the poem is an "attempt at turning a process of passive suffering... into an outlet for creative energy." Thus the prisoner exalts her suffering: "Yet I would lose no sting, would wish no torture less;...If it but herald Death, the vision is divine." This "solution," which owes

Pain: False Transcendence

much to the nineteenth-century Romantic exaltation of pain as "what transforms mere minds into souls," taking us "toward a higher level of experience," seems distant enough from our time, but in fact, the romance of pain and suffering remains potently seductive.[40]

Elizabeth Wurtzel's memoir of depression, for example, is also a romantic tale of a flirtation with death. Though depression is classified as a disorder of mood, or emotion, Wurtzel describes it in terms of physical pain that plays a role like that of Alicia's migraines. Depression, she says, "involves a complete absence" of affect; what takes its place, "to fill up the empty space," is "a mass of the most fucking god-awful excruciating pain like a pair of boiling hot tongs clamped tight around my spine and pressing on all my nerves." Although the book recounts her desperate attempts to be cured of this pain, she also confesses, "In a strange way, I had fallen in love with my depression....I thought depression was the part of my character that made me worthwhile. I thought...that the one thing that justified my existence at all was my agony." She believed that the melodramatic, blackly humorous persona she developed to present herself as a depressive in public "was what my friends liked about me"; only after she got better did she learn that it was, rather, what they felt they had to put up with to be her friend.[41] Child of the nineties that she was, Wurtzel believed no less than the nineteenth-century invalid that sickness made her desirable.

In Suzanne Stutman's experience, too, physical and emotional pain intermingled to create a kind of high. Stutman, who was fifty-six when I spoke to her, had been sexually abused by her uncle between the ages of three and nine. "I was constantly in fear and often in physical pain," she told me. "I was angry with my mother because she didn't save me and she wouldn't see—plus we had no relationship, she closed me off. I was so emotionally deprived and neglected and abandoned. I was sexually abused but everybody turned away. They don't believe me yet, and they never will."

Stutman did not remember this abuse until she was over fifty, when she had to confront an enormous reservoir of pain that had become a part of her. "I was totally in love with my pain," she told me; it was "the aphrodisiac," "the reward for the guilt"—that is, pain, guilt, anger, and sexual pleasure were all mixed up together. As a poem she wrote put it, "Pain is a rush"—the same image we saw Amy use in Chapter 1. For Stutman, this rush of pain was a deadly beast, ready to "spring / and devour / the / quivering, / succulent / lust."[42] The pain, she said, was both "attraction and repulsion"; love was "being hurt."

The exaltation of pain takes other forms as well. Karen, the political activist described in Chapter 3 who equated sacrifice with risk, was a modern version of Weil and Dickinson, similarly impelled to challenge the powers that be. Coming as she did from a family of atheists, religious excitement for Karen, as she said, took the shape of a duty to change the world, but she too went about it in the conviction that pain was a necessary part of the process. Growing up among hard-working immigrants who made do on very little, and with a mother whose family had died in Auschwitz, Karen saw sacrifice as "tied into the theme of risk, and sacrifice and survival under terribly stringent circumstances was my way of proving myself." Only after she realized that she was not required to put herself on the line every time an issue presented itself, but had a choice, could she stop being self-destructive about her advocacy work. "And the tougher I've gotten about that," she noted, "the less physically ill I've been. I've had terrific problems with sickness since I was about fifteen." For her too, physical pain mediated engagement with the world.

Pain Is Powerlessness

Pain can also be a practical response of sorts to an impossible situation. Mary Catherine, the out-of-wedlock daughter of a poor Irish Catholic mother who beat her when she was a child, was married to a violent, alcoholic husband and lived with the constant fear that he would start abusing their daughter. Since he made too little money to support them—partly because he spent so much on liquor—she was forced to take a dead-end, low-paying job she detested. Even so the family had to live with her mother, whom she hated and who treated her like a servant. Mary Catherine feared as well that in her own periodic outbursts of rage she herself would lose control and hit her daughter, duplicating her mother's behavior.

In the depths of this despair—repeating another pattern of her mother's—she began getting such terrible migraines that she was driven to lock herself into her room and sleep. Despite the financial consequences, she quit her job, and decided she could not do housework or cook either. Disregarding the family's lack of health insurance, she consulted pain specialists—who were unable to cure the headaches—and insisted that her husband and mother pay for these visits.

Mother and husband not only took over the housework but became sympathetic and even affectionate; her husband stopped drinking. "They treat me the way I have to be treated—considerate," Mary Catherine told Arthur Kleinman, who interviewed her after five years of these headaches. "If they are not, I'll kill somebody!... Everyone stays out of my way when I have a headache and that's what I want them to do." At the time of the interview the headaches had diminished in intensity, except during times of stress.

For someone who lives in "a world without security," Kleinman notes,

> the normal, everyday routinization of misery...can be experienced as bodily pain....The confluence of this source of pain and bodily pathology makes it impossible for the afflicted person to determine what "causes" pain to worsen and what will limit or remove it....Pain... becomes the bodily component of so fundamental an experience of suffering that the local world becomes a world of suffering.

Because she lacked any other resources, Mary Catherine wound up using pain itself as "a kind of solution" to her difficulties—but at the cost of periodic physical suffering. Kleinman's word "afflicted" is appropriate here, for the combination of physical abuse, degradation inflicted by her mother, and despair that Mary Catherine had experienced is exactly what Simone Weil was talking about. Like Weil and Dickinson, yet very differently, Mary Catherine made power out of pain. And as the preponderance of chronic pain among women as well as the examples above suggest, even those who are not so trapped by circumstance have been conditioned by the "local world" they inhabit to use what Kleinman calls "this 'weapon of the weak.' " [43] It is an equivocal weapon, though, for it also wounds those who employ it. This was true of Dickinson, who never published her poems; and of Weil, who achieved none of her political goals and died before she had the chance to do what could perhaps have been more influential, mature work in postwar France; and it is true of all the headache sufferers (or low-back-pain or TMJ sufferers) whose lives never expand to their fullest potential. That too is a form of sacrifice.

Pain Is Political

Though we can't eliminate pain, we can reconceptualize it. Scholar Elaine Scarry has provided an antidote to the romanticization of pain. Her sweeping theory of pain's role in civilization is a strange but enormously provocative analysis that makes remarkable sense of some of the reactions to pain that I have described. For example, Alicia's feeling that making her pain tangible would restore her sense of reality was a response to a cardinal feature of pain: its ability, according to Scarry, to destroy "the world"—our perception of everything that surrounds us. Intense physical pain, she explains, obliterates the entire contents of the mind; the sufferer experiences either the universe contracting "down to the immediate vicinity of the body" or "the body swelling to fill the entire universe." (Scarry asserts that this wiping out of mental content is actually the purpose of self-flagellation by religious ascetics; the intense physical sensation cancels the contents of the mind, leaving "the path...clear for the entry of an unworldly, contentless force.")[44] Once psychological content is gone, so is reality, as well as language (one's "voice") and the self.

Yet at the same time, pain itself possesses an ultimate, absolute realness, because it "resides in the human body, the original site of reality." This is why Dalzell's patient Sarah in Chapter 6 cut her arms in order to feel real; but less drastically, anyone who makes decisions or assesses people or situations according to "gut reaction" has experienced the body as the site of reality. Scarry maintains that pain's attribute of realness can be imaginatively transferred to an external or intangible object and will give that object a reality, or validity, that it would not otherwise have. Sealing an oath with blood is one example; the compelling vividness of the pain sensation produced by the wound is experienced as verifying the binding force of the words. This, Scarry suggests, is how the covenant with Yahweh was repeatedly made real to the ancient Hebrews, whose faith suffered so many lapses. Failures of belief lead to scenes of wounding and hurt; the resulting pain in the people's bodies enables them to apprehend God's realness. Thus he sends floods, plagues, fire, and brimstone; he unsheathes his sword against the people (as in, for example, Ezekiel 21). In fact, says Scarry, the Old Testament represents the relationship between the people and their God by an "image of a colossal weapon that traverses the space between them...whose one end is on the ground and whose other end is in heaven."[45]

And in this colossal weapon, we recognize the same image that Simone Weil conceived as a huge nail. Apparently the vision of humanity at the mercy of a cosmic source of pain was not purely the product of her idiosyncratic genius but has deep roots in Judeo-Christian culture. But whereas for Weil pain is an eternal constant, for Scarry the need to make belief in a Creator real by inflicting pain represents an evolutionary phase that Western civilization subsequently transcended. The weapon evolved into a tool used to create an artifact that makes God real by giving him tangible form—in an image, or an altar—through the work of the imagination. Thus Scarry visualizes the creative process of making things as reversing the image of the weapon, for in creation the tool is used to lift pain out of the body (as she puts it), externalizing pain in the form of all the artifacts of civilization. Each layer of objects we surround ourselves with—from clothing to houses to books—is another shield against the body's vulnerability to physical pain.

Creation thus constitutes an expansive movement "out into the world which is the opposite of pain's contractive potential."[46] The expansion may take many forms: work, education, risk-taking, adventure. Suffering—or we might say affliction—then becomes the result of a lack of capacity for such self-extension into the world; the person is reduced to nothing but the body, nakedly vulnerable to pain. This is what happened to Weil in the factory, as she put herself in the situation of the worker trapped there by inadequate pay and no alternative, and also to Alicia, lying in bed behind her blackout curtains.

I like Scarry's theory because it brings pain down to earth, tying it to the material reality of our lives as bodies. In Brontë's poem, the prisoner's visions of death come at night, when her "spirit's sky was full of flashes warm." When she wakes and inhabits her body again, "dreadful is the check—intense the agony— / When the ear begins to hear and the eye begins to see...."[47] The Romantic vision, which linked suffering with a disembodied spiritual exaltation while disparaging everyday material reality, saw the highest art being created out of suffering.[48] Scarry, by contrast, makes creativity a power that relieves pain. For the same reason, though I admire Weil and Dickinson and admit that their visions of salvation make sense for them, given who they were and when they lived, I shudder at the notion of embracing pain for purposes of transcendence myself. While it's true that a sense of pervasive pain was the core of my identification with the Little Mermaid—which in turn was the embryo of this book—

Pain: False Transcendence

my intention is to leave her behind as a source of inspiration and turn instead to that potential for expansion.

Two narratives of ordinary women will ground pain for us along the lines of Scarry's analysis. Kleinman gives the history of Stella Hoff, a thirty-one-year-old biochemistry researcher who suffered "exhausting, wretched, unbearable, agonizing" continuous pain after an automobile accident. None of the health-care professionals she consulted could relieve it. Suffering made her joyless, full of rage, and suspicious of other people, and she was diagnosed as clinically depressed. She continued her laboratory work despite her pain, but fell behind in her career and had no social life because she spent so much time in bed. She had always been extremely ambitious, but already before her accident had felt "serious doubts" about her ability to become "a great researcher"; afterward, she began to wonder whether her condition were not "a disguised form of avoiding failure." Finally, she confided what she called "the spiritual side" of her pain. "Suffering that has no meaning, that brings nothing good with it," she declared, is "an evil.…My spirit is hurt, wounded. There is no transcendence. I have found no creativity, no meaning in this… entirely horrible experience. There is no God in it.…I came from a religious family, French Protestants. I was taught to put faith in God. All I was taught…has been shattered."[49]

The other woman is Gail Johnston, a political science professor, who suffered migraines and pain in her jaw, neck, hip, and shoulder blade, all related to temporomandibular joint syndrome, although it took years and visits to numerous practitioners before she got this diagnosis. Many failed treatments later, she at last discovered TMJ specialists who could help her. Meanwhile, she had learned to cope with headaches using meditation. Unlike Hoff, Johnston felt that her experience of chronic pain had "re-created" her into "freedom to be a whole person."

"I think of pain as extended consciousness of your body," she explained. "I think that most normal people…are not at all aware of their bodies....Pain restores us to what every aborigine or tribal person in the ancient world used to have, which is a sense of their internal universe." Realizing that she had to stop living "this disembodied life of the mind...and start living as a human being," she, like Hoff, ultimately relinquished her initial ambition to be a "leader in her field" who would "set the world on fire," but she did so because she had discovered there were "bigger things than status." She now centered her life on the painting she had used along with meditation to release her pain, in hopes of helping others. "I feel as though those of us who walk in shadow [live in pain] every day, and find a path through it and try to live normally with some integrity and some hope, that we have something very special to say to...people who don't have pain, and to the...medical establishment." Her goal was that "people look at my painting and say, 'God, what suffering, but what hope.'...I can't help but feel like...not that there's a purpose to my pain, but that I haven't let it triumph....I've made it into a way to make connections to people." [50]

Both of these profoundly antiromantic experiences confute the suffering-is-noble ideology. Hoff's pain destroyed a sense of transcendence that she had already believed she possessed. And Johnston's ability to give her pain meaning follows Scarry's paradigm: instead of soaring into some heavenly realm, she was brought deep into the interior of her own body; and rather than seek salvation through the self-obliteration of pain, she found it by developing her talent in order to reach out to help others. And as, with her art, she regained the power of self-expression (the "voice") that pain deprived her of, as well as the ability to connect with other people, she moved into the realm of power and the political: for political power necessarily involves the ability to describe oneself and to articulate one's own needs. [51]

Johnston's experience suggests something else. To the extent that pain is an affliction caused by external circumstances restricting self-expansion—as in Mary Catherine's case, where physical pain was so closely linked to financial and physical insecurity and emotional distress that they were hard to differentiate—one tactic for eliminating it involves action, moving out into that world. If the habit of taking on pain entails a kind of sacrifice because it contracts the self, the antidote is not to leave the self behind by transcending it, but rather to stay with it and expand it out into the world.

9

Sacrifice and Power

ONE FALL AFTERNOON, AS A NERVOUS, BRAND-NEW VOLUNTEER AT the homeless women's shelter, I took Rose, a seventy-three-year-old Hungarian Jewish refugee whose family had been killed by the Nazis, to the Hungarian consulate on Manhattan's Upper East Side. The idea was to see if Rose could get some kind of papers that would enable her to return to Hungary. It was a fool's errand, but I was too young and dumb to know that. In any case, we got there too late, and the consulate was closed.

We stood on the sidewalk for a while as I tried to get Rose, who had no place to spend the night, to decide to do something. It was almost five o'clock, and the wealthiest people in the city were passing by on their way home from work, eyeing us. Finally Rose agreed to return to the shelter. As we walked down the block toward Fifth Avenue, the doormen of the posh buildings watched us, as though if we didn't keep moving they would hustle us away as unfit to loiter near their entrances.

Sacrifice and Power

We boarded the Fifth Avenue bus to go downtown. As we sat down I looked up—and there directly across from us was Fay, a woman I knew from an office where I had worked several years before. It took me some moments to recognize her because this previously rather mousy person had evidently been to a beauty establishment and gotten a total makeover. So she recognized me first, and just as I was deciding this really was Fay, she got up and changed her seat. The bus was nearly empty; she moved only to avoid having to acknowledge me—no doubt because Rose looked so weird.

Rose was not dirty or ragged, but she was quite shabby, wore sneakers (which old ladies didn't do in Manhattan in 1977), and held her head perpetually tilted to one side. Sitting beside her, I began to look at Fifth Avenue not as a person whose mother used to take her shopping at Saks, but as one of society's outcasts—as though Rose had a condition that was catching. The rest of the ride was excruciating, as the bus filled up and each new passenger looked askance at the two of us. I was never so glad to get back to the seedy neighborhood of the shelter, where Rose didn't look so out of place.

These feelings are still vivid to me, though I think now that I made the whole thing up. Probably nobody was passing judgment on Rose and me—most likely they hardly noticed us. And maybe Fay changed her seat because she didn't want *me* to see *her*—maybe she felt ambivalent about her makeover. In any case, why would it matter what anyone thought? I was doing something useful and compassionate. What strikes me now is how easily my sense of identity was contaminated by the image of being an outsider and a victim. But in a culture that validates suffering as ours does, it's not so difficult to slip into an identification with the victimhood of marginal people—especially if you are engaged in a mission of serving them. And when you do, unfortunately, you take on the liabilities of victimhood. If the consulate had been open, and I had had to advocate for Rose, I would have felt too downtrodden to be forceful and effective.

Another of those liabilities burdened Diane, the theater director and performer. She had chosen to work with groups that focused on social issues because the Catholic theology she was raised on "dove-tailed with political activism" to make her feel "guilty about the state of the world."

"Why guilty?" I asked.

Taken aback, Diane paused. "That's a very good question," she responded finally, "because feeling guilty supposes that we have power to change the circumstances, when in fact our access to this power, I came to realize, is very distant. I don't have instant access to changing the lives of homeless people. There's a sort of naive assumption that I have this power and if I'm not advocating, then these people will go homeless. The guilt comes from not acknowledging the true political situation."

Perhaps because of this guilt, doing political theater gave Diane "a very dark picture of life. It made me afraid. If I was doing a piece about the torture of Guatemalan Indians, I would take it very personally. Psychologically I would assume some of their suffering," and become depressed. "How can you feel good about anything if you're literally taking on the suffering of an oppressed people? It was only later that I really began to see that I was hurting myself doing this. There's a difference between helping oppressed people and identifying with oppressed people. I discovered that for my own survival, much of my life needs to be involved with positive people and positive experiences."

Arlene fell into a more subtle snare. Writing an essay that reflected on her thirteen years as a political activist, she found herself describing an "image I had really strongly in my head" of a woman being tortured. It was an illustration in a children's Bible. "My father used to read to us from this Bible every night. It was the scariest thing in the world, because it was all filled with God punishing people—at least, if there were loving stories in there, I didn't take them in." The picture showed a woman with "her arms crossed over her head, she has no shirt on, so she's like—her breasts—it's almost a cartoon. And these men are cutting off pieces of her flesh, literally—'cause she's a sinner."

Political activism—work Arlene had deliberately chosen—felt like having her flesh stripped from her body? At the time she wrote the essay, it really did, Arlene affirmed.

> I always felt a lot of guilt about doing something just because I wanted to, because it was fun or satisfying. It was always: you do what needs to be done. Otherwise you're not really working, you're doing something else—you're playing or something. There's a lot of guilt about doing something just because you want to. Over the years I've gotten to the point where I can do it more, but I'm still not all that comfortable with it.

As we saw in Chapter 3, Arlene had given up the more introverted, creative work she felt drawn to in order to pursue "big political activity." The very fact that political work felt unsatisfying, she said, was partly what made her feel she should be doing it. Not surprisingly, then—although she did enjoy some aspects of it, and it had helped her overcome her shyness and develop new abilities—it also sometimes felt like "being bled." Only now, a couple of years after writing the essay, was she beginning to think about pursuing work she really wanted to do instead of what she thought she ought to do.

Another problem was that, despite the expertise she had acquired, Arlene encountered a frustrating barrier in all her jobs. "I've never looked at my career in terms of name visibility or promotion, but I have looked at it in terms of authority," she explained. Although the various nonprofit organizations she had worked for—as a writer, program director, and administrator—gave her a great deal of responsibility, she had never been able to gain decision-making authority or direct access to people who controlled funding. In one job, at planning sessions for national conferences, she repeatedly found herself in the classic position of being put in charge of coffee arrangements while the men decided the program content; then they asked her to chair the meeting. (The chair, of course, facilitates exchanges among everyone else but does not get to speak herself.) At first, Arlene invented reasons for accepting this division of labor: "It's what the organization needs and I'm here to serve the organization." Finally she told her boss directly that she hated being relegated to coffee provider. He was "somewhat responsive" and asked her to prepare part of the next meeting's content.

Yet Arlene remained uncertain whether this issue was "worth fighting over....The fact that I can talk about it and have it acknowledged makes it not feel as bad." For she knew that if she didn't do the coffee, no one would (she being the only woman in the office). The men, she said, were "just not going to do it. I've been experiencing that since my first political activities. You plan the march and the men just cannot think about having sandwiches on the bus for the people who will miss a meal at the shelter. I've always made the decision that I'm just going to do it, because I think it's important." In the same way, "It bothers me if we have a conference and the food is crummy, or there's no food. There is something in me that feels like I want everybody to be happy, to be taken care of. I get some satisfaction from that."

But Arlene did not want to make people happy only out of an impulse to put "what the organization needs" before her own needs. She knew that the people who go hungry at a demonstration will be less likely to show up for the next one, and that a meeting fueled by a reliable supply of coffee and decent food will run better than one where people are conscious of physical needs unfilled. But engaging in the low-status activity of providing these creature comforts meant sacrificing the very authority—or power—within the organization that she sought.

Arlene's experience demonstrates the inverse relation between sacrifice and power: self-sacrifice is incompatible with wielding authority. Women engaged in other forms of action out in the world also discover this equation. Some, like Arlene, consciously accept a trade-off; others remain stuck in the comfortable routines of self-sacrifice without realizing that they are giving up the chance at power.

"A lot of women are very uncomfortable with power," said consultant Renée Karas, describing the businesswomen she advises. Thirty years ago, Karas recalled, she read Michael Korda's book *Power! How to Get It, How to Use It* and was "shocked that he was talking about it in public. I thought it was something you had to keep hidden." She still sees a similar reaction among her clients: power is "a bad thing, it's harmful, people aren't going to like me if I exercise power, people are going to be threatened by it"—since taking power means relinquishing the enabling, self-sacrificing attitude that "my role is to advance my husband, my child, my boss."

"Exercising power," explains psychologist Jean Baker Miller, "conflicts with the lifelong messages [women] have received about devoting their energies to enhance the power of others."[1] Like Catherine, the bank vice president described in Chapter 3, who was resentful that she had "paid my dues" but was then taken for granted while men at her level got faster promotions and bigger raises, they may expect their self-sacrifice to be rewarded and feel hurt and angry when it isn't. As Karas pointed out, women don't realize that sitting back and waiting for their sacrifices to be appreciated is not enough; self-assertion is what gets raises. But more fundamentally, women often lose out in organizational settings—whether nonprofit or commercial—because their hierarchical power structure is a manifestation of the same dualism that originally made self-sacrifice women's business.

Hierarchical power—power exerted *over* another person, the prevailing model in Western culture—derives from the basic dualism of self and other. In the classic liberal model, the isolated, autonomous individual, or subject, by definition male, protected his personal sovereignty and independence by dominating nature and other people. Women, however, as we saw in Chapter 4, were originally left out of the social contract and so could not be subjects. They were objectified, which in practical terms meant being relegated to the domestic sphere and to lives of self-sacrifice. In other words: self-sacrifice was inherent in their status as objects.

Despite all the changes in women's political and social status, so that today they can own property, vote, have careers, and hold office, the power structure of domination remains largely intact. And since, as Chapter 7 explained, most boys grow up into subjects and most girls into objects, the structure is continually reproduced, with the man zealously protecting the autonomy of his ever-threatened self, while the woman gives away pieces of hers.

The relationship of domination is inherent in the structure of organizations and therefore determines the behavior of their members, superseding reactions arising from personal characteristics. This relationship is evident, for example, in the faint paternalism that people (of whatever age or gender) at upper management levels often display toward employees at lower levels, even those to whom in a social situation they would feel obliged to show respect. Indeed, says Jessica Benjamin, the fact that some individuals do manage to conduct their personal relationships according to a different model has not weakened the overall structure of domination:

> Woman's increasing participation in the public, productive sphere of society...has no effect on its rules and processes. The public institutions and the relations of production display an apparent genderlessness, so impersonal do they seem. Yet it is precisely this objective character, with its indifference to personal need, that is recognized as the hallmark of masculine power. It is precisely the pervasive depersonalization, the banishment of nurturance to the private sphere, that reveal the logic of male dominance, of female denigration and exclusion.[2]

This abstract pronouncement can be telescoped into a concrete incident. One morning, in the ladies' room at the office where I worked, I ran into the sales manager, frenzied and desperate. She was having an extremely heavy period (as happened when she was under stress, which was all the time) and would have to sit all day in meetings with male executives who considered taking a bathroom break an unacceptable acknowledgment of weakness. Preserving her precarious status (she was the first ever female sales manager in the company) required that she too maintain that image of perfect self-sufficiency and "indifference to personal need," and she was terrified that no amount of sanitary protection would last until lunch.

The problem, then, is not only that on a personal level women substitute self-sacrifice for self-assertion, but that within the power structure present in almost all institutions (not to mention many families), self-sacrifice automatically puts them on the powerless-object side of the divide. Arlene's desire to provide sandwiches for demonstrations or food for meetings arose from a realistic assessment that feeding people would further the organization's goals. But because the institutional culture of a nonprofit organization (or even of a political group organizing a march of homeless people), deeply imprinted with polarized thinking, associated serving food with the objectified domestic sphere, none of the men would do it. And when Arlene did it, she was perceived as low status and therefore powerless. Consequently her decision to provide coffee involved a real sacrifice of her career goals.

Arlene's impulse to feed people exemplifies what some social thinkers call an "ethic of care." For people who operate according to this ethic, morality is based not on abstract principles of what is uniformly "right" but on a feeling of responsibility and caring that responds to actual needs of particular people in specific situations. The "ethic of care" is especially associated with Carol Gilligan's description of how women make moral judgments differently from men, as a result of the different ways the sexes are raised. But other writers associate this ethic not just with women but with groups of people—composed of both genders—who lack power in society, including African-Americans and other minorities. In fact, caring has been called a characteristic "response to subordination." Not only, as in Arlene's case, does caring itself entail self-sacrifice, but the people who do the most sacrificing tend to be those with the least power.[3] Unfortunately our cultural absorption with victimhood obscures this basic power imbalance.

Victimhood and Power

In 1996, amid intense debate over welfare reform, Joe Klein revealed in his *Newsweek* column the "secret truth" that the majority of unmarried pregnant teenagers were not "just amoral, premature tarts" but victims of child abuse by older men. This fact upsets conservatives (among others), Klein asserted, because "it posits another victim class"—given that defining these girls as victims makes it much more difficult to justify cutting off their welfare benefits.[4]

Actually, this "truth" was no "secret"; long known to welfare experts and advocates, it had not reached wide public awareness because of the power of what Klein himself called the "prevailing mythologies about teen pregnancy." In order to promote the solution he championed, therefore, Klein turned to an image that packed a punch of its own: the victim. The potency of this image is widely recognized, which is why people who are shut out from the dominant model of power often take refuge in it. Jill Johnston, whom I quoted in Chapter 7 as proclaiming that all women are victims whether they think so or not, notes approvingly "the tremendous outbreak of victim consciousness in America, arising from the political consensus developed by the civil rights and women's movements."[5]

The emergence of previously discriminated-against groups waging political battles on behalf of their disregarded interests is part of the finest American democratic tradition. But, although for many, as

Benjamin notes, "the role of 'the other'...is their only moral refuge and political hope," hailing the legacy of these movements as "victim consciousness" is problematic.[6] For one thing, a hallmark of those movements—even when they did not fully achieve their goals—was that they enabled their adherents to stop feeling like victims. And more to the point here, cultivating such a consciousness is self-defeating tactically; for victimhood, based as it is on pain, has an alien-ating effect. Just as pain creates personal isolation, dwelling within the victim identity damages social cohesion.

Certainly assertions of victimhood, instead of evoking sympathy, often irritate people and allow them to trivialize the claims of the self-identified victims. Christopher Leighton, director of the Institute for Christian-Jewish Studies, told the Baltimore *Sun* in 1994 that "in some ways, the philosophy that undergirds that show [*Queen for a Day*] has won the day.... What's of greatest concern is that suffering is increasingly translated into a kind of moral calculus: The person who can lay claim to having suffered the most can also lay claim to being owed the most by the society that damaged them." Historian Joseph Amato similarly lamented, "It seems everyone wants to maximize their victim status.... We see a growth of representatives of the vari-ous causes of suffering which vie for public space. You could almost say there's a stock market of pity, with fashionable and unfashionable victims depending on the period." One group that has remained "fashionable," he added, evidently with regret, is women: "They've had general victim status for the last twenty-five years." Amato's per-ception that victimhood is fashionable is bolstered by the *New York Times* reporter who, seeking insight about a rash of hunger strikes that occurred in 1996, turned not to a political scientist or a religious authority but to a marketing consultant specializing in consumer psy-chology. Not only was it "fashionable to be a victim in our culture," this expert informed him, but "self-deprivation and extreme dietary control have become idealized," as evidenced by the photos of "skele-tal supermodels" in fashion magazines.[7]

A more substantive objection, expressed by liberal as well as conservative commentators, is that achieving victim status relieves people of personal responsibility. Political theorist Jean Bethke Elshtain, criticizing what she calls the routine portrayal of women "as debased, victimized, deformed, and mutilated" by certain feminists, objects that "by construing herself as a victim, the woman...seeks to attain power through depictions of her victimization. The presumption is that the victim speaks in a voice more reliable than that of any other."[8] When not a power play, Elshtain continues, the voice of the victim is used to evade responsibility; and she gives the example of a trial in Nashville of a battered wife whose infant son died of neglect. The woman's defense was "battered woman syndrome"—a condition said to result from long-term abuse by her husband that impaired her ability to care for the child. To Elshtain, battered woman syndrome exemplifies victimization claims run amok.

Her objection to battered woman syndrome is reasonable in itself, although recourse to this legal defense is not, apparently, as widespread as she implies.[9] But her focus on the essentially flimsy power of the victim allows a more pernicious injustice, the power imbalance that traps women into battering situations in the first place, to get lost. Two other critics of "victim consciousness" do address this issue.

In her book *I'm Dysfunctional, You're Dysfunctional,* social critic Wendy Kaminer attacks "the recovery movement and other self-help fashions" as being based on "a fascination with victimhood as a primary source of identity" that allows people to evade accountability for their behavior even as they feel entitled to sympathy.

> Like contestants on *Queen for a Day,* Americans of various persuasions assert competing claims of victimhood, vying for attention and support. The intense preoccupation with addiction and abuse reflects an ominous sense of powerlessness that infects gender and race relations, and notions of justice and heroism, as well as our view of

the self.... The cult of victimhood reflects a collective sense of resignation. It responds to widespread feelings of helplessness in the face of poverty, crime, disease, pollution.[10]

Kaminer objects as much as Elshtain to the avoidance of responsibility but, unlike her, focuses on the true condition of victimhood, which is powerlessness. Psychologist Carol Tavris goes further, connecting the feeling of victimization to the social factors that are often its primary causes. The recovery movement, she maintains, teaches women to regard themselves as codependent "enablers" of their husbands' alcoholism, focusing on their own "disease" instead of looking outward at "the social and economic realities" that may have contributed to their victimization, such as the unemployment that drives many men to drink. Playing out "a classic aspect of the female role... the woman takes on the guilt and the responsibility for fixing things."[11] Such women then develop a voluptuous fascination with their own "sickness" that perpetuates their victimization.

In a similar way, Tavris continues, women with a history of sexual abuse are often drawn, through participation in sexual-abuse survivor support groups, "to incorporate the language of victimhood and survival into the sole organizing narrative of their identity." Such groups, confirms psychiatrist William Weber, often reinforce the victim identity by leading survivors to dwell on their anger at the perpetrator and on blaming him, which makes it much more difficult to "get past the experience of being a victim." Judith Herman notes that survivors of trauma sometimes develop "a grandiose feeling of specialness" that "compensates for self-loathing and feelings of worthlessness. Always brittle, it admits of no imperfection" and "carries with it a feeling of difference and isolation with others."[12] This grandiosity, compounded of self-righteousness and fueled by anger, often characterizes people who present themselves as victims. It is easy to fall into it, for when you feel powerless, the virtue accorded

Slaying the Mermaid

the victim seems the only route to some form of respect and to a feeling of entitlement.

The sense of being righteous and special is part of what makes the
role of the victim so attractive that, according to Tavris, even women
who may not have suffered such severe abuse may be drawn to it.
"For some women, the sexual-victim identity is appealing because it
is a lightning rod for the inchoate feelings of victimization they have
as a result of their status in society at large.... 'Sexual abuse' is a
metaphor for all that is wrong in women's lives."[13] But by locating the
problem within individuals—the codependent woman, the psychologically disturbed male offender—the focus on victimhood keeps
women confined to that same sphere of the personal which was the
locus of self-sacrifice and powerlessness in the first place.

Some women, like my college roommate Evelyn, create a kind of
bogus victimhood that provides a reliable, ongoing sense of virtue.
Former nun Mary Gilligan Wong realized that one thing the "valuable currencies" of suffering and self-sacrifice had bought her was
freedom from social responsibility:

> As far as the suffering of fellow human beings was con-
> cerned, I...learned that their pain obligated me to do my
> fair share of suffering—that if they hurt, my first oblig-
> ation was to hurt too. If my burden of self-torture
> seemed heavy at first, I eventually found that it ulti-
> mately freed me from any real responsibility for my
> world: it wasn't necessary that I *do* anything about the
> problems of the world, about hunger and war and
> poverty, only that I feel guilty. Guilt became, in the end,
> a comfortable refuge.[14]

And "guilt," says Audre Lorde, "is only another form of objectifica-
tion," for when you simply retreat into guilt instead of trying to adjust
your behavior, those who are the objects of the guilt become mere
functions helping you to construct your own comfort.[15]

The most gratifying component of victimhood, however, is anger. Like pain, anger is seductive, and for the same reason: it gives you a high. Physiologically, anger releases adrenaline, which produces a surge of energy that feels like power. That is why Amy, the community activist in Chapter 1, felt hooked on the adrenaline rush evoked by resentment over doing grunt work—an "addiction" she also connected to chronic physical pain from whiplash. Physical and emotional pain are both associated with adrenaline release, which is why Suzanne Stutman wrote that "pain is a rush." The high feels like a form of transcendence, so it is hardly surprising that people get hooked on it.

But the combination of the high with the self-righteousness of victimhood can be disastrous. Jessica Benjamin, for example, speaks of the "euphoria of righteousness" that makes political idealists—intent on relieving their own or someone else's victimization—light-headed enough to lose touch with reality. In a union campaign I took part in, righteous indignation—in response to real inequities in the office—blinded organizers to their coworkers' degree of distaste for the blue-collar image of unions and for communal action in general. Consequently the organizers failed to recognize how effective were management's tactics in opposing the union. Unable to evaluate the balance of power accurately, they called an election too soon and lost it.

In a series of poems Adrienne Rich, who has suffered for many years from arthritis, describes how the pain she experienced after surgery seemed indistinguishable from the pain felt by victims of torture and political killings all over the world. She struggles to find a way to connect these two pains "without hysteria"—without, that is, the light-headed assumption of equal victimhood that would allow her to evade the reality of her own more privileged political position and her social responsibility in the light of that difference (poem #18). She concludes that, though "The body's pain and the pain on the streets / are not the same," that there is a place where their edges blur together (#29).[16] In that space, insight can arise—deriving perhaps from the sympathetic imagination that one's own experience of pain makes possible.

Through some such mechanism, perhaps, we can perceive why for someone who is powerless, anger may supply the only consistent feeling of strength she experiences. I recall hearing stories from homeless women who, riding a wave of fury, told off bureaucrats, caseworkers, or doctors who were treating them like dirt. For the moment, they salvaged their self-respect, but at the price of losing the resource that the other controlled.

A particularly nuanced appreciation of what anger means for the powerless is that of Audre Lorde, who calls it a "powerful fuel." To a white woman who accused her of unfairly trading on her victim status as "Black and Lesbian...to speak with the moral authority of suffering," Lorde responded, "What you hear in my voice is fury, not suffering. Anger, not moral authority....Black women are expected to use our anger only in the service of other people's salvation or learning. But that time is over...." That is, she will no longer hide her anger to spare the white woman guilt. But she also knows that "anger, like guilt, is an incomplete form of human knowledge....In the long run, strength that is bred by anger alone is a blind force which cannot create the future." It is only not destructive when its expression is used to "transform difference [as between black and white] through insight into power."

Lorde speaks from that experience of double sacrifice described in Chapter 5, in which "Black women," as she says, "traditionally have had compassion for everybody else except ourselves," sacrificing a great deal for their men and their children.[17] As Antonia Cottrell Martin explained, "When men can't find employment in a climate of racism, it's harder to hold families together, and the burden can fall largely on the women. So everybody gets sacrificed in the black community."

With these remarks we turn a corner in this discussion. Beyond it a wider landscape spreads out, of which women's sacrifice forms only one piece. Other people out there are making sacrifices, too; or more precisely—as becomes clear once the entire scene is visible—they are themselves being sacrificed. What they all share—what puts these different groups in the sacrificer category—is that they lack power. All are part of a pattern in which the most powerless people are made to sacrifice for everyone else.

Scapegoating and Power

This pattern is quite ancient. Its prototype is the ceremony of the scapegoat in the biblical book of Leviticus, which the Lord instructs the ancient Israelites to perform as part of the elaborate sacrificial ritual for the Day of Atonement (Leviticus 16). The high priest, laying his hands upon the head of a live goat, confesses over it all the sins of the people. Bearing their iniquities, the goat is then driven off into the wilderness. Today we still drive scapegoats into a "solitary land" (Leviticus 20:22)—the margins of society, where they become outcasts, sacrifices for the well-being of everybody else; only because we have no formal, named ritual, it is not so obvious what is happening.

To get at the connection between scapegoating and individual women's self-sacrifice, we must look again at the significance of pain. But to understand the relation of pain to the social form of sacrifice that constitutes scapegoating, we need the help of two new images.

The first is supplied by psychologist David Bakan, who regards pain as a manifestation of the breakdown of a harmoniously functioning whole, whether individual body or social organism. When a part succumbs to dis-ease of some sort, it falls out of harmony, and pain is the signal of this separation. Pain is, in fact, "the characterizing experience of the human organism torn out of a larger [whole]," says Bakan. With this image of pain as a sign of the loss of wholeness—physical and spiritual alike—we approach the central mystery of sacrifice.

When pain afflicts the individual body, Bakan says, restoring harmony requires that the self perceive the affected part as "not-me" so that part can, if necessary, be sacrificed to enable the rest to be made whole, as in having a tooth pulled. "That which is 'me' is made into something which is 'not-me,' and...that 'not-me' is sacrificed in order that 'I' might continue to live."[18] On the social level, I suggest, when there is dis-ease within the social body—anxiety, conflict, economic insecurity—the ancient mechanism kicks in and the "goat" is sacrificed to preserve the soundness of the community. The scapegoat becomes "not-us," an other.

We have seen how women became the other—nurturers and self-sacrificers—that enabled men to be rationalist, competitive, invulnerable strivers while preserving the health of the social organism. But to explain how the burden of sacrifice is further extended to the powerless, we need Elaine Scarry's analysis of pain as the engine of creation, which uncovers the relation between pain and power.

As Chapter 8 explained, Scarry sees the creation of any material object as a form of self-extension that relieves the pain of sheer raw physical existence by sheltering (houses, clothing) or in other ways supporting (chairs, eyeglasses) the body. Creation, Scarry continues, reverses the isolation of the pain experience by making pain visible: a coat is an expression of the body's vulnerability to cold; an aspirin tablet is a statement that people get headaches.[19] If pain can be made real to other people in this way, she contends, it can also be represented politically. This statement is both metaphoric and literal. For Scarry, the making of a chair is of the same order as the writing of a book like this one: both are forms of representation, of self-extension, that carry with them a certain measure of power.

But often the people who make objects are unable to enjoy their benefits, as when, for example, sweatshop workers manufacture coats they could never buy themselves. Their creation affords no self-extension, and they suffer the physical and spiritual pains of poverty. Whereas for an individual, pain destroys mental content and language, for a group it destroys political power, which depends on the power of self-description.

Thus young Asian women work under degrading, painful conditions for very low wages so that I can buy a coat or a pair of running shoes for a price I am willing to pay, while the company that sells them to me makes what it considers an adequate profit and its shareholders receive a dividend that supports the price of the stock. In Scarry's terms, the Asian women's pain literally becomes our power. In other words, the gender split by which women became the sacrificers doing the suffering for everyone else is only one element of a wider cultural pattern that takes in groups of both genders. Therefore the dilemma of the middle-class woman who feels trapped in what appears to be a purely personal compulsion always to put her own needs last bears a kinship with the painful experiences of women (and plenty of men) who may seem quite remote. We need to recognize this kinship, because ultimately coming to terms with both personal sacrifice and social scapegoating will require the sense that all these groups are interconnected.

Nevertheless, we cannot forget that the burden of sacrifice is unequally distributed. The rest of this chapter illustrates how the scapegoating of two groups of women recapitulates the issues inherent in individual self-sacrifice.

Contemporary Scapegoats

What always puzzled me about the debate over unmarried teenage mothers was the attribution of tremendous destructive power to people who—as I knew from teaching them and other volunteer work—had almost no power at all. "Illegitimacy is a threat to the survival of our nation and our culture," proclaimed Sen. John Ashcroft of Missouri in 1995. Lisa Schiffren, a former speechwriter for Dan Quayle, agreed that "America faces no problem more urgent than our skyrocketing illegitimacy rate." And Diane Sawyer, introducing a segment about teenage mothers on *Primetime Live,* told her audience that "to many people, these girls are public enemy number one." *The New York Times* evoked the "sense of 'otherness'" felt by suburban voters toward the "urban underclass" (mistakenly assumed to include the majority of women on welfare) by quoting two Republican House members who asserted during debate over a welfare bill that, as with wolves and alligators, "unnatural feeding and artificial care creates dependency."[20]

Yet government figures demonstrated not only that the teenage birth rate was lower than it had been in the 1950s but also that—far from "skyrocketing"—it was actually falling among teenagers aged eighteen and nineteen, and showed no increase among those fifteen to seventeen.[21] Why then should these beliefs persist in the face of such strong evidence against them—to the point where young women on welfare are perceived as predatory wild animals?

A young unmarried mother from a minority group—especially if she is African American—is a lightning rod for a whole slew of social issues that evoke tremendous dissension: race, poverty, single-parent families, female sexuality, contraception, abortion, dependency. These issues are all extremely difficult to confront, first because they touch deep insecurities and needs in everyone, and second because addressing them would involve radical shifts in that same power imbalance I have described. Rather than face the discomforts of such change, we load all the blame on the back of the "welfare mother" and cast her out into the wilderness.

Joe Klein, for example, advocated requiring all pregnant teens who wanted government assistance to live in "second-chance homes," otherwise known as orphanages. Although he presented these institutions as offering protection, "structure and support," and training in "motherhood and morality," their essence would more likely be— as has been true of all publicly funded institutions for the poor, literally for centuries—punishment.[22] But that is the point. Forcing these young women out into the margins of society—for to be on welfare is to be an outcast—provides a measure of relief for everyone else, as though chastising them absolves us from confronting the disturbing social issues they embody.

At the same time, the choice of these teenage mothers as scapegoats is also a function of women's traditional role of self-sacrifice within a culture based on dualistic thinking. The very nature of welfare as a "culture of dependency," as politicians like to describe it, is rooted historically in a determination to preserve that same dependency within the separate sphere of domesticity. From the beginning, historian Linda Gordon points out, "worry about single mothers and their children was a major influence on the development of modern welfare policy," which was intended to prevent single mothers "from being too comfortable on their own." Since the values represented by the domestic ideal and the Angel in the House made single mothers morally suspect, early-twentieth-century reformers working to get state legislatures to enact "mother's aid pensions" for poor single mothers emphasized the Victorian image of the homebound, self-sacrificing mother to argue that these women deserved help.[23]

Eventually social welfare advocates developed three different arguments on which to base claims for assistance. One asserted that citizens had a natural right to adequate income and shelter, education, and other benefits of society. A second claim was based on compensation for service to the state, such as a lifetime of labor. The third argument was based on need: that the state had a responsibility to fulfill human needs. Advocates argued this third claim by appealing not to law, as with the rights claim, but to public sympathy and compassion for self-sacrificing motherhood; they portrayed assistance to these needy mothers as charity, not an entitlement.[24]

The New Deal social welfare legislation passed in the 1930s reflected these claims differently for men and for women. Programs that benefited mostly men—Social Security, unemployment compensation—were based on rights and service claims. Tied to the level of wages and to military service, the benefits these programs provided were considered entitlements and set as fixed amounts. But since motherhood was not seen as service to the state, the main women's program—Aid to Dependent Children, or "welfare"—relied on

Slaying the Mermaid

claims of need, which meant that its benefits were seen as charity. While recipients of entitlements were considered to deserve their benefits, those who received charity constantly had to prove their deservingness to caseworkers who had discretion to increase or reduce their stipend—which itself was always lower than those provided by the entitlement programs.[25]

The distinction between charity and entitlement underlies our attitudes today toward young mothers on welfare. Programs like Social Security and unemployment insurance "appear as rights and deserved benefits that increase a citizen's self-esteem and feeling of entitlement," says Gordon, while "public assistance recipients are daily told that they are parasites." Welfare "embodied a lack of national social citizenship," expressed in inadequate grants and the humiliation recipients had to undergo. What has been added to the issue of welfare since the 1930s, when the problem of single mothers was conceptualized in terms of white women's experience, is the element of race, as African-American single mothers became more visible in northern cities, and welfare as a whole was reconceptualized as a problem particularly involving African Americans.[26]

Welfare is thus a primary mechanism by which unmarried mothers have become the others for our entire society. In the dynamic between self and other, Jessica Benjamin notes, the autonomous subject can only recognize another person's individual needs (as opposed to that person's abstract, generalized rights) if that other person is defined as an object: "Only the other...who does *not* have the same rights as I do, and against whom I do *not* compete, may claim respect for needs—in this category we find the helpless wife, the child, the deprived."[27] This is another reason why being on welfare automatically thrusts people out into that wilderness of otherdom where they have no rights. What is more, stigmatizing the welfare mother "as the cause of her own poverty and that of African-American communities," as sociologist Patricia Hill Collins puts it, "shifts the angle of vision away" from other causes such as the disappearance of jobs for black men due to the changing nature of the economy, leaving them financially unable to support families. At a time when downsizing and wage stagnation left the working poor and even the middle class increasingly insecure, it was easier to attack these female others who had already been made "not-us" than to blame the powerful men whose decisions made the jobs disappear. In the words of two women living in a community that sheltered homeless families, the scapegoats could "carry the rage and fear of the people out into the wilderness to die. Someone must be punished to relieve the constant stress of fear." [28]

The second scapegoat group, battered women, have oddly enough been blamed for their own battering almost as much as teenage mothers have been blamed for having sex. Battered women of all races and economic levels, according to writer Ann Jones, are "sacrificed to preserve the 'family' and 'society'" much as prostitutes always were. In the thirteenth century St. Thomas Aquinas concluded that prostitution was a social evil that had to be tolerated, for like a sewer in a palace, it drained off "pollution" that would otherwise infect all the inhabitants; the prostitute was a scapegoat who enabled other women to remain chaste. In the same way, battered women (like African-American women, in Toni Morrison's account) absorb the rage that men might otherwise self-destructively turn against more powerful forces in society. These women also, says Jones, serve as "a conduit to carry off the political energy of other women who must care for them, an exemplum of what awaits all women who don't behave as prescribed, and a pariah group to amplify by contrast our good opinion of ourselves." [29]

Battered woman syndrome, from this perspective, is a concept invented—though no doubt not consciously—for the purpose of scapegoating. "I don't think there is a battered woman syndrome. I would call it post-traumatic stress disorder. What happens is not peculiar to battered women....It's a consequence of severe and prolonged battery; it's not something women are naturally afflicted with," commented Jones in an interview. And Judith Herman points

Slaying the Mermaid

out that the "tendency to misdiagnose victims was at the heart" of the controversy over the definition of "self-defeating personality disorder" in the APA diagnostic manual. "For too long," says Herman, "psychiatric opinion has simply reflected the crude social judgment that survivors 'ask for' abuse. The earlier concepts of masochism and the more recent formulations of addiction to trauma imply that the victims seek and derive gratification from repeated abuse. This is rarely true." "Crude social judgment" is also evident in the fact that the conviction rate for women (particularly women of color) who kill batterers is "higher than that of male murderers, even though women usually have more and better self-defense justifications."[30]

At this level of scapegoating, battered women are absorbing not simply individual men's rage but everyone else's discomfort with the prospect of altering a set of social conditions in which men are allowed to respond to their own frustration and despair by turning to violence. Applying sanctions to this male behavior amounts to dismantling the power structure of domination, which is why there has been such resistance to proposals to do so. Consequently even battered women who successfully negotiate the complexities of the courts and the agencies that provide shelter feel as though they are being punished, especially if they are unable to return home because the man is stalking them: "He committed a crime," they say, "and his punishment is he gets to keep the apartment, while I get to be homeless. It's my legs that were broken, I'm the one who was shot, I'm the one who was knifed. I didn't do this to myself, but I'm the one being treated as a criminal."[31] If she gets the blame, we don't have to feel the responsibility.

The wrongness in the assumptions behind the blaming of battered women becomes evident in the saga of one battered wife who escaped. Reva grew up in Berkeley, California, and married when she was twenty-two, partly to get away from her strict family and partly because her stepfather told her that if she didn't get married she

Sacrifice and Power

would turn into an old maid. She expected to have many babies and a "beautiful marriage....I was overweight; I felt good because this good-looking man wants to marry me. To me I wasn't attractive, 'cause nobody told me, I had low self-esteem. I thought it was an honor to marry this man."

After two miscarriages, Reva's first daughter was born, and eventually she had four children. "When I was carrying them he was nicer than he was ordinarily. He didn't abuse me, he respected a woman that was carrying a baby"—for otherwise he did abuse her, mostly "with the mouth" at first, but also physically. Since he was a veteran on disability, he was home all day. To avoid being there with him, Reva refused to accept Social Security for herself and instead worked as an aide at the Catholic school her children attended. "We didn't have the money for tuition, but Sister let me work it out, doing the cleaning. Oh, Lord—I cleaned toilets, I did the whole nine yards." She became president of the PTA; she was a Girl Scout leader; and when the Black Panthers set up their first free breakfast program at her church, in a poor neighborhood of Oakland, she helped in the kitchen—all to escape the verbal and physical violence at home, where her husband kept reminding her that she could never leave him. "What are you going to do, nobody gonna hire you, you don't even know how to dress," he would say. And in fact she had no decent clothing, since all her money went to her children's needs. Since he considered her job a joke, her husband never asked for her paycheck, so she could save a bit. He drank, gambled, and often disappeared for two or three days at a time, leaving her without funds. "If it was just enough for the kids, they ate and I didn't, 'cause they were more important than me."

But during all this time, her community activities "made me stronger," and Reva began to believe she could escape. She had an aunt in Portland who told her to come there, but she was afraid to leave, until one night her husband threw the TV set at her thirteen-year-old daughter and the police came.

It was one black, two white policemen. The black one
came down [from talking to her husband upstairs] and
talked to me, and told the white ones, "This is a little
family thing." One white policeman said, "No, this goes
beyond. I made several calls to this house." The black
policeman [had the attitude that] it's okay if I got my ass
whupped, I'm a woman. But the white policeman, God
bless his soul, he said, "Ma'am, do you have someplace
you can go tonight to kind of think this over?"

Reva spent the night with a friend in Berkeley, and within a couple of
weeks, with help from her friend and the nuns at the school, made it
to Portland. Not long after, she had another job as a school aide.

Once she was safe, Reva's latent talents emerged. She got involved
in a community development corporation that started out remodeling
one fourplex into low-income housing and by 1997 owned 174 units.
She became an advocate for seniors, ran neighborhood meetings for
local women, visited homeless shelters. "I belong to everything in
Portland," the sixty-four-year-old Reva told me.

I feel like I have accomplished a lot, fund-raising and
housing—I raised a lot of money. Fund-raising is my
thing—I can beg real good and make people feel good
about it. I used to be shy, because this man made me shy.
I didn't speak up—everything I said was wrong. But
now I go to different places and speak, and get money
for the organization, and I speak with mayors—I'm
going to a mayor's cocktail party tonight; the mayor is
honoring all the housing people. I'm very well-known in
my community, people call me for advice.

During all the years that Reva was victimized by her husband, she
never knew she had such abilities.

My esteem was so, so low. I had no self-esteem and I had
no encouragement. Just the sisters encouraged me. But I
had nobody to say—not even my mom—that you can do
anything if you try [her voice wavered here with emo-
tion]. That's why I try to tell the young women now, and
my girls, "You don't have to take the things that you
take—you don't have to take this abuse. And you think
you're the onliest woman it happens to, but you're not.
It's all over.

What makes me feel sad is that I stayed in this abuse
for so long and didn't tell anybody. I just feel real sad that
I didn't have enough confidence in myself, that I didn't
feel that I was self-worthy. 'Cause I'm a strong woman. I
am a very strong woman. Where was this Reva many
years ago, this person that didn't believe in herself?

She was, in fact, surrounded by influences that conspired to keep
her feeling like a victim: the attitude of her culture and her family
that a woman was nothing if she did not marry and have children; her
husband's constant verbal abuse; her mother, who told her to stay
with him anyway "because he's bringing the money in"; even (except
for the good fortune that his colleague disagreed) the policeman who
figured it was okay for a woman to be beaten. What finally gave Reva
the strength to rescue her children and herself was her own community work. There she found a part of herself that wasn't a victim, that
could act. Through action, she found power. And later, when her
career as a community activist blossomed, she used that power to
empower other women.

My community needs me; so many things need to be
done. I need to get out there and get other women that
have low self-esteem, and we need to save our children.
So many women stay there and take the bullshit because

they have children. They don't want to take their children away from their only home and only father that they have. They have the mistaken impression that they should be there with this father.

It's the grandmothers that's making the difference. The grandmothers tell the young women, "You don't lay up and have babies for men just because they say they love you." I advise anybody to marry at thirty-five. You're a mature person. And you don't have to have babies right away.

Redefining Power

Attempts to generalize about "all women" risk allowing people to disregard differences among groups, especially specific harms inflicted on some women and not others. Therefore I have stressed the scapegoating of certain women over and above the sacrifices they make in common with women generally. But it is also true that without a sense of commonality we will never discover a sense of connection, and without that connection the changes that will diminish people's need to scapegoat teenage mothers or other groups are unlikely to occur. Looking through the lens of sacrifice, and the experience of being other, is one way to focus our vision so we can perceive this commonality.

That is why I emphasize that the same dilemma—always putting her needs after everyone else's—that an individual woman experiences as a personal, apparently psychological problem manifests on a social level as the scapegoating of entire groups. In both cases, polarized thinking creates a split between self and other. An individual woman may function as other for a single man—as, say, Bernice, the ex–Hollywood wife, did for her husband. Evidently she represented to him the entire domestic realm of maternal nurturing, which is why he exploded into rage when she stepped out of it and left him. Or a group may represent the negation of the domestic ideal for an entire society—as teenage mothers came to do. In both cases, the fundamental mechanism is the same.

The question, then, is how to counter these tendencies both to individual self-sacrifice and to scapegoating. If sacrifice is the inverse of power, clearly we must redress the power imbalance—but not by simply reversing the polarity and seizing dominance. As Benjamin cautions, people who have been subjugated, whose "acts and integrity are granted no recognition," may wind up identifying with the powerful who subjugate them, so that even after being freed from domination, they "remain in love with the ideal of power that has been denied to them." Instead, she says, to break the pattern of domination, "women must claim their subjectivity," not by jumping to the other side of the polarity but by evolving a way to interact so that everyone is a subject.[32] This requires redefining power so that it does not mean being one up over someone else.

Writers on women's spirituality and Green politics, as well as some environmental activists, have already done this, formulating concepts in which, instead of power being *over* another, as traditionally conceived in Western culture, power is *for* oneself or *with* others. Power, that is, can inhere in affiliation and be synergistic; among people who mutually possess power as equals, a reciprocity occurs that enhances the power of all.[33]

This concept of power is not new. It has been practiced for a long time, but invisibly, because the practitioners were those very groups whose reality disappeared when they were cast as other. For example, African-American women active in civil rights movements in the nineteenth and twentieth centuries followed traditions deriving from West African culture that did not involve hierarchical models of authority, explains sociologist Patricia Hill Collins. Activist Septima Clark "sent a letter to Dr. King asking him not to lead all the marches himself, but instead to develop leaders who could lead their own marches." His staff laughed at this idea, but Clark and other women activists believed "that teaching people how to be self-reliant fosters more empowerment than teaching them how to follow." Their approach grew out of African models of community based on extended female networks that included both blood mothers and women called othermothers who shared child-care responsibilities. These "models of community stress connections, caring, and personal accountability" and see power as "a creative power used for the good of the community, whether...one's family, church, community, or the next generation." Strengthening the community in this way also empowers individuals.[34]

Reva's practice embodied these principles. In her poor neighborhood plagued by drugs, she told me, the children were falling under the dealers' influence.

> You can't fault the parents for some of these kids. Because they're probably in an abusive situation. These kids are out there because they have no other home to go to that's a safe haven. I've started grassroots meetings in my neighborhood, leadership to get these kids off the street. We have women that have lost control of the children. I invite them to come to give them support, let them know there's a better way. We'll help you claim your children back.

This is not the social service model of the expert taking charge, which is based on the hierarchical form of power; it is a model of empowerment.

Even more intriguing, related concepts of nondominating power appeared even at the very center of the mainstream as women began entering it. "Power is the ability to make things happen" is what Renée Karas says to make her clients more comfortable with the idea of wielding it. "Power is the ability to advance your agenda. Power is neither good nor bad; it depends on the way you use it." Her advice to businesswomen is echoed by the voices of women politicians.

> I like being powerful. I hope it doesn't go to my head. If somebody's going to have it, it might just as soon be me....I don't think women have enough of those power levers in their hands. It is a little scary, but I'd like to use the power that comes from this office to help other people and to really make our state and the world better. I think it's the only reason one should want power. It shouldn't be for one's self-enrichment or to make your ego feel better. I really believe that power should be used to serve other people. If it can't be, then it should be taken away.

This was the response of Mary Landrieu, then state treasurer of Louisiana, subsequently elected United States Senator, to a survey of twenty-five female elected officials carried out by Dorothy W. Cantor and Toni Bernay. These researchers, and others as well, found that female politicians not only sought office for different reasons than did men, as Chapter 3 explained, but generally had a different concept of power. One investigator "suggested that women...are more interested in doing things for the public good than in simply expanding their own sphere of power." As then-Congresswoman Olympia Snowe put it, "Some people just like to acquire power, but they do nothing with it." Cantor and Bernay conclude that power seen "through feminine eyes" is "a caring kind of power. It's not self-serving, instead, it's directed toward advancing an agenda."[35]

It would be foolhardy to take the earnest assurances of any politician completely at face value, but it is encouraging to hear women politicians even talking about power in this mode. And the consistency of their responses across political parties and generations (since both younger and older officials spoke of power this way) at least allows for some hope that a new element has been introduced. What it needs is reinforcement, so that in practical terms women who hold these views can maintain their positions in a high-stakes environment like the U.S. Congress.

Power that empowers is creative; it helps people grow. "It's just like a plant," said Reva, "a seed you plant in soil, and then you go back and you see how healthy it is and how it comes up and you're proud of it. People are like plants. If you give them the love and the understanding, they'll grow. If you give them the abuse, and they have no esteem, they wither."

To extend her image, power is the sap rising up the stem. Enforcing sacrifice on oneself or another is like puncturing the stem, so that (to go back to Arlene's image) the plant is being bled. When it bleeds too much, it droops and withers. Yet there are people who maintain a seemingly inexhaustible supply of energy that flows out to nourish others without depleting the source. To them we can look to discover when and how self-sacrifice can be not only appropriate but transforming.

10

The Lost Side of Sacrifice: Connection

THIS IS WHAT I TELL MY STUDENTS: I DON'T LEAVE. I COME
with a lifetime guarantee. If they need me beyond, and
beyond, and beyond, I'll be there. I don't expect from them
anything, beyond the obligation of the classroom. For me,
not leaving is the nature of sacrifice.

Suzanne Stutman, who teaches literature at a state college in
Pennsylvania, gives her unlisted home phone number to all her students and tells them, "If you need me, call me. If you have questions,
if you're not sure about a paper, if you have a crisis, call me." To one
young woman she helped, who felt guilty for taking up so much of
her time, Stutman explained, "Nobody was there to save me, so I
want to save everybody. What I would like to be—and have really
always wanted to be, but now it's much more conscious, and deeper,
if anything, and more firm—I want to be a catcher in the rye."

Stutman, as we saw in Chapter 8, was sexually abused by her uncle and emotionally abandoned by her mother, who refused to believe that the abuse had occurred. Before Stutman herself recalled it, she was a classic case of the woman constantly giving away pieces of herself. "If your self-esteem is low," she explained, "then you can never do enough. To get people to love you, you have to be a good girl, an overachiever, you have to be the best of the best of the best, but it still doesn't work, so you have to keep doing more. That's very much a part of women's sacrifice." Accordingly she felt compelled to "make it perfect" for her own children. "If I was holding a full basket and one of my kids needed me for something, I would just drop the basket. I just knew that I had to—from my heart—had to do everything, everything, everything in my power for them."

In time she learned to say no more often to requests for her time and energy, but still refused to turn her back on students or others whose need she recognized.

> Because having been invisible myself, I know what that is. And I've determined that I don't look away, that no one should be invisible, and that whenever I can act to do something for anyone, that's what I will try to do.
>
> Knowing what it is to be voiceless, I teach multicultural literature, I bring voices into the mainstream. I try not to make anyone invisible. I believe that pain is an incredible and excellent window—one's own pain is a window into the pain of others. If the anger and the pain can be consciously used and turned toward eliminating injustice, then something constructive comes from something terrible.

As therapy uncovered excruciating layers of pain surrounding her abuse, instead of sitting statically inside it feeling like a victim, Stutman transmuted it, as if alchemically, into a power of compassion and channeled it outward into her teaching, "trying to save the children so that the next generation will be stronger."

> Because I had no family, the world became my family, and that's a form of transcendence. It's just a sense of universality. And I understand that when one gives, one gets back much more than one gives. It's an exquisite luxury to be able to help people. Because it's like a square root. Everybody you make stronger can then go out and make somebody else stronger.

Stutman made her pain a bridge out of the isolation the pain itself had imposed. Although she sometimes still went overboard helping everyone who crossed her path and exhausted herself, by and large the sacrifices of her time and energy became transformative instead of self-defeating—transforming not only her own being but her students' lives.

Stutman's achievement returns us to the ancient ideal of sacrifice in which the offering that is made feeds into a stream of life that flows outward into a larger circuit. Hers is our first example of positive, appropriate sacrifice. I will define this type of sacrifice not by trying to specify external conditions that make it "right" but by describing what it feels like from inside. Thus this chapter asks: What is the nature of the self whose sacrifice is appropriate? Most of the evidence derives from stories told by women I interviewed. It turned out that these women had all, like Suzanne Stutman, consciously devoted their careers to service of some kind, which in itself suggests part of the answer to our question. Most gave the impression of a stable, centered self that made choices instead of being at the mercy of whatever happened—even when, as in Stutman's or Josephine's case, terrible things happened. These women also emanated the opposite of the victim's anger, guilt, and self-righteousness: pleasure, joyfulness, and gratitude.

The Boundary of the Self

Certainly Josephine, as we saw in Chapter 3, felt "grateful for my life" despite her own illnesses, despite even the death of her daughter Cheryl. Just before Cheryl was diagnosed with pulmonary hypertension, Josephine herself had spent months recovering from major abdominal surgery, followed by a second episode of blindness. Then she had to watch Cheryl's condition deteriorate—since they lacked the resources to obtain the organs she needed to live—while nursing her, working to pay the bills, and caring for Cheryl's children. During this period Josephine found herself buying clothes that were three or four sizes too large. "I realized I was carrying such a burden that I thought I was at least three sizes bigger than I was," she explained. "I had to give all those clothes away because I couldn't wear 'em. I was so filled up that I needed to have this room to fit my burden in." The clothes went into an exchange system Josephine had created.

> It started out with my friends and then it was my daughter's friends and her. They were networking clothing to help one another. If the clothes were too small, we would pass them on to the kids. It became a lifestyle for us for over twenty years. I started something a long time ago as a seed and it snowballed into a very, very big thing. Not for gain, but for friendship and because you care about another person. I developed a network with other women who needed things rather than going to find Joe Blow who had this great job to support me [she laughed ironically] and turn out to be disappointed.

What prompted Josephine to describe this network was reciting to me the message on the last birthday card her daughter had sent her: "Mom, you have touched many people's lives. Everywhere you go, you spread love to people. Keep spreading love." For Josephine, circulating clothes—and food, at times, or other things people needed—was spreading love. Her network of single mothers was another type of sacred circuit, and the sense of being replenished and sustained by this constant stream of nurturance was, perhaps, one source of her gratitude.

Yet Josephine could be tough-minded. "I've had people come and ask me for some help. No problem. If I can do it I will. But you have to know how far to take it. You can't just go in your pocket and give somebody a bundle of cash because they came in with a story." Instead, you tell them where to go to get help. "So that way they're feeling they're controlling their own lives," Josephine concluded, following the tradition of empowerment. "Feeling responsible for other people is very, very difficult. I can't use [any] more responsibility!"

For Josephine as for Suzanne Stutman, giving was both intimately related to the traumas of her life and had a transcendent dimension. The Lord, she told me, "was always there, carrying me through all these different circumstances, sheltering me from some very negative situations. I would never have been able to do half of what I did or successfully made it through without a scar if it wasn't for the Lord."

This transcendent aspect is always present in constructive sacrifice, though not necessarily in conventionally religious terms. Wendy, the community artist, experienced it in relation to her art. Art originally saved her from becoming a sacrifice to her family's need for a scapegoat, then became the vehicle for her own giving. Her earliest happy memories, she recalled, were "connected with—with God, for want of another way to put it."

> I have strong memories of being very, very little and feeling a kind of spiritual rapture, that I was in the presence of something much greater than myself or any of these people around me. It was a much more significant con-

nection and one entirely invested in my well-being. And the primary ways of reconnecting with this presence were through nature and through my art—drawing, painting, sculpting, singing, dancing, making up stories. I kept sitting back down at the piano or taking out that pencil and drawing. Or even going to a movie or a play. It didn't even have to be my own expression—through art I would be reminded that there was something finer being asked of me than what this family was asking. And that it was more my obligation to remain whole and connected to God through art than to remain connected to my family through self-destruction.

Wendy had not quite achieved Josephine's sense of boundaries; she still, you will recall, had to consciously resist her mother's voice in her head, telling her that with her gift of being comforting and supportive, she should do her community arts work for little or even no pay. This is a tricky line to draw when the work you donate is also the way you make a living; and Wendy took a rather muddled position, insisting that she wanted to be paid not by the people she worked directly with but by the agencies that sent her into their communities—as though removing the direct transfer of money made her work more pure, even though being paid was still a condition of her doing it. Though she could set limits on her giving in practice, she could not quite accept that she deserved to set them.

This issue of setting limits, another crucial component of constructive sacrifice, brings us back to my original question, in Chapter 1, of where to draw the line. Buried beneath this question is a deeper one: Where is the boundary of the self? In its widest application—which Stutman expressed when she said, "The world became my family, and that's a form of transcendence"—the question is a spiritual one, and it returns us to the quest for salvation that Chapter 1 identified as a central motive of self-sacrifice. So in answering it I turned first to two women who had confronted the question in an explicitly spiritual context.

Margaret, who grew up in a devout Polish Catholic home, was clearly marked by that vision Mary Gordon described of the directed, singular life devoted to an ideal. Coming of age in the sixties, she threw herself into protesting the Vietnam War, which she did as part of the Catholic Worker movement. She was attracted to the way this group—founded in 1933 by Dorothy Day, a left-wing journalist and recent convert to Catholicism, and Peter Maurin, a French peasant-scholar—"put together their religious ideals with practical action in the world" to work for social justice. Catholic Workers live in independent "houses of hospitality," adopting voluntary poverty in order to share the lives of the poor, to whom they offer food and shelter, no questions asked. Voluntary poverty, they say, frees them to respond to militarism, economic injustice, and racism "in the spirit of Christian nonviolence with the weapons of the Spirit, prayer, penance and self-sacrifice." They are consciously part of the political tradition of Gandhi, Martin Luther King, Jr., and Cesar Chavez.[1]

At the time I worked with the nuns, the Catholic Worker house in Manhattan was one of the very few places that sheltered homeless women. Encounters both then and later with members of the movement always evoked in me an uncomfortable mixture of admiration for their dedication to living their principles, combined with guilt, especially since a certain self-righteousness I detected in some of them exacerbated my uncertainty about my own level of giving. They remained for me the ultimate representatives of that question of where to draw the line, so when I found myself committed to answering it, I turned to two of them.

After graduating from college in the early 1970s, Margaret joined a small community of nuns, priests, and a few laypeople whose goal was "truly to live in common just like the first apostles, share resources, and do good works, like in the Book of Acts."

Slaying the Mermaid

We did draft counseling, I managed the office, there was a tutoring program for kids after school, a breakfast program for a while. In a real sense, if you want to talk about sacrifice, there was something very freeing about it. Because you were sharing income, you were freed to be more generous. You did have less material things, but in an odd way you also had less material worries, because there was more than just you. That's a tough model, I think, because you have less as an individual.

After seven years the community folded and she got her first paying job, at a settlement house that was part of a church. She continued to work for not-for-profit service organizations and now, at forty-nine, was associate executive director of a different settlement house in New York City. Although Margaret liked working in a religious context that eliminated the distance between professional service provider and client—a setting where "that poor homeless person is Christ, so you're all one body," as she put it—she wound up choosing settings much less radical than her original community, for she had discovered that

I like beauty, I like pleasure, I like flowers, I like gourmet food, and so I became a little more—I would still label it self-indulgent. But I enjoyed those things and I have enough joie de vivre to allow myself to enjoy them. Earlier in my life I thought, If *I* had *this,* that meant *you* didn't. If I were to buy something luxurious [I would think], Gee, I could have given that money away. I didn't last too long in that. Part of me thinks, in a way the Catholic Workers are right. And on the other hand, they're so unembracing of good things. As a young woman Dorothy Day said something I still think is pretty haunting: she wanted the abundant life, and she wanted it for others, too. She didn't say she wanted the depriving life.

Yet when I asked, "What does sacrifice mean to you?" Margaret responded:

> I think it's gotta mean going beyond what is comfortable. Somehow the idea of Christianity is that you're to push yourself a little bit further than you might naturally feel inclined to do. It's easy to extend yourself to someone you find attractive and you want to love, but...So maybe it's the effort, the unnaturalness of it, in a sense, what I think maybe we're called to do if we want to call ourselves Christians. I don't think I do that kind of hard loving.

Some years back she had taken a part-time job while trying to make a documentary film. "I probably could have stayed a lot poorer and continued to work on it, but it was becoming an untenable project for other reasons and also I was getting frightened of having so little income. Had I been really pure, maybe I could have lived the life of the struggling documentarian—which I did for a while—but it reached an uncomfortable point." At the same time, Margaret added, "I never would be comfortable having tons of money, though. I think I have internal barometers that say, 'That's too much, now.'"

These comments have multiple resonances. Margaret's lingering feeling that it might be "purer" to remain poor, or more Christian to push yourself beyond comfort, echoes an assertion in the *Catholic Worker* newspaper that "sacrifice and suffering are part of the Christian life."[2] But more broadly, her thoughts reflect the Puritanical streak that runs through our society. The implicit assumption that willed discomfort is integral to some kind of salvation is shared by a variety of people, ranging from my former roommate Evelyn to artists devoted to the old ideal of starving in a garret—who fear that making decent money means selling out—to political activists (especially on the left) who flaunt their own self-deprivation—recall Vera's assertion that "your desires can't come in the way of other people's needs"—to the dieters who accept constant hunger in order to achieve thinness.

Margaret herself believed, she told me, that she wasn't "sure how much self-sacrificing I've done in my life," since she hadn't really ever gone "beyond what is comfortable."

"Living in poverty in your community wasn't self-sacrifice?" I asked.

"Well, we weren't direly poor, we were just simple," she responded. That is, she hadn't felt uncomfortable in that situation—which I would have myself, as I imagine many others would—so it didn't *feel* like self-sacrifice. When asked directly about the virtue of discomfort, Margaret responded:

> Uncomfortable for what? I think you can fall in love with the means. I personally don't think in and of themselves, these things have much virtue. Maybe I'm not spiritual enough, but I don't see the point. If it's uncomfortable because if I extend myself a little more, this person's going to be helped, okay. The point is not to suffer for the sake of suffering, it has to be something more positive. But maybe that sometimes gets lost. Also, maybe it's really harder to be happier.

"Why?" I asked.

> Well, maybe on some level we don't really value ourselves or understand that we're entitled to be happy. I'm just thinking of women and the lack of self-worth. If we really believe that God is good, then wouldn't that goodness be there in abundance? We come from a deprived

model of what's out there. In my own life I've had a sense that there were these dichotomies: that there was good, there was bad, there was only so much to go around. Maybe in a material sense that's true, but maybe in a spiritual sense grace abounds—your having some happiness does not mean you're depriving someone else from being happy. That there's enough. That doesn't mean that one glibly forgets that there's suffering. The point is not to be miserable, the point is to be full of life.

I concluded that despite her doubtful thoughts about what being a true Christian might require, she had found a balance that was appropriate, for her.

For Patricia, a different balance was appropriate; with her husband, she had lived as part of a Catholic Worker community for nearly twenty years. In response to my question about the virtue of discomfort, she remarked thoughtfully, "I don't think you accomplish much when your goal is to be uncomfortable." Yet her life had been characterized by what many would consider extreme self-denial. "For many years," she told me, "in order not to be paying into the part of the economy that gets used for weapons and warfare, we had lived below a taxable income, which is a *very* modest way of living." But she did not feel deprived. "It felt for me like a gift," Patricia explained. "I felt a great sense of blessing to be able to live in such a context. Living in a community and doing work that is clearly direct service, the voluntary poverty was part and parcel of that, it freed you to do that." At the same time she stressed the importance of "a constant refreshing of the spirit" through prayer and solitude and also through beauty: "Go to the botanical garden and look at the flowering cherry trees; turn the radio on to hear the opera." And she noted that her strong, happy marriage gave her tremendous support in living that lifestyle.

Patricia was completely without that edge of self-righteousness that had disturbed me in the past. As she spoke I realized this was because she recognized that, as she put it, "We're not called to stark-ness or to harshness for their own sake. One does not seek sacrifice; sacrifice is not an end in itself. I learned a lot about that from Dorothy and the Catholic Worker." The secret is to discover "what my voca-tion is—for us, What is God asking me to do?—both in terms of the events in my life right now, but also in terms of who I am, what my talents are, what my temperament is, what am I able to contribute? There's a traditional Christian teaching that grace builds on nature."

Here Patricia touched the heart of the question this book seeks to resolve. "Dorothy used to say," she went on, "that you will know your vocation by the joy you experience." This joy is what makes such sac-rifice as hers possible. It was Patricia who made me understand that even the most "selfless" service does not leave the self behind, and that everyone must make her own decision about where to draw the line. But what clinched it for me was hearing the same message from Ruth, the high-school teacher.

In addition to teaching and caring for her parents, Ruth was a community activist. "The projects I chose had to be with groups that were very caring and connected. I never got involved in party-building or sectarian stuff," she told me.

> I do some very tangential electoral work, but mostly I'm involved in local community groups. And the commu-nity association in my neighborhood is a pleasure, because these are neighbors, and our quality of life depends on the relationships we build with our neigh-bors. So it's a joy to be around people who are thinking, How can something be more beautiful? How can we look after each other?

She was never tempted by a secular version of voluntary poverty.

> I always felt I wanted to live well in the way that I felt all people had a right to live. I never wanted to bring myself

down to the level of suffering in order to share the suffering of the masses. I always wanted to be an example of a good life, a creative life, a community life, that I would like to offer as a model for others. Because I'm not greedy. I've always had a generous nature. And I don't need a lot. I enjoy the give-and-take of exchanging gifts, being invited and inviting back—that's the greatest pleasure for me, not how elaborate the meal is.

A third aspect of constructive self-sacrifice, then, is that it entails self-respect and a commitment to self-care. (Literally: Stutman's mother, a beautician and manicurist, had made her feel physically ugly. Part of restoring her self-esteem, she said, was "to reclaim my whole physical self and learn to love it." Then she looked down at her hands and said, "I have to go get a manicure, in fact, because I'm letting my nails go, and for me that's symbolic.")

What I learned from these women is summarized by Carol Pearson's useful distinction between the rudimentary "martyrdom" described in Chapter 7—a bargain made in the hope of salvation—and a more developed form, in which the sacrifice is intended to save not self but others. Martyrdom undertaken before a person knows who she is and (especially) what her desires are, says Pearson, is a form of self-abnegation—what I have called giving away pieces of yourself—whose "results are bitterness, manipulation, and a general sense of guilt and dis-ease"—that is, the victim mentality. This was the form practiced by the Little Mermaid, and if she did not feel bitter and victimized, it was only because her story really was a fairy tale. Sacrifice made freely, on the other hand, marks a transition out of the victim mentality. As Pearson says, "genuine sacrifice is transformative and not maiming"; it not only "feels compatible with your identity" but deepens and solidifies your sense of self.[3] Appropriate sacrifice, she too affirms, is life-giving and joyous. Because people are different, it is impossible to define it in terms of externals; what felt like a blessing to Patricia would have felt cramped and self-denying to Margaret.

But it certainly is possible to evolve toward fuller participation in the sacred circuit.

An Expansive Self

In appropriate sacrifice, then, the self maintains a solicitude for itself amid caring for others; thus Patricia emphasized solitude and other forms of replenishment, while Josephine spoke of needing "some sort of playtime" to "rekindle your selfness." This self also feels a strong connection to other people; thus Stutman did not allow her pain to enclose her in solitude but made it a window into other people's feelings. Third—and perhaps growing out of the balance between caring for self and other simultaneously—it can accept other people as they are. Such acceptance is implicit when Patricia speaks of needing to consider "who I am," for if she accepts who she is, she is also willing to accept who others are, without needing to judge them for choosing differently.

Here we reach the question at the core of the issue of women and sacrifice: how to "have a compassionate connection to others and still retain a powerful sense of self."[4] This phrasing comes from Anne Carolyn Klein, an American student of Buddhism, who has applied its teachings with illuminating aptness to the issues of self that Western women confront. Buddhism (at least in the forms popular among Westerners) is a religion without a divinity, offering not theology but rather a conceptualization of self and of the nature of reality that can be used to reconsider the problematic Western constructs discussed in previous chapters, without interfering with Western belief systems.

Buddhist concepts are extremely helpful in reconstituting that sense of self which, as I have shown, has been damaged in Western women. In particular, Buddhism focuses directly on the question of suffering but—far from giving suffering any intrinsic value, as we do when we make it into a virtue—Buddhism teaches how to end suffering. Suffering is said to result from desires of all types and from the belief that there is anything we can hold on to as stable and permanent. We cling to this belief out of ignorance of the true nature of reality. Buddhism therefore provides a method of practice that leads to an understanding that everything is in a state of flux. This recognition releases us from the anxiety, frustration, and other painful states of mind that result from seeking security and permanence where none exists.[5] Just in itself, the goal of ending suffering comes as a tremendous relief, a wonderful antidote to the deeply ingrained assumption that suffering ennobles.

The prescribed method involves what appear to be a series of sacrifices: the giving up of all sorts of desires and attachments, ultimately to one's own ego as a stable, substantive entity. But just like the constructive sacrifices I've described, this giving-up process is said to open one up to a more expansive state of mind that is "both buoyant and deeply joyful." Life's difficulties do not evaporate, but one becomes able to live with them "freely and compassionately."[6]

This Buddhist approach can be extremely liberating for someone seeking a way out of dualistic conceptualizations of self and other. Possibly that is one reason why, of the numerous Americans who felt its appeal during the 1990s, so many were women. (Though in the cultures where this tradition arose and developed, women were relegated to a secondary position, in the West they have played a major role in shaping its transition to our culture.) Klein and other Western women who began studying Buddhism in the 1960s and 1970s have applied its teachings to issues of women's selfhood and agency, and it is their thinking I rely on here.

Klein is particularly interested in using Buddhist concepts to support new models of selfhood that combine agency with compassion while preventing that "loss of self in relationship" to which Western women are so prone. The "core problem" in making relatedness compatible with "a sense of powerful agency," she says, is the opposition between autonomy and relationship that is so central to Western thought. Insistence on autonomy makes relatedness a threat, while defining the self completely in terms of relationship and compassion (or self-sacrifice), as women were trained to do, diminishes the status of the self and prevents appropriate self-care.[7]

From a Buddhist perspective, however, this Western autonomous self is actually quite fragile, by virtue of its very isolation. In contrast Buddhism sees the self not as separate and independent but as interdependent, embedded in an intricate living matrix. This perception is based on the central Buddhist concept of dependent (or interdependent) co-arising, which simply means that everything in the universe is fundamentally connected to everything else. The Vietnamese Zen monk and peace activist Thich Nhat Hanh coined the term "interbeing" to refer to this relationship, in which everything depends on everything else for its very existence.

It is not necessary to take up a Buddhist practice to accept this doctrine and appreciate its psychological and social ramifications, for it is actually being confirmed by modern science in the form of systems theory, which describes living forms, from single cells to ecosystems, as open systems. As Joanna Macy, a social and ecological activist who first came into contact with Buddhist teachings while working for the Peace Corps in a Tibetan community in India, explains, "Living systems evolve...through interaction with each other" and therefore "require openness and vulnerability in order to process the flow-through of energy and information." These systems are self-organizing; that is, order is implicit within them and does not need to be imposed from above in the form of our familiar power structure of domination.

Awareness of "the interdependence of all phenomena," Macy says, completely changes one's perception of the nature of the self, and consequently of the type of power it can access. Interdependent co-arising "knock[s] down the dichotomies bred by hierarchical thinking, the old polarities between mind and matter, self and world"—that is, self and other. Without polarities and hierarchy, power no longer involves domination. Instead of issuing "forth from its possessor, who is able to affect others without being affected in return," power arises not from separation but from connection. This vision of interaction contrasts sharply with the "Western…notion of social contract," which "assumes a free association between individuals who remain basically distinct and unaltered by such association." In the Buddhist view, "self, society, and world are reciprocally modified by their interaction, as they form relationships and are in turn conditioned by them." These interactions between open systems "bring into play new responses and new possibilities not previously present, increasing the capacity to effect change. This interdependent release of fresh potential is called synergy. It is like grace, because it brings an increase of power beyond one's own capacity as a separate entity."[8] When Stutman said that "when one gives, one gets back much more than one gives," she was describing synergy.

It is the "knocking down" of dichotomies that shifts us out of dualism. One effect of thinking in polarities is that the self is defined in opposition to the other, which means that to feel secure in who it is, it needs others to be different. One way we create and maintain that difference is by scapegoating, whose basis is projecting characteristics we consider negative onto other people. From the perspective of interdependent co-arising, on the other hand, self and other, subject and object, "are experienced as mutually defining"; "'you' and 'I' may retain our different identities without becoming the dominated, subjected, or objectified other." Even more important, "insight into the radical interdependence of all phenomena" leads to awareness "that it is not a battle between good guys and bad guys, but that the line between good and evil runs through the landscape of every human heart."[9] It is, in other words, impossible to draw a complete line of separation between yourself and even the people of whom you most disapprove, since all belong to this same matrix and are not fundamentally separate. Where duality does not reign, you cannot polarize your enemies into a category of absolute otherness—though you can still disapprove of what they do and take steps to counteract it.

Slaying the Mermaid

Interconnectedness, Macy goes on, also changes the experience of pain. "We are, as open systems, sustained by flows of energy and information that extend beyond the reach of conscious ego." The ability to cope with pain springs from this "great matrix of relationships in which we take our being," which "reconnects us with our fellow beings and our deep collective energies." For example, Macy's passionate concern with the well-being of the natural environment means that she feels deep grief for the planet and its future. But the doctrine of interdependent co-arising "led me to see that even my pain for the world is a function of this mutual belonging, like a cell experiencing the larger body. Because it shows that causality, or power, resides in relationships rather than in persons or institutions, it offers the courage to resist conformity and to act in new ways to change the situation." When the self is experienced in this expansive way, furthermore, individual pain does not "consum[e] one's identity"; it is only a part of one's experience.[10] In other words, the victim identity does not take over.

Macy here uses exactly the same image for pain as David Bakan: an experience felt by one part of a larger whole that signals a breakdown of harmony in the whole. Bakan also draws the analogy of a single cell. "It is helpful," he writes, "to think of the processes which precede...cellular fission as formally the same as those which, in the higher organism endowed with consciousness, make for pain." That is, the division of a single cell into two is an archetypal pattern for the existential human condition of separateness, of which pain is the archetypal experience. For Bakan, a Freudian deeply wedded to the concept of autonomous individualism, the restoration of harmony, as we saw, requires making the diseased part "not-me" so it can be sacrificed. One manifestation of this habitual Western thought pattern is the making "not-us" that constitutes scapegoating. Macy, however, draws from the image of the cell a completely opposite conclusion. For her the entire "intricate web of co-arising" *is* "me," and far from cutting any part of it off, she embraces it as a source of strength that can issue in action—action that will not rely on polarizing certain groups as other, for she does not need an other.[11]

This Buddhist logic brings us back to Jessica Benjamin's assertion that a relationship of equals requires the ability to tolerate paradox and maintain a tension between self-assertion and mutual recognition. Benjamin's term for this balance between two contradictory forces, "intersubjectivity," expresses her view that "the individual grows in and through the relationship to other subjects"—what might be called the developmental-theory analogue of interdependent co-arising. In similar language Macy speaks of "our interactive presence to each other as beings—not pawns, not victims—engaged in a dance." Both achieve a perspective in which self and other are not in opposition and do not threaten to undermine each other.[12]

The self described by these writers is expansive. Awareness of interdependence, says Macy, leads to "a shift in identification, a shift from the isolated 'I' to a new, vaster sense of what we are"—the same shift that "every major religion has sought to offer." This larger self, she adds, "serves to empower effective action." Klein points out further that Buddhists traditionally considered relatedness "magnificently self-empowering," believing that repaying "in kind what one has already received in plenty is empowered giving, quite different from giving out of a need for approval, or to fulfill a role one has inherited but not chosen."[13] Self-sacrifice does not diminish this expanded self.

Interdependence in Practice

Interdependence is already part of many people's experience, although since we lack a conceptual category for it—and because the people most familiar with it belong to minority populations—it has gone unvalued and even unrecognized in society at large. But once I looked at my interview transcripts through this frame of reference, hidden configurations jumped out at me. The most dramatic example was Joyce, the African-American woman whose awareness that her mother's and grandmother's self-sacrifices had made her own privileged position possible was tinged with a certain poignancy. "Mine was not completely a typical black experience," she explained. Listening to stories of her mother's and grandmother's youth that were imbued with their sense of purpose and determination, she envied them, feeling

> that I have lost something in having had some of the educational opportunities that I had. There's sort of a disconnect between me and some of my peers, because part of me was raised with that American typical white standard, and so there's a lack of community that I wish I had sometimes.
>
> Life was really hard for them, but they had the benefit of being able to struggle for something. I really think that having a purpose and having something to fight for—I've never put this into coherent thought, but I swear I think having something to fight for—Martin Luther King did say this—there's such a value to that in terms of having a life that's worth something.

We had met at a party, where Joyce, with her mother's and grandmother's sacrifices of their personal dreams in mind, had said she thought of sacrifice as negative; she could not see herself doing what they had done. "My life has been about finding myself. That does not compute in my family," she remarked. But as she recounted those family stories during our interview, her feelings began to shift. "In a way," she mused, "I don't feel that there's anything, whether it's a value or a quest or a purpose, that I don't have that I am aiming for." And this she felt as a lack. "But now that I'm thinking like this," she went on,

I think absolutely that were there something that's worth dying for, that's worth living for, that's worth fighting and struggling for, any sacrifice would be worth it to achieve that. Any sacrifice would be worth achieving that. On a big level, I think that's why the folks who did the whole civil rights thing were willing to put their lives down for it. That was something that was big. And I'm sure with all other communities all over the world—things that are worth fighting for, worth dying for...I hear these clichés, but now I understand what they're talking about, through this conversation.

At this point there is a long pause on the tape, with only the sound of my typing, as Joyce assimilated this conviction rushing in on her. Then she continued,

I think individuality run amok leads to that place where you're not willing to fight for anything, because the stake isn't big enough...I mean, in a way other people or something larger than you has to be involved in it. Earlier I was saying how horrible it would be to give up your dream to be a writer for a family, as women had to do. I saw it as not being able to self-actualize. I heard people say the whole time I'm growing up, you give something up but you get something in return. My grandmother's generation worked real hard and they struggled, but although being happy wasn't an end result, there was a certain contentment and peace that they had with themselves and with their lives that to me seems unthinkable, because they couldn't do the things they wanted to do. But maybe in return what they got out of it was closer to what I think of in terms of being happy than this state of being completely free that I think about sometimes as what would make me happy. And I don't know if that's true. I don't know.

But part of her did know, for the next thing she said was, "I feel different." She laughed, then in a quieter tone repeated, "I feel different." We both felt something had happened, without being quite sure what it was. So I asked her to keep talking.

> It's inherent in sacrifice that the individual is always going to lose something. So if you are not a part of a community that has value to you, then that thing you're going to be gaining, either you can't comprehend it or it's not worth it to you. From a completely individual standpoint, with individual freedom being the highest value, it's not worth it to you to sacrifice. And that's the way I was thinking about it. That there's not anything I'm connected to enough that would be worth it to me to sacrifice. In a way you have to be a part of something larger—whether it be a family, or having a child, or a big social cause. That's the thing that you gain. Lose something to gain something greater. But there's got to be a connection to something else.

What had happened was that, as she talked, Joyce suddenly opened up to that expansive, transcendent dimension. She had generated her own shift out of autonomy and separateness—the state where "freedom's just another word for nothing left to lose"—and into interdependence. She had discovered the sacred circuit.

That sense of community which Joyce felt she had lost has been an important part of the culture of minority groups in this country. Among African Americans it derived from "African worldviews" in which the self is defined as "'we.' Embedded in this 'extended self' is an individual's connectedness with others." Africans brought to

The Lost Side of Sacrifice: Connection

America as slaves extended the concept of kin beyond blood relatives to the entire community of black people.[14] Versions of this extended community (such as the communal child-care networks described in Chapter 9) continued to sustain them through the twentieth century.

Nor have Latino cultures completely assimilated the European model of the autonomous self. For Chicanos, "personality is defined by the community of which the individual is a part. Identity is defined in relationship to others: not to belong to a group is not to exist."[15] Maria, the social service administrator whose background is Puerto Rican, spoke of her experience of family in similar terms. "The message is always to better your condition," she explained, but in a way that brings everyone along together. Maria, whose grandparents were sharecroppers in Puerto Rico, was one of the few in her generation to go to college. "As I moved forward," she said, "I did the best I could to help my brothers. And sometimes I had no money or anything, so the only thing I could do was pray for them that they would find their way."

At the same time Maria, as we saw, remained alert to avoid the sacrifice of self-development her culture traditionally imposed on women.

> If you can move yourself forward, and help the rest of your family moving forward, it's not sacrifice. It's trying to do the best you can with the resources that you have. You're still able to take care of what you need and go toward your goals. When you leave yourself out of the picture and help everybody else move forward, that's where the sacrifice is.

Maria knew that, as Klein puts it, women must include themselves "in the circle of care" to create "a compassion that is self-empowering."[16] With that principle as a guide, the balance can tip within a fairly wide range without becoming self-destructive. When

Maria married her husband, she consciously took on responsibilities toward his three children, then in elementary school and junior high. She had finished college but not yet gotten her master's degree, and there was not enough money to send the children to college and her to graduate school. So she did not begin her master's program until they finished college. "I made that choice—my husband didn't expect it—but I felt it was a sacrifice, for sure. I was torn between what I wanted for me but what I knew I needed to do for them." Still, making that choice was less of an emotional struggle since it was "reinforced by my inner being that was well ingrained into sacrificing, both from my cultural and my religious background."

Though disregarded, therefore, interdependence is not so foreign as the use of Buddhist terminology to define it might suggest. But putting a name to it can generate a focus and intention that will support both more positive sacrifice and more powerful selves.

Heart of Compassion in South Carolina

One more remarkable example of constructive sacrifice brings all its attributes together, in a woman who would have lived a completely obscure life were it not for a driven photojournalist with a passion for social issues. In 1951 W. Eugene Smith, a renowned photographer for *Life* magazine, decided to do a photo essay about a nurse-midwife practicing in a poor rural county in South Carolina. His account of her, in both words and photos, reveals the core quality of the self engaged in constructive sacrifice.

The facts alone give Maude Callen, a fifty-one-year-old African-American woman, heroic stature. Almost single-handedly responsible for ten thousand people's health care, she treated all kinds of illnesses and injuries, gave vaccinations, tracked contagious diseases, delivered babies, and taught uneducated people the rudiments of good diet. She worked day and night, driving over thirty-six thousand miles a year on muddy back roads to visit patients in their homes, hold clinics in churches and schools, and teach classes for mid-wives and new mothers. Married but without children of her own, she had apparently raised several foster children. During her brief periods at home—where her husband had to resign himself to coming second to her work—she saw patients at all hours in a clinic attached to her house. Because of the poverty of the district, as well as the state government's reluctance to spend money on health care for black people, she had to pay for some equipment herself and construct other necessities from makeshift materials—for example, making an incubator for a premature baby out of a cardboard box and old whiskey bottles filled with warm water. Callen also functioned as an unofficial social worker, handling relief checks, helping people get on welfare, paying bills for the disabled, passing along donations of clothes (or buying new ones herself), posting bond for someone in jail (also out of her own pocket).[17]

These are impressive facts, but what brings them to life is the reaction of Smith, an intense, idealistic man possessed by the desire to reveal profound human truths through his art, to the personal presence of this woman and her "life of complete devotion to others." After a month of accompanying Callen on her rounds, Smith wrote an emotional research report for his editors:

> There beats a heart, surrounding that heart is the sturdy body of a woman and in that body is a strong clear mind educated in nursing, in obstetrics; and in that mind is more than medical knowledge, for, from the woman pours forth, a quiet, eversurging, powerful flow of dedicated work that is more than technical competence; by reason of tremendous depth of compassionate understanding, a complete, unselfish love of humanity—the all that is the stature of this person; a truly noble realization of the human potential to good, so seldom found.

The slightly skewed syntax reflects the pressure of Smith's effort to convey an ineffable quality that he could not quite capture in words. Throughout the report recurs the theme of Maude Callen's refusing to admit how tired she obviously is and moving on to the next delivery, the next round of vaccinations. No doubt Smith's emphasis on her exhaustion is a reflection of the strain of keeping up with her. "Maude, dear Maude," he wrote in a letter home, "it's legal to admit being tired! A scant forty-five minutes or so after we flopped into bed, the beloved, wonderful, indefatigable voice chipped through our sleep, 'Let's go! get up, let's go!' We staggered out of bed, jerked to alertness, and eight minutes later back into the road. It was another delivery."

After the baby arrived, Callen carried on until the next evening without more sleep. "Tears cut deeply and hot through me," wrote Smith. "No story could translate justly the life depth of this wonderful, patient, directional woman...and I love her, do love her with a respect I hold for almost no one. Humble, I am in the presence of this simple, complex, positive greatness....The uninteresting routine is vast in its drama when placed in relationship to the undramatic giving of this grand person." In an almost stream-of-consciousness passage that reflects his own exhaustion, the report concludes:

> But Maude, is not tired—she says she isn't. But what holds her up at a time like this when it seems that all 10,000 need her in the space of four days?...The car wobbles close to the ditch, but no, Maude isn't sleepy.... She has had one hour's sleep back thru days. Oh, a little headache maybe, really it's nothing...granite, blood shot eyes staring ahead—now I'll cook a little something for you to eat. I'm sorry it's so little—please sit down while I do the dishes before I work for an infinity more.

The photographs provide a fuller sense of what Smith's piled-up adjectives are striving at. Maude Callen in his portraits possesses a calm, solid, attentive presence, as though nothing she encounters, among the tragedies and successes of her practice or the wide variety of human situations, could fundamentally disturb her equilibrium— certainly not the presence of a photographer with cameras hanging all over him. In the opinion of Smith's assistant, who carried his film and equipment, "She was not performing for us."[18]

One goal of Buddhist meditation practice is a calm, concentrated state of clear awareness called mindfulness. "A person who is mindful is present, accepting, focused, and clear.... To be mindful...is to acknowledge and accept plurality without being disrupted by it," including "weakness, defect, or confusion in oneself or others." As Klein points out, this is not a specifically Buddhist quality; many Westerners have it, but without recognizing it since we have no name for it. Such people emanate a quality of "there-ness," like rocks sitting in the middle of a stream quite unaffected by the eddies of water rushing past. That is the quality evident in Maude Callen. "Her drive was religious as well as moral and intellectual, although her feet were very much on the ground," Smith's assistant reported, and this "drive" I think is what Smith means by his odd word "directional."[19] Her single-minded purpose carries her in the direction she has chosen.

Despite her constant exhaustion, the need to supplement the inadequate transportation funds provided by the state and county with her husband's pension money, being forced to swallow much injustice (Smith says she handled race relationships "with magnificent intelligence and grace"), and never being able to take a vacation since there was no one to replace her, Maude Callen in Smith's portrayal does not give an impression of self-destructive self-denial. Rather it seems that the work she did was simply an outgrowth of who she was, a fulfillment of her nature. Over thirty years later, Smith's biographer, Jim Hughes, interviewed the eighty-four-year-old Callen, who "was still serving her people, driving a van to bus them to and from a center for the elderly."[20]

Making Sacred

At the end of Chapter 7 I noted that what happened to the nuns was the result of a sacrifice of self for the sake of an ideal by women who lacked the strong selfhood that is necessary to pursue an ideal successfully. Ideals are useful in enabling us to create a vision of positive personal or social change. However they are problematic, cautions Klein, because they may become a vehicle for controlling people who, lacking that strong self, can become alienated from their own feelings if those feelings "do not measure up to the ideal with which [they] prefer to identify." Ideals also "foster an oppositional or divided sense of self," since the ideal identity one strives for is always cast in opposition to the self one actually is.[21]

From this perspective it is clear that the nuns, socialized by a culture that held self-sacrifice up as the feminine ideal, then indoctrinated by a religious tradition epitomizing that ideal, under John's influence became literally possessed by it and almost completely alienated from their own feelings and experience of reality. Yet all along, the constructive aspect of sacrifice was also present, and it was this that saved them.

Not until years after my experience at the shelter did I come to understand that at its heart—which was what made it so powerful and central an experience for me—it was a community of spirit, founded on the connection that the sisters had created among themselves. This connection persisted even as John extended his control over them. During that whole period, Elizabeth recalled,

> the one thing we did that remained basic to us was our own prayer. But it was less and less. It was constantly more interrupted. Every time we were in a group together—the five of us—he would interrupt us. He would come up for a very legitimate reason—somebody sick downstairs, a lady needs you, a volunteer needs you,

something. So we had less and less time. Our prayer was one of the last things to go. He didn't too easily interrupt that—initially.

One offshoot of this powerful connection among the five nuns was the loyalty of the regular volunteers, who did a great deal of work in the shelter and also shared their devotional life (not being Catholic, I was outside this circle). These volunteers arranged to give the sisters a gift—a weekend retreat away together, during which the volunteers would run the house. As it happened, the scheduled weekend was the one following the Monday of that meeting described in Chapter 1, at which the nuns decided to say good-bye to their families.

That was a week of tremendous pressure, from distressed relatives, from their own feelings, from the usual business of the house, and from John himself, who badgered them to let him go with them. In the middle of one excruciating confrontation, Sister Catherine burst into tears and cried out that she couldn't take it anymore—she had to get out, although she didn't know where to go. But the others insisted, "No, you're not going anywhere. We're going together." "That was the one clear strong point: we're going to work this thing through together," Elizabeth recalled. John continued pestering them to let him go, but Elizabeth said no, and the others backed her up. "I think for me it was Catherine," she said. "I knew we were going to lose Catherine if he went." So they got in the car without him and left.

At the retreat house, many rooms were available but, afraid to be away from one another, they all crowded into two. For the umpteenth time, Elizabeth began talking about her persistent doubts regarding John and his supposed message. "Suddenly it was like: We *have* been brainwashed. We have been *brainwashed*. It was like *relief*." They jumped up, ran outside and called their families, bought cigarettes, then went to a pizza parlor, ate pizza, and smoked. On Sunday, when they returned to the shelter, they told John to leave.

"For me," said Elizabeth, "it was, I think, the distance together away from the house, and beginning to talk about the doubts," that released them from John's control. Later she learned that, because she had doubted him the most, John had been trying to get the others to make her leave the shelter. "But they wouldn't let me go. And that's why I truly believe it was our relationship and community that kept us together."

That community is an example of Joanna Macy's point about synergy: that the whole generates a sum of energy greater than its parts can individually. For in certain ways the individual nuns, as I realized in retrospect, were not very strong at all. I recalled incidents revealing that these women who seemed so powerful to me—after all, they had created the shelter from nothing and ran it on their own—had no concept of their true strength, nor any acceptance of their own needs. Monica, for example, who was a powerhouse, whose very presence in the house during those shaky early days gave me courage to cope with all sorts of exigencies that were totally foreign to my experience, was quite unaware of her enormous charisma and the aura she projected of almost limitless strength; she was repeatedly astonished when I mentioned it. She once confessed, describing some tension between herself and a volunteer, that she felt she had no right to ask anything, even the most basic recognition of her own humanity, of anybody she did not love. "The impulse toward sacrifice," I wrote in a note at the time, "is the same as saying 'I don't have needs.'"

Yet, though unable to be strong separately, as a group they were—in Macy's terms—"sustained by flows of energy and information that extend beyond the reach of conscious ego," from which they drew the fortitude to resist John. What he could not destroy was the sacred circuit.

If inappropriate self-sacrifice reflects a self that is reduced to other in a world of polarities, constructive sacrifice is the expression of a self that expands to encompass both self and other. What shifts is the sense not simply of what self is but of what self-interest is. And the most marvelous aspect of this shift is that it releases us from the sense of moral obligation traditionally attached to self-sacrifice, as well as the associated burden of guilt. Macy quotes the Norwegian philosopher Arne Naess, who says that in the process of developing a more expansive sense of self,

> notions such as altruism and moral duty are left behind.... Altruism implies that the ego sacrifices its interests in favor of the other, the alter. The motivation is primarily that of duty. It is said we *ought* to love others as strongly as we love our self. There are, however, very limited numbers among humanity capable of loving from mere duty or from moral exhortation.

People don't like being told they must make sacrifices to preserve the environment, he goes on, but in fact, this isn't necessary. "All of that would flow naturally and easily if the self were widened and deepened so that the protection of nature was felt and perceived as protection of our very selves."[22] If nature itself can be experienced as part of the expanded self, certainly fellow humans can, which means that—for example—by supporting services for teenage mothers I am taking care of myself, because we are part of the same social body. If a part of that body becomes diseased, sacrificing it diminishes me. Healing it strengthens me.

As we evolve into the twenty-first century, the old mode of sacrifice derived from dualism becomes increasingly inappropriate. Women, mandated since Eve to redeem humanity by not eating the fruits of life, have been the ones most afflicted by that sacrificial ideal. At the same time, more comfortable with connection and less encumbered by the benefits of power as domination, they are particularly equipped to invent an effective balance between holding on to personal selfhood and recognizing the selfhood of the other. Through such a shift in consciousness may we expand the circuit of what is "made sacred."

Notes

1. Sacrifice and the Feminine Ideal

1. Joseph A. Amato, *Victims and Values: A History and a Theory of Suffering* (New York: Praeger, 1990), quotes on 43, 46; 48, 62.

2. Quoted in Karen Armstrong, *A History of God: The 4000-Year Quest of Judaism, Christianity and Islam* (New York: Ballantine Books, 1993), 277. On Buddhism, Walpola Rahula, *What the Buddha Taught,* 2d ed. enl. (New York: Grove Weidenfeld, 1974), 28.

3. Mary Lou Randour, *Women's Psyche, Women's Spirit: The Reality of Relationships* (New York: Columbia University Press, 1987), 17–18.

4. Caroline Walker Bynum, *Holy Feast and Holy Fast: The Religious Significance of Food to Medieval Women* (Berkeley and Los Angeles: University of California Press, 1987), 24–26.

5. Bonnie S. Anderson and Judith P. Zinsser, *A History of Their Own: Women in Europe From Prehistory to the Present,* vol. 2 (New York: Harper & Row, 1988), 130, 144.

6. Bram Dijkstra, *Idols of Perversity: Fantasies of Feminine Evil in Fin-de-Siècle Culture* (New York and Oxford: Oxford University Press, 1986), 8–9; Anderson and Zinsser, vol. 2, 130, 144.

7. Dijkstra, 8f.

8. Quoted in Dijkstra, 13.

9. Both quoted in Barbara J. Berg, *The Remembered Gate: Origins of American Feminism, The Woman and the City, 1800–1860* (New York: Oxford University Press, 1978), 86.

10. Quoted in Dijkstra, 19.

11. Virginia Woolf, "Professions for Women," in *The Death of the Moth and Other Essays* (San Diego: Harcourt Brace & Co., Harvest Books, 1970), 237.

12. Gini Kopecky, "Born to Please," *Redbook,* February 1993, 90, 102.

13. *Women's Health,* supplement, November 1995.

14. Noreen Seebacher, "Femme Financial," *Detroit News,* February 27, 1995, 10F.

15. Dr. Susan Forward and Craig Buck, *Money Demons: Keep Them from Sabotaging Your Relationships—and Your Life* (New York: Bantam Books, 1994), 54–55.

16. Ibid., 80–85.

17. Harriet Goldhor Lerner, *The Dance of Deception: Pretending and Truth-Telling in Women's Lives* (New York: HarperCollins, 1993), 58; Susan L. Taylor, "Reflections on Motherhood," *Essence,* May 1994, 69.

18. Peggy Orenstein, in association with the American Association of University Women, *Schoolgirls: Young Women, Self-Esteem, and the Confidence Gap* (New York: Doubleday, 1994), 35, 37–38.

19. Claudia Bepko and Jo-Ann Krestan, *Too Good for Her Own Good: Breaking Free from the Burden of Female Responsibility* (New York: Harper & Row, 1990).

20. Lerner, 49–50, 59.

21. Michele Hoffnung, "Motherhood: Contemporary Conflict for Women," in Jo Freeman, ed., *Women: A Feminist Perspective,* 5th ed. (Mountain View, Calif.: Mayfield Publishing Co., 1995), 164, 165, 169.

22. One exception is Carol S. Pearson, *The Hero Within: Six Archetypes We Live By,* expanded ed. (San Francisco: HarperSanFrancisco, 1989), Chapter 5, "The Martyr." However, Pearson presents "transformative sacrifice" largely as an aspect of individual psychological development, without relating it to a social and historical background.

23. Hans Christian Andersen, *The Complete Fairy Tales and Stories,* tr. Erik Christian Haugaard (Garden City, N.Y.: Doubleday, 1974), 68, 70.

24. Ibid., 66.

25. Ibid., 75–76.

26. *Waiting for God,* quoted in David McLellan, *Utopian Pessimist: The Life and Thought of Simone Weil* (New York: Poseidon Press, 1990), 104.

27. David Bakan, *Disease, Pain, and Sacrifice: Toward a Psychology of Suffering* (Chicago and London: University of Chicago Press, 1968), 64.

2. Queen for a Day: The Rewards of Virtue

1. Maxene Fabe, *TV Game Shows* (Garden City, N.Y.: Doubleday, 1979), 176; Les Brown, *Les Brown's Encyclopedia of Television* (New York: New York Zoetrope, 1982), 344. Episodes are still being offered for sale in video catalogs.

2. Cynthia Kling, "'I'll Do Anything': How to Break the Yes Habit," *Mademoiselle,* July 1995, 105–7.

3. Lillian B. Rubin, *Worlds of Pain: Life in the Working-Class Family* (New York: Basic Books, 1976), 40.

4. Sharon Hays, *The Cultural Contradictions of Motherhood* (New Haven and London: Yale University Press, 1996), 8–18.

5. Ron Taffel, "Three Sacrifices Moms Shouldn't Make," *McCall's,* April 1996, 122–24; Gail E. Hudson, "Nurturing Number One," *Parents,* April 1994, 67.

6. Judith Lorber, "Choice, Gift, or Patriarchal Bargain? Women's Consent to *In Vitro* Fertilization in Male Infertility," *Hypatia* 4, no. 3 (fall 1989):23–36; Judith Lorber and Lakshmi Bandaluni, "The Dynamics of Marital Bargaining in Male Infertility," *Gender & Society* 7, no. 1 (March 1993):32–49.

7. Mary Catherine Bateson, *Composing a Life* (New York: Penguin Plume, 1990), 54, 200.

8. Dee Wedemeyer, "His Life Is His Mind," *The New York Times Magazine,* August 18, 1996, 22–25; letters in issue of September 8, 1996, 14.

9. Jeanette Rodriguez, *Our Lady of Guadalupe: Faith and Empowerment Among Mexican-American Women* (Austin: University of Texas Press, 1994), 81, 159; quotes on 73, 164.

10. Elaine M. Brody, "Parent Care as a Normative Family Stress," *The Gerontologist* 25, no. 1 (1985):19–29.

3. Global Responsibilities

1. Lillian B. Rubin, *Worlds of Pain: Life in the Working-Class Family* (New York: Basic Books, 1976), 42.

2. Susan Carroll, interview, January 28, 1997, and Ruth B. Mandel, *In the Running: The New Woman Candidate* (New Haven and New York: Ticknor & Fields, 1981), 166.

Notes

4. A Good Woman Is a Sacrificing One

1. Shel Silverstein, *The Giving Tree* (New York, Evanston, and London: Harper & Row, 1964).

2. The previous two paragraphs are based on the following sources: "Rites and Ceremonies, Sacred," *Encyclopaedia Britannica,* 15th ed. (Chicago: Encyclopaedia Britannica, Inc., 1993), vol. 26, p. 791; Godfrey Ashby, *Sacrifice: Its Nature and Purpose* (London: SCM Press, 1988), 6, 11–15; and Bruce Lincoln, *Death, War, and Sacrifice: Studies in Ideology and Practice* (Chicago and London: The University of Chicago Press, 1991), 202.

   This list of theories is not exhaustive; others include that of Freud, which is based on the Oedipus complex, and that of René Girard, who sees sacrifice as a way of channeling male violence to a victim in order to preserve the social order.

3. Nancy Jay, *Throughout Your Generations Forever: Sacrifice, Religion, and Paternity* (Chicago and London: The University of Chicago Press, 1992), xxiii (quote), xxiv, 35–39, 148–50. "The post–Vatican II Church," she notes, demonstrates "the difficulty of maintaining a sacrificial cult and a sacred hierarchy in an industrialized, democratic, pluralistic world where structures of domination are not organized as descent systems" and which lacks "social structures that allow sacrificial ideology to be taken for granted" (113).

4. "Rites and Ceremonies, Sacred," 791.

5. Ashby, *Sacrifice,* 15, 16 (quoting G. van der Leeuw, *Religion in Essence and Manifestation* [London: Allen & Unwin, 1938], 357); Henri Hubert and Marcel Mauss, *Sacrifice: Its Nature and Function,* tr. W. D. Hall (1898; Chicago: The University of Chicago Press, 1964), 43–44.

6. "Sacrifice," *Encyclopaedia Judaica* (Jerusalem: Keter Publishing House, 1971–72), vol. 14, p. 613.

7. "Sacrifice," *Encyclopaedia Judaica,* 614; Ashby, *Sacrifice,* 52; Frances M. Young, *Sacrifice and the Death of Christ* (Philadelphia: Westminster Press, 1975), 10, quoted in Inna Jane Ray, "The Atonement Muddle: An Historical Analysis and Clarification of a Salvation Theory," *Journal of Women and Religion* 15 (1997): 31; "Sacrifice, IV," *New Catholic Encyclopedia* (Washington, D.C.: Catholic University of America, 1967), vol. 12, quote on 837; Ashby, *Sacrifice,* quote on 54; "Sacrifice, IV," 839.

8. Ray, "Atonement Muddle," 32–33; Ashby, *Sacrifice,* 62; John Bowker, *Problems of Suffering in Religions of the World* (Cambridge: Cambridge University Press, 1970), 16, 34, 28; Ashby, *Sacrifice,* 62-63; Bowker, *Suffering,* 74, 76.

9. Ray, "Atonement Muddle," quote on 63; Caroline Walker Bynum, *Holy Feast and Holy Fast: The Religious Significance of Food to Medieval Women* (Berkeley and Los Angeles: University of California Press, 1987), 418n., 54.

10. Bynum, *Holy Feast,* 13; Rudolph M. Bell, *Holy Anorexia* (Chicago and London: University of Chicago Press, 1985), 57, 100; Bynum, *Holy Feast,* 25, 26, 76, 94–95, 167–69; Bell, *Holy Anorexia,* 52; Bynum, *Holy Feast,* 86.

11. Bynum, *Holy Feast,* 211–12, 165.

12. Ibid., 25, 191, 276, quotes on 296, 25.

13. Bonnie S. Anderson and Judith P. Zinsser, *A History of Their Own: Women in Europe from Prehistory to the Present,* vol. 1 (New York: Harper & Row, 1988), quotes on 254, 432; Bynum, *Holy Feast,* 214, 216–17.

14. Bell, *Holy Anorexia,* 172, 174–75, 178.

15. Ibid., 178; Anderson and Zinsser, *History of Their Own,* 238–39, 253–54, quote on 253; Adrienne Rich, *Of Woman Born: Motherhood as Experience and Institution* (1976; New York: Bantam Books, 1977), 118; Anderson and Zinsser, *History of Their Own,* 260; Rich, *Of Woman Born,* 117; Elisabeth Badinter, *Mother Love, Myth and Reality: Motherhood in Modern History* (New York: Macmillan, 1981), 236; Rich, *Of Woman Born,* 162.

16. Nel Noddings, *Women and Evil* (Berkeley: University of California Press, 1989), 36; Anderson and Zinsser, *History of Their Own,* 78.

17. Bonnie S. Anderson, "Making Angels," Chapter 2 of *Joyous Greetings: The First International Women's Movement* (New York: Oxford University Press, forthcoming), 18, 14, 11, 16, 23. I thank Bonnie Anderson for allowing me to read and quote from this manuscript.

18. Ibid., 6–7.

19. Barbara Ehrenreich and Deirdre English, *For Her Own Good: 150 Years of the Experts' Advice to Women* (New York: Doubleday Anchor Books, 1978), 9–10.

20. Stephanie Coontz, *The Way We Never Were: American Families and the Nostalgia Trap* (New York: Basic Books, 1992), 44–53.

21. Ehrenreich and English, *For Her Own Good,* 19, 24–25; Coontz, *Way We Never Were,* 58, quote on 61.

22. Charlene Spretnak, *States of Grace: The Recovery of Meaning in the Postmodern Age* (San Francisco: Harper SanFrancisco, 1991) 119, 253–54; Karen Armstrong, *A History of God: The 4000-Year Quest of Judaism, Christianity and Islam* (New York: Ballantine Books, 1993), 301.

23. Badinter, *Mother Love,* 215–16; Alfred, Lord Tennyson, "The Princess," part VII, lines 301–2, quoted in Jessie

Bernard, *The Future of Motherhood* (1974; New York: Penguin Books, 1975), 4.

24. Quoted in Bram Dijkstra, *Idols of Perversity: Fantasies of Feminine Evil in Fin-de-Siècle Culture* (New York and Oxford: Oxford University Press, 1986), 10–11.

25. Ann Douglas, *The Feminization of American Culture* (New York: Alfred A. Knopf, 1977), 44, 128–29; Dijkstra, *Idols of Perversity,* 14.

26. Ibid., x.

27. Ibid., 23; Ehrenreich and English, *For Her Own Good,* 103–4, 105–7; Dijkstra, *Idols of Perversity,* 27–28; quote from Douglas, *Feminization,* 92.

28. Harvey Green with Mary-Ellen Perry, *The Light of the Home: An Intimate View of the Lives of Women in Victorian America* (New York: Pantheon Books, 1983), 114; Susan Sontag, *Illness as Metaphor* (New York: Farrar, Straus & Giroux, 1978), 30.

29. Dijkstra, *Idols of Perversity,* 29; Ehrenreich and English, *For Her Own Good,* 103, 109, quote on 120.

30. Dijkstra, *Idols of Perversity,* 23.

31. Ehrenreich and English, *For Her Own Good,* 105, 106–7.

32. Ibid., 113–14.

33. Ellen Ross, *Love and Toil: Motherhood in Outcast London, 1870–1918* (New York and Oxford: Oxford University Press, 1993), 55.

34. Ibid., 35, 55.

35. Dijkstra, *Idols of Perversity,* 101.

36. Gwen Benwell and Arthur Waugh, *Sea Enchantress: The Tale of the Mermaid and Her Kin* (New York: Citadel Press, 1965), 14, 28, 44, 81; Beatrice Phillpotts, *Mermaids* (New York: Ballantine Books, 1980), 6, 10, 20–22, 38.

37. Benwell and Waugh, *Sea Enchantress,* 130; William Makepeace Thackeray, *Vanity Fair,* quoted in Nina Auerbach, *Woman and the Demon: The Life of a Victorian Myth* (Cambridge and London: Harvard University Press, 1982), 90; George Eliot, *Middlemarch* (New York: Washington Square Press, 1963), 427; Dijkstra, *Idols of Perversity,* 258–69.

38. Hans Christian Andersen, "Notes for My Fairy Tales and Stories," in *The Complete Fairy Tales and Stories,* tr. Erik Christian Haugaard (Garden City, N.Y.: Doubleday, 1974).

39. Hans Christian Andersen, "The Little Mermaid," in ibid., 69.

40. Ibid., 71, 72.

41. Wolfgang Lederer, *The Kiss of the Snow Queen: Hans Christian Andersen and Man's Redemption by Woman* (Berkeley: University of California Press, 1986), 153, 158, 163; Elias Bredesdorff, *Hans Christian Andersen: The Story of His Life and Work* (New York: Charles Scribner's Sons, 1975), 280–81.

5. The Mermaid's Tail

1. Thomas Mann, *Doctor Faustus,* tr. H. T. Lowe-Porter (New York: Random House, 1948; Vintage Books, 1971), 230, 342, 500; Wolfgang Lederer, *The Kiss of the Snow Queen: Hans Christian Andersen and Man's Redemption by Woman* (Berkeley: University of California Press, 1986), 166.

2. Harvey Green with Mary-Ellen Perry, *The Light of the Home: An Intimate View of the Lives of Women in Victorian America* (New York: Pantheon Books, 1983), 114.

3. Molly Haskell, *From Reverence to Rape: The Treatment of Women in the Movies* (New York: Holt, Rinehart & Winston, 1974), 40, 160–61.

4. Fannie Hurst, *Imitation of Life* (1933; New York: Harper & Row Perennial Library, 1990), 164.

5. Ibid., 259.

6. Lina Mainiero, ed., *American Women Writers: A Critical Reference Guide from Colonial Times to the Present* (New York: Ungar, 1979), vol. 2, 362.

7. George Ferguson, *Signs and Symbols in Christian Art* (New York: Oxford University Press, 1959), 9; Caroline Walker Bynum, *Holy Feast and Holy Fast: The Religious Significance of Food to Medieval Women* (Berkeley and Los Angeles: University of California Press, 1987), 270–72; Phyllis Rose, *Woman of Letters: A Life of Virginia Woolf* (New York: Oxford University Press, 1978), 157.

8. Sharon Hays, *The Cultural Contradictions of Motherhood* (New Haven and London: Yale University Press, 1996), 41, 44.

9. Ibid., 45–46.

10. Bonnie S. Anderson and Judith P. Zinsser, *A History of Their Own: Women in Europe from Prehistory to the Present,* vol. 2 (New York: Harper & Row, 1988), 219; Helene Deutsch quoted in Barbara Ehrenreich and Deirdre English, *For Her Own Good: 150 Years of the Experts' Advice to Women* (New York: Doubleday Anchor Books, 1978), 272; Elisabeth Badinter, *Mother Love, Myth and Reality: Motherhood in Modern History* (New York: Macmillan, 1981), 272–73.

11. Ehrenreich and English, *For Her Own Good,* 270; Badinter, *Mother Love,* 277.

12. Ibid., 272, Deutsch quoted on 273.

13. Winnicott quoted in ibid., 273.

14. Coontz, *Way We Never Were,* 36.

15. Marilyn French, *Her Mother's Daughter* (New York: Summit Books, 1987), 171, 12.

16. Alix Kates Shulman, "A Mother's Story," *Ms.,* May/June 1996, 53–55.

17. M. Rivka Polatnick, "Diversity in Women's Liberation Ideology: How a Black and a White Group of the 1960s Viewed Motherhood," *Signs: Journal of Women in Culture and Society* 21 (spring 1996): 690.

18. Alix Kates Shulman, interview, April 10, 1997.

19. Ibid.

20. Patricia Hill Collins, *Black Feminist Thought: Knowledge, Consciousness, and the Politics of Empowerment* (New York and London: Routledge, 1991), 71.

21. Frances E. W. Harper, *Minnie's Sacrifice,* in *Minnie's Sacrifice, Sowing and Reaping, Trial and Triumph: Three Rediscovered Novels by Frances E.W. Harper,* ed. Frances Smith Foster (Boston: Beacon Press, 1994), 91–92. It is not clear exactly who murders Minnie, for the novel was published only as a serial in a periodical, and the episode describing her death is missing.

22. Paula Giddings, *When and Where I Enter: The Impact of Black Women on Race and Sex in America* (1984; New York: Bantam Books, 1985), 45–49, 88, 89, quote on 201.

23. Giddings, *When and Where,* 356; Collins, *Black Feminist Thought,* 124, 47, 49–50.

24. Audre Lorde, *Sister Outsider: Essays and Speeches* (Freedom, Calif.: Crossing Press, 1984), 150; Toni Morrison, *Sula* (Penguin Books, 1973), 67, 69.

25. Collins, *Black Feminist Thought,* 54–55, quote on 55.

26. Quoted in Giddings, *When and Where,* 310.

27. Polatnick, "Diversity in Women's Liberation Ideology," 680, 684, 696.

28. Ibid., 680, 685, 701, 686.

29. Hays, *Cultural Contradictions of Motherhood,* 86, 87, 78; Jill McLean Taylor, Carol Gilligan, and Amy W. Sullivan, *Between Voice and Silence: Women and Girls, Race and Relationship* (Cambridge and London: Harvard University Press, 1995), 82.

30. Ibid., 170, 169.

31. John Gray, *Mars and Venus Together Forever: Relationship Skills for Lasting Love* (New York: HarperCollins, HarperPerennial paperback, 1996), 22–23, 28, 12, 39, 21, 42.

32. Ibid., 23, 92.

33. Ibid., 25.

34. Letters from Readers, *Commentary,* June 1996, 3–4.

35. Ibid., 6–7.

36. Dalma Heyn, *The Erotic Silence of the American Wife* (New York: Turtle Bay Books, 1992), 55, 73–74.

37. Ibid., 147.

38. Ibid., 266.

39. Ursula K. Le Guin, "The Fisherman's Daughter," in Diane Apostolos-Cappadona and Lucinda Ebersole, eds., *Women, Creativity and the Arts: Critical and Autobiographical Perspectives* (New York: Continuum, 1995), 180.

40. Ibid., 182.

41. Elizabeth Wurtzel, *Prozac Nation: Young and Depressed in America* (Boston and New York: Houghton Mifflin, 1994).

42. Dan Hofstadter, "Frida Kahlo: Victim Status," *The New York Times Magazine,* November 24, 1996, 96.

43. Hayden Herrera, *Frida: A Biography of Frida Kahlo* (New York: Harper & Row, 1983), 76, 73.

44. Deborah Solomon, "Saint Frida," *New Republic,* September 30, 1991, 28–31.

45. Judd Tully, "The Kahlo Cult," *ArtNews,* April 1994, 126, 127; Solomon, "Saint Frida"; paraphrased admirer is Jill

Johnston, "Self-Portrait," review of *The Diary of Frida Kahlo,* in *Art in America,* March 1996, 31–33.

46. Tully, "Kahlo Cult," 127; Laura Shapiro, "Cookin' Up Good Times with Frida," *Newsweek,* December 12, 1994, 76; Irving Howe, "The Plath Celebration: A Partial Dissent" (orig. pub. 1973), in Harold Bloom, ed., *Modern Critical Views: Sylvia Plath* (New York and Philadelphia: Chelsea House Publishers, 1989), 5; Elizabeth Frank, "A Long Romance with Death," review of Ronald Hayman, *The Death and Life of Sylvia Plath,* and Paul Alexander, *Rough Magic, The New York Times Book Review,* October 6, 1991, 14; Andrea Sachs, "Poets in Suicide Sex Shocker!" *Time,* April 18, 1994, 74.

47. Anne Lamott, "Sylvia Plath: The Literary Girl's Elvis," *Mademoiselle,* November 1991, 82; following quote from Frank, "Long Romance," 14.

48. Alicia Ostriker, "The Americanization of Sylvia," in Linda W. Wagner, ed., *Critical Essays on Sylvia Plath* (Boston: G. K. Hall & Co., 1984), 98–99.

6. Disappearing Acts

   1. Le Anne Schreiber, "A Talk with Mary Gordon," *The New York Times Book Review,* February 15, 1981, 26–27.

   2. Mary Pipher, *Reviving Ophelia: Saving the Selves of Adolescent Girls* (New York: G. P. Putnam's Sons, 1994), 39; Lyn Mikel Brown and Carol Gilligan, *Meeting at the Crossroads: Women's Psychology and Girls' Development* (1992; New York: Ballantine Books, 1993), 58–59.

   3. Ibid., 61, 176.

   4. Ibid., 21, 3; Pipher, *Reviving Ophelia,* 257.

   5. Brown and Gilligan, *Meeting at the Crossroads,* 5, 168.

6. Ibid., 106; Laura Ring, "Sexual Harassment and the Production of Gender," in *Differences: A Journal of Feminist Cultural Studies* 6 (1994):138.

7. Brown and Gilligan, *Meeting at the Crossroads,* 226.

8. Jill McLean Taylor, Carol Gilligan, and Amy M. Sullivan, *Between Voice and Silence: Women and Girls, Race and Relationship* (Cambridge and London: Harvard University Press, 1995), 61, 62, 41.

9. Ibid., 77.

10. Joan Jacobs Brumberg, *Fasting Girls: The Emergence of Anorexia Nervosa as a Modern Disease* (Cambridge and London: Harvard University Press, 1988), 42, 78–85, 99, 98.

11. Ibid., 112, 128, 113.

12. Ibid., 175, 180, 182, 184, 188.

13. Ibid., 185, 242, 7.

14. Ibid., 265–66; Naomi Wolf, *The Beauty Myth: How Images of Beauty Are Used Against Women* (New York: Doubleday, Anchor Books, 1992), 197.

15. Brumberg, *Fasting Girls,* 112, 142, 216–17, 229.

16. Ibid., 39.

17. I. R. Tofler et al., "Physical and Emotional Problems of Elite Female Gymnasts," *New England Journal of Medicine* 335 (July 25, 1996):281; Joan Ryan, *Little Girls in Pretty Boxes: The Making and Breaking of Elite Gymnasts and Figure Skaters* (New York: Doubleday, 1995), 10.

18. Marc Bloom, "Running and Winning the Race Against Anorexia," *The New York Times,* April 5, 1996, B15.

19. Wolf, *Beauty Myth,* 204–5, 215.

20. Brumberg, *Fasting Girls,* 12.

21. Taylor, Gilligan, and Sullivan, *Between Voice and Silence,* 220, n. 11.

22. Patricia Hill Collins, *Black Feminist Thought: Knowledge, Consciousness, and the Politics of Empowerment* (New York and London: Routledge, 1991), 79–80.

23. Brown and Gilligan, *Meeting at the Crossroads,* 203.

24. Heidi Dalzell, "Feminism, Reality and Eating Disorders," *Eating Disorders: Journal of Treatment and Prevention* 5 (summer 1997):165. Quotes in this paragraph and the preceding one are from this article; all others are from an interview, March 19, 1997.

25. Elizabeth Wurtzel, *Prozac Nation: Young and Depressed in America* (Boston and New York: Houghton Mifflin, 1994), 40–41.

26. Pipher, *Reviving Ophelia,* 157–58.

27. "Rites and Ceremonies, Sacred," *Encyclopaedia Britannica,* 15th ed. (Chicago: Encyclopaedia Britannica, Inc., 1993), vol. 26, 793; Godfrey Ashby, *Sacrifice: Its Nature and Purpose* (London: SCM Press, 1988), 20.

28. Georg Lukács, "On Poverty of Spirit," in *The Lukács Reader,* ed. Arpad Kadarkay (Oxford, U.K., and Cambridge, Mass.: Blackwell, 1995), 50.

29. "Rites and Ceremonies, Sacred," 796.

30. Mary Gordon, *The Shadow Man* (New York: Random House, 1996), 63–64.

31. Ibid.

32. Toni Morrison, *Sula* (New York: Penguin Books, 1973), 53–55.

33. Quoted in Nancy Jay, *Throughout Your Generations Forever: Sacrifice, Religion, and Paternity* (Chicago and London: University of Chicago Press, 1992), 62.

34. Morrison, *Sula,* 101, 93.

7. Victimhood and Identity

1. Anne Wilson Schaef, *Meditations for Women Who Do Too Much* (New York: Harper & Row, 1990), unpaged. Quotes from introduction and March 31 meditation.

2. Linell Smith, "No-Fault Behavior: Have Excuses Replaced Personal Accountability?" *The Sun* (Baltimore), August 7, 1994, 1J.

3. Mary Gilligan Wong, *Nun: A Memoir* (San Diego: Harcourt Brace Jovanovich, 1983), 140–41.

4. Dick Francis, *Longshot* (New York: Fawcett Crest, 1990), 106.

5. Guy Garcia, "Lord Sting, at Peace in His Fields of Gold," *The New York Times,* March 10, 1996, section 2, p. 34.

6. Joyce Carol Oates, *On Boxing* (1987; Hopewell, N.J.: Ecco Press, 1994), 73.

7. Jill Johnston, "Fictions of the Self in the Making," *The New York Times Book Review,* April 25, 1993, 29.

8. Sara Paretsky, *Killing Orders* (New York: William Morrow, 1985), 287–88.

9. Judith Lewis Herman, *Trauma and Recovery* (New York: Basic Books, 1992), 106.

10. Dr. Dan Kiley, *The Wendy Dilemma: When Women Stop Mothering Their Men* (New York: Arbor House, 1984), 18, 96.

11. Carol S. Pearson, *The Hero Within: Six Archetypes We Live By,* expanded ed. (San Francisco: HarperSanFrancisco, 1989), 101–2.

12. Claire Bloom, *Leaving a Doll's House: A Memoir* (Boston and New York: Little, Brown and Co., 1996), 158, 203.

13. Patricia Bosworth, "Goodbye, Connecticut" (review of Bloom, *Leaving a Doll's House), The New York Times Book Review,* October 13, 1996, 7.

14. Dalma Heyn, *The Erotic Silence of the American Wife* (New York: Turtle Bay Books, 1992), 151.

15. Erica Jong, "Hillary's Husband Re-Elected! The Clinton Marriage of Politics and Power," *The Nation,* November 25, 1996, 14, 15.

16. Natalie Shainess, *Sweet Suffering: Woman as Victim* (Indianapolis and New York: Bobbs-Merrill, 1984), 1–3.

17. Paula J. Caplan, *The Myth of Women's Masochism* (New York: E. P. Dutton, 1985), 9.

18. Audre Lorde, "Eye to Eye: Black Women, Hatred, and Anger," in *Sister Outsider: Essays and Speeches* (Freedom, Calif.: Crossing Press, 1984), 146, 152.

19. Herman, *Trauma and Recovery,* 178.

20. Ibid., 113; Carol Tavris, *The Mismeasure of Woman: Why Women Are Not the Better Sex, the Inferior Sex, or the Opposite Sex* (New York: Simon & Schuster, Touchstone, 1992), 320.

21. Joan Jacobs Brumberg, *Fasting Girls: The Emergence of Anorexia Nervosa as a Modern Disease* (Cambridge and London: Harvard University Press, 1988), 142.

22. Deborah Franklin, "The Politics of Masochism," *Psychology Today,* January 1987, 54; Jessica Benjamin, *The Bonds of Love: Psychoanalysis, Feminism, and the Problem of Domination* (New York: Pantheon Books, 1988), 261, n. 9.

23. Susan Faludi, *Backlash: The Undeclared War Against American Women* (New York: Crown Publishers, 1991), 358; Herman, *Trauma and Recovery,* 117.

24. Faludi, *Backlash,* 356–62; Franklin, "Politics of Masochism," 54–56.

25. Faludi, *Backlash,* 359.

26. Benjamin, *Bonds of Love,* 7.

27. Ibid., 12, 49.

28. Ibid., 77, 23, 214, 82.

29. Ibid., 78, 76.

30. Ibid., 78–79.

31. Ibid., 81, 172, 187.

32. Ibid., 81.

33. Schreiber, "Talk with Mary Gordon," 26.

34. Bloom, *Leaving a Doll's House,* 9, 60.

35. Heidi Dalzell, "Feminism, Reality and Eating Disorders," *Eating Disorders: Journal of Treatment and Prevention* 5 (summer 1997):165; following quote from interview.

36. Benjamin, *Bonds of Love,* 86, 122, 117, 218.

37. Ibid., 111, 116.

38. Lyn Mikel Brown and Carol Gilligan, *Meeting at the Crossroads: Women's Psychology and Girls' Development* (1992; New York: Ballantine Books, 1993), 148, 151, 152.

39. Benjamin, *Bonds of Love,* 117.

8. Pain: False Transcendence

1. Simone Weil, "Factory Journal," in *Formative Writings,* ed. Dorothy Tuck McFarland and Wilhelmina Van Ness (Amherst: University of Massachusetts Press, 1987), 211.

2. Simone Weil, letter to Joë Bousquet, in *Simone Weil—An Anthology,* ed. and introduced by Sîan Miles (New York: Weidenfeld & Nicolson, 1986), 262.

3. Simone Pétrement, *Simone Weil: A Life,* tr. Raymond Rosenthal (New York: Pantheon Books, 1976), 204.

4. Ibid., 8, 99–100, 227, 79–81.

5. Ibid., 215.

6. Weil, "Factory Journal," 225; Simone Weil, "The Love of God and Affliction," in George A. Panichas, ed., *The Simone*

Weil Reader (Mt. Kisco, N.Y.: Moyer Bell Ltd., 1977), 452, 443; Weil, "Factory Work," in ibid., 56.

7. David McLellan, *Utopian Pessimist: The Life and Thought of Simone Weil* (New York: Poseidon Press, 1990), 186; Weil, "Affliction," 452; McLellan, *Utopian Pessimist,* 231.

8. Pétrement, *Simone Weil,* 515, 482.

9. Ibid., 420; Simone Weil, "Forms of the Implicit Love of God," in *Waiting for God,* trans. Emma Crawfurd (New York: Harper & Row reprint of 1951 Putnam ed.), 166; Robert Coles, *Simone Weil: A Modern Pilgrimage* (Reading, Mass.: Addison-Wesley, 1987), 28; Michele Murray, "Simone Weil: Last Things," in George Abbott White, *Simone Weil: Interpretations of a Life* (Amherst, Mass.: University of Massachusetts Press, 1981), 53.

10. Caroline Walker Bynum, *Holy Feast and Holy Fast: The Religious Significance of Food to Medieval Women* (Berkeley and Los Angeles: University of California Press, 1987), 206.

11. McLellan, *Utopian Pessimist,* 268.

12. Weil, "Factory Journal," 224; Pétrement, *Simone Weil,* 262; McLellan, *Utopian Pessimist,* 135; Pétrement, *Simone Weil,* 70.

13. Ibid., 261.

14. Margaret R. Miles, "The Courage to Be Alone," in Mary E. Giles, ed., *The Feminist Mystic and Other Essays on Women and Spirituality* (New York: Crossroad, 1982), 98.

15. Cynthia Griffin Wolff, *Emily Dickinson* (New York: Alfred A. Knopf, 1986), 194, 103.

16. Adrienne Rich, "Vesuvius at Home: The Power of Emily Dickinson," in *On Lies, Secrets, and Silence: Selected Prose 1966–1978* (New York: W. W. Norton, 1979), 160; Wolff, *Emily Dickinson,* 147.

17. Citations of Dickinson's poems are from *The Complete Poems of Emily Dickinson,* ed. Thomas H. Johnson (Boston: Little, Brown, Back Bay Books, 1960); Wolff, *Emily Dickinson,* 215–16.

18. Ibid., 194.

19. This interpretation is based on comments by Barbara Antonina Clarke Mossberg, "'Everyone Else Is Prose': Emily Dickinson's Lack of Community Spirit," in Paul J. Ferlazzo, ed., *Critical Essays on Emily Dickinson* (Boston: G. K. Hall, 1984), 234.

20. Wolff, *Emily Dickinson,* 210–11; Coles, *Simone Weil: A Modern Pilgrimage,* 28–29.

21. Kenneth D. Craig, "Emotional Aspects of Pain," in Patrick D. Wall and Ronald Melzack, eds., *Textbook of Pain,* 3d ed. (Edinburgh: Churchill Livingstone, 1994), 261; Ivan Illich, *Medical Nemesis: The Expropriation of Health* (New York: Pantheon Books, 1976), 147–48, 150.

22. Craig, "Emotional Aspects of Pain," 262.

23. Oliver Sacks, *Migraine,* rev. ed. (Berkeley: University of California Press, 1992), 301.

24. Ibid., 299, 301; Bynum, *Holy Feast and Holy Fast,* 245.

25. Harvey Green with Mary-Ellen Perry, *The Light of the Home: An Intimate View of the Lives of Women in Victorian America* (New York: Pantheon Books, 1983), 115.

26. Patrick D. Wall, "Introduction," in Wall and Melzack, *Textbook of Pain,* 2–3; H. Merskey, "Pain and Psychological Medicine," in ibid., 916.

27. Mary-Jo DelVecchio Good et al., "Epilogue," in Mary-Jo DelVecchio Good et al., eds., *Pain as Human Experience: An Anthropological Perspective* (Berkeley: University of California Press, 1992), 203.

Notes

28. Natalie Angier, "Yet Another Sex Difference Found: Gaining Relief from a Painkiller," *The New York Times*, October 30, 1996, C12; Suzanne M. Skevington, *Psychology of Pain* (Chichester and New York: John Wiley & Sons, 1995), 75, 276, 74, 275.

29. Craig, "Emotional Aspects of Pain," 265.

30. Skevington, *Psychology of Pain*, 146; Craig, "Emotional Aspects of Pain," 266; Skevington, *Psychology of Pain*, 110; Matisyohu Weisenberg, "Cognitive Aspects of Pain," in Wall and Melzack, *Textbook of Pain*, 278.

31. Craig, "Emotional Aspects of Pain," 265; Skevington, *Psychology of Pain*, 146.

32. Craig, "Emotional Aspects of Pain," 266.

33. Merskey, "Pain and Psychological Medicine," 906.

34. Skevington, *Psychology of Pain*, 138–40; Weisenberg, "Cognitive Aspects of Pain," 278, 281.

35. Skevington, *Psychology of Pain*, 148.

36. Arthur Kleinman, "Pain and Resistance," in Good et al., *Pain as Human Experience*, 172.

37. Sacks, *Migraine*, 208–9, 212.

38. Jill McLean Taylor, Carol Gilligan, and Amy M. Sullivan, *Between Voice and Silence: Women and Girls, Race and Relationship* (Cambridge and London: Harvard University Press, 1995), 96, 97.

39. K. M. Rowat and K. A. Knafl, "Living with Chronic Pain: The Spouse's Perspective," *Pain* 23 (1985):265; H. Flor et al., "Relationship of Pain Impact and Significant Other Reinforcement of Pain Behaviors: The Mediating Role of Gender, Marital Status and Marital Satisfaction," *Pain* 38 (1989):46; J. M. Romano et al., "Sex Differences in the Relationship of Pain Patient Dysfunction to Spouse Adjustment," *Pain* 39 (1985):293.

40. Bram Dijkstra, *Idols of Perversity: Fantasies of Feminine Evil in Fin-de-Siècle Culture* (New York and Oxford: Oxford University Press, 1986), 23; David B. Morris, *The Culture of Pain* (Berkeley: University of California Press, 1991), 208–9.

41. Elizabeth Wurtzel, *Prozac Nation: Young and Depressed in America* (Boston and New York: Houghton Mifflin, 1994), 19, 289, 290.

42. Suzanne Stutman, *Broken Feather: A Journey to Healing* (Philadelphia: Manor House Publications, 1996), 45. I am grateful to Suzanne Stutman for allowing me to quote this poem.

43. Kleinman, "Pain and Resistance," 186, 174.

44. Elaine Scarry, *The Body in Pain: The Making and Unmaking of the World* (New York and Oxford: Oxford University Press, 1985), 35, 34.

45. Ibid., 121, 127, 201, 183, 173.

46. Ibid., 169.

47. Dijkstra, *Idols of Perversity,* 22.

48. Morris, *Culture of Pain,* 211.

49. Kleinman, "Pain and Resistance," 176, 179.

50. Linda C. Garro, "Chronic Illness and the Construction of Narratives," in Good et al., *Pain as Human Experience,* 126, 129, 130.

51. Scarry, *Body in Pain,* 279.

9. Sacrifice and Power

1. Quoted in Dorothy W. Cantor and Toni Bernay with Jean Stoess, *Women in Power: The Secrets of Leadership* (Boston: Houghton Mifflin Co., 1992), 52.

2. Jessica Benjamin, *The Bonds of Love: Psychoanalysis, Feminism, and the Problem of Domination* (New York: Pantheon Books, 1988), 187.

3. Patricia Hill Collins, *Black Feminist Thought: Knowledge, Consciousness, and the Politics of Empowerment* (New York and London: Routledge, 1991), 216; Joan C. Tronto, *Moral Boundaries: A Political Argument for an Ethic of Care* (New York and London: Routledge, 1993), 89, 154.

4. Joe Klein, "The Predator Problem," *Newsweek,* April 29, 1996, 32.

5. Jill Johnston, "Fictions of the Self in the Making," *The New York Times Book Review,* April 25, 1993, 29.

6. Benjamin, *Bonds of Love,* 220.

7. Linell Smith, "No-Fault Behavior: Have Excuses Replaced Personal Accountability?" *The Sun* (Baltimore), August 7, 1994, 1J; David Wallis, "Starving for Attention," *The New York Times,* June 30, 1996, section 4, p. 2.

8. Jean Bethke Elshtain, "Battered Reason," *New Republic,* October 5, 1992, 25.

9. Linda Gordon, "Killing in Self-Defense," review of Donald Alexander Downs, *More Than Victims: Battered Women, the Syndrome Society, and the Law, The Nation,* March 24, 1997, 26.

10. Wendy Kaminer, *I'm Dysfunctional, You're Dysfunctional: The Recovery Movement and Other Self-Help Fashions* (New York: Random House, Vintage Books, 1993), 27–28, 152, 158.

11. Carol Tavris, *The Mismeasure of Woman: Why Women Are Not the Better Sex, the Inferior Sex, or the Opposite Sex* (New York: Simon & Schuster, Touchstone, 1992), 201, 198.

12. Ibid., 329; Judith Lewis Herman, *Trauma and Recovery* (New York: Basic Books, 1992), 204.

13. Tavris, *Mismeasure of Woman,* 321.

14. Mary Gilligan Wong, *Nun: A Memoir* (San Diego: Harcourt Brace Jovanovich, 1983), 141.

15. Audre Lorde, "The Uses of Anger: Women Responding to Racism," in *Sister Outsider: Essays and Speeches* (Freedom, Calif.: Crossing Press, 1984), 132.

16. Benjamin, *Bonds of Love,* 293, n. 56; Adrienne Rich, *Your Native Land, Your Life: Poems* (New York: W. W. Norton, 1986), 100, 111.

17. Lorde, *Sister Outsider,* "Eye to Eye: Black Women, Hatred, and Anger," 152; "Uses of Anger," 131; "Sexism: An American Disease in Blackface," 62.

18. David Bakan, *Disease, Pain, and Sacrifice: Toward a Psychology of Suffering* (Chicago and London: University of Chicago Press, 1968), 59, 125.

19. Elaine Scarry, *The Body in Pain: The Making and Unmaking of the World* (New York and Oxford: Oxford University Press, 1985), 290–91.

20. Robert Pear, "Dole Courts Conservatives with Changes on Welfare," *The New York Times,* August 10, 1995, B6; Lisa Schiffren, "Penalize the Unwed Dad? Fat Chance," *The New York Times,* August 10, 1995, A19; Laura Flanders and Janine Jackson, "Public Enemy No. 1?" *FAIR,* May/June 1995, 13; Robin Toner, "Resolved: No More Bleeding Hearts," *The New York Times,* July 16, 1995, section 4, p. 1.

21. Kai Erikson, "Scandal or Scapegoating?" review of Kristin Luker, *Dubious Conceptions: The Politics of Teenage Pregnancy, The New York Times Book Review,* September 1, 1996, 12; "Rate of Births for Teen-Agers Drops Again," *The New York Times,* September 22, 1995, A18; see also Margaret

Notes

L. Usdansky, "Single Motherhood: Stereotypes vs. Statistics," *The New York Times,* February 11, 1996, section 4, p. 4.

22. Klein, "Predator Problem," 32.

23. Linda Gordon, *Pitied But Not Entitled: Single Mothers and the History of Welfare, 1890-1935* (New York: Free Press, 1994), 7, 27, 39.

24. Ibid., 160–61, 167.

25. Ibid., 7, 295, 299.

26. Ibid., 303, 34–35.

27. Benjamin, *Bonds of Love,* 195.

28. Collins, *Black Feminist Thought,* 77; Rosemary Haughton and Nancy Schwoyer, "Welfare Reform and National Scapegoating: The Politics of Fear," *Cross Currents,* spring 1995, 80–94.

29. Ann Jones, *Next Time, She'll Be Dead: Battering and How to Stop It* (Boston: Beacon Press, 1994), 208; Vern L. Bullough and Bonnie L. Bullough, *The History of Prostitution* (New Hyde Park, N.Y.: University Books, 1964), 24; Jones, *Next Time,* 205, 207.

30. Gloria Jacobs, "Where Do We Go from Here? An Interview with Ann Jones," *Ms.,* September/October 1994, 60; Herman, *Trauma and Recovery,* 117, 112; Gordon, "Killing in Self-Defense," 25.

31. Stephanie Golden, "Beaten Out of a Home," *New York Newsday,* December 20, 1988, 60.

32. Benjamin, *Bonds of Love,* 220, 221.

33. Riane Eisler, *The Chalice and the Blade: Our History, Our Future* (San Francisco: Harper & Row Perennial, 1987), 193; Joanna Macy, *World as Lover, World as Self* (Berkeley, Calif.: Parallax Press, 1991), 35. See also Starhawk, *Truth or Dare:*

Encounters with Power, Authority, and Mystery (San Francisco: Harper & Row, 1987), 9–10.

34. Collins, *Black Feminist Thought,* 157, 223, 224.

35. Cantor and Bernay, *Women in Power,* 64, 58, 56.

10. The Lost Side of Sacrifice: Connection

1. Tom Cornell, "A Brief Introduction to the Catholic Worker Movement," posted on the Catholic Worker Web site, http://www.catholicworker.org.

2. *The Catholic Worker,* May 1996, posted on Catholic Worker Web site.

3. Carol S. Pearson, *The Hero Within: Six Archetypes We Live By,* expanded ed. (San Francisco: HarperSanFrancisco, 1989), 99, 105.

4. Anne Carolyn Klein, *Meeting the Great Bliss Queen: Buddhists, Feminists, and the Art of the Self* (Boston: Beacon Press, 1995), 89.

5. Rita M. Gross, *Buddhism After Patriarchy: A Feminist History, Analysis, and Reconstruction of Buddhism* (Albany, N.Y.: State University of New York Press, 1993), 7–8; Charlene Spretnak, *States of Grace: The Recovery of Meaning in the Postmodern Age* (San Francisco: HarperSanFrancisco, 1991), 48.

6. Ibid., 51; Gross, *Buddhism After Patriarchy,* 8.

7. Klein, *Bliss Queen,* 196, 101, 102.

8. Joanna Macy, *World as Lover, World as Self* (Berkeley, Calif.: Parallax Press, 1991), 35, 54, 59, 99, 35.

9. Klein, *Bliss Queen,* 154–55; Macy, *World as Lover,* 180. See also Klein, 102.

10. Macy, *World as Lover,* 21, 24, 63; Klein, *Bliss Queen,* 200.

11. David Bakan, *Disease, Pain, and Sacrifice: Toward a Psychology of Suffering* (Chicago and London: University of Chicago Press, 1968), 29; Macy, *World as Lover,* 63.

12. Jessica Benjamin, *The Bonds of Love: Psychoanalysis, Feminism, and the Problem of Domination* (New York: Pantheon Books, 1988), 221, 19–20; Catherine Ingram, "Joanna Macy," in *In the Footsteps of Gandhi: Conversations with Spiritual Social Activists* (Berkeley, Calif.: Parallax Press, 1990), 160; Klein, *Bliss Queen,* 143.

13. Macy, *World as Lover,* 33, 185; Klein, *Bliss Queen,* 89, 97.

14. Tracey Robinson and Janie Ward, "'A Belief in Self Far Greater than Anyone's Disbelief': Cultivating Resistance Among African American Female Adolescents," *Women and Therapy* 11 (1991):91, quoted in Jill McLean Taylor, Carol Gilligan, and Amy M. Sullivan, *Between Voice and Silence: Women and Girls, Race and Relationship* (Cambridge and London: Harvard University Press, 1995), 30; Patricia Hill Collins, *Black Feminist Thought: Knowledge, Consciousness, and the Politics of Empowerment* (New York and London: Routledge, 1991), 49.

15. Jeanette Rodriguez, *Our Lady of Guadalupe: Faith and Empowerment Among Mexican-American Women* (Austin, Tex.: University of Texas Press, 1994), 77.

16. Klein, *Bliss Queen,* 96.

17. "Nurse Midwife: Maude Callen Eases Pain of Birth, Life, and Death," photos by W. Eugene Smith, *Life,* December 3, 1951, 134–45. Quotations of Smith's comments about Maude Callen in the text are from "Nurse Midwife, Research by W. Eugene Smith," a twenty-three-page typescript, including text and captions, submitted by Smith to *Life.* I would like to thank Jim Hughes, Smith's biographer, for telling me about Maude Callen and providing me with a

copy of this typescript, and Kevin Smith, W. Eugene Smith's son, for allowing me to quote from it.

18. Jim Hughes, *W. Eugene Smith: Shadow and Substance: The Life and Work of an American Photographer* (New York: McGraw-Hill, 1989), 277.

19. Klein, *Bliss Queen,* 81; Hughes, *Smith,* 277.

20. Ibid., 570.

21. Klein, *Bliss Queen,* 77.

22. Quoted in Macy, *World as Lover,* 191.

Index

Index

Index

About the Author

Stephanie Golden is an independent scholar and writer. She is the author of the acclaimed book *The Women Outside: Meanings and Myths of Homelessness,* which was a finalist for the Robert F. Kennedy Award. Her work has appeared in *New York Newsday,* the *San Francisco Chronicle,* and *Yoga Journal,* among other publications. She lives in Brooklyn, New York.